UNIVERSITY PRESS OF FLORIDA

Florida A&M University, Tallahassee
Florida Atlantic University, Boca Raton
Florida Gulf Coast University, Ft. Myers
Florida International University, Miami
Florida State University, Tallahassee
New College of Florida, Sarasota
University of Central Florida, Orlando
University of Florida, Gainesville
University of North Florida, Jacksonville
University of South Florida, Tampa
University of West Florida, Pensacola

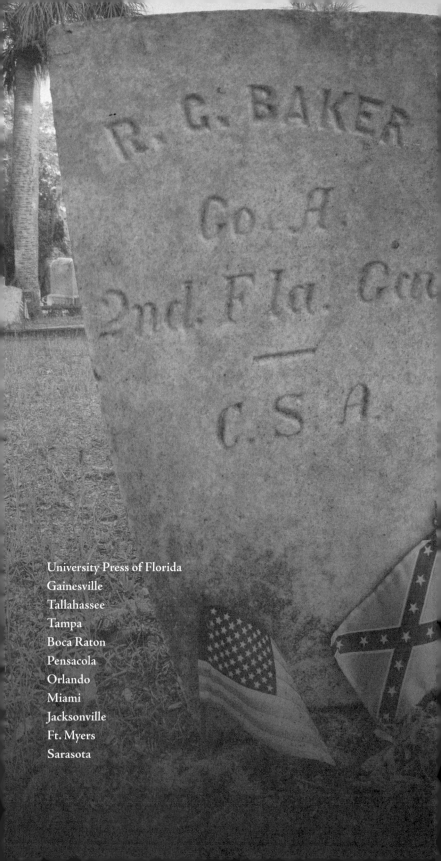

University Press of Florida
Gainesville
Tallahassee
Tampa
Boca Raton
Pensacola
Orlando
Miami
Jacksonville
Ft. Myers
Sarasota

LOLA HASKINS

FIFTEEN FLORIDA CEMETERIES

STRANGE TALES UNEARTHED

16 15 14 13 12 11   6 5 4 3 2 1

LIBRARY OF CONGRESS CATALOGING-IN-PUBLICATION DATA
Haskins, Lola.
Fifteen Florida cemeteries : strange tales unearthed / Lola Haskins.
p. cm.
Includes bibliographical references and index.
ISBN 978-0-8130-3572-7
    1. Cemeteries—Florida—Anecdotes. 2. Florida—History, Local—
Anecdotes. 3. Florida—Description and travel—Anecdotes. 4. Haskins,
Lola—Travel—Florida—Anecdotes.. 5. Florida—Biography—Anecdotes.
I. Title.
F312.H37   2011
363.7'509759—dc22   2010040995

The University Press of Florida is the scholarly publishing agency for the
State University System of Florida, comprising Florida A&M University,
Florida Atlantic University, Florida Gulf Coast University, Florida Interna-
tional University, Florida State University, New College of Florida, Univer-
sity of Central Florida, University of Florida, University of North Florida,
University of South Florida, and University of West Florida.

University Press of Florida
15 Northwest 15th Street
Gainesville, FL 32611-2079
www.upf.com

CONTENTS

PREFACE

I've been thinking about why so many of us are attracted to cemeteries full of strangers. In some cases, the appeal is obvious—a picturesque church or a parklike vista. But that can't be all there is to it, because even graveyards surrounded by seas of car dealers and fast food restaurants retain their interest.

Maybe it's the stories that draw us in, the ones we get to make up as if we were children again. A particularly eloquent inscription may set us off, or a small angel holding a flower, or an embedded daguerreotype that shows us how Martha wore her hair. Or maybe it's something apparently out of place—a tableau of plastic action figures, an enormous fire hydrant—that starts us dreaming.

Or maybe what brings us in is simply kinship, not the blood kind but the human kind. After all, the only difference between these people with stone names and us is that their time came but ours hasn't yet. And there's something oddly comforting that all these others came before us. And poignant too, for cemeteries make it clear how easily a man can vanish—his inscription, even his name, weathered gone. Besides, every time we go, given our commonalities with those who lie under our feet, how can their sorrows not move? I wanted so much to comfort the mother who lost her twelve-year-old to drowning, the siblings of the child who died at four, the sister of the man killed in wartime.

And there's something else about cemeteries as well, something wider: that to stand among the dead is to stand on the grass that has overgrown the times in which these people lived. In other words, cemeteries are repositories not just of individuals, but of history. The 1918 flu epidemic, for instance, comes alive in five graves behind a small white church overlooking the Santa Fe River: four children and their mother, dead within a week of each other. In a cemetery near Olustee, the site of an important battle during the Civil War, if you shut your eyes you can smell the acrid smoke, the rot of the dead lying in the relentless sun. You can experience the faith of early Catholic missionaries too, via the four-hundred-year-old remains of nuns laid to rest by their shell-studded chapel in St. Augustine.

This is probably a good time for a disclosure. I'm not a trained historian, nor even an experienced nonfiction writer. I am, though, an amateur in the original sense of that word. I wrote this book for love: because I love my state and its history and because I love stories. And one more revelation: since over the years, I've published several books of poems, I can't always keep my poet's mindset from creeping into my prose.

That said, here's how I approached this project. I started with two goals: to reflect Florida's past, especially parts of it most people don't know, and to tell the most interesting stories I could find. Honoring that, I've written two essays for each cemetery. In the first, I'll fill you in on the history of the area and share with you what I noticed when I went there. I don't intend these first essays to amount to guided tours. For one thing, some of the cemeteries I've written about have their own, very good, tours already, so in those cases I'd be duplicating what was already available. More fundamentally, I decided that rather than make this book into the usual look-here-look-there, it would be more fun for me, and hopefully for you, if I gave you a general-cum-idiosyncratic sense of each place then let you loose to discover it for yourself.

The second essays I've written for each cemetery are intended as spotlights: each tells the story of someone or something buried there. My thought for those was that then when you go, you'll know someone.

Once I'd settled on my format, I set about choosing cemeteries. Certain cities were givens: Pensacola and St. Augustine, because they're the state's oldest; Miami because it's so important today, and Key West because (*a*) it's such a wild town and (*b*) so many people visit it.

Once I'd found burial grounds in each of those places, I added others whose clientele represent parts of Florida history many people don't know. Here are some questions you'll find answered in this book: Why did the first territorial legislature, slated to convene in 1821 at Pensacola, have to move out of town (the same reason that in 1878 all U.S. mail leaving Florida was quarantined)? Why are there so many central Floridians of Swedish descent? Why did the great hurricane of 1928 kill so many people?

After I settled this second history-triggered tier, I trolled through the Department of State's registry of historic cemeteries for interesting, out of the way, places. I augmented the list with a few more recent graveyards because their origins interested me—Manasota, for example, because it was founded by Charles Ringling of the Ringling Brothers Barnum and Bailey Circus.

Finally, I decided the book wouldn't be complete without animals, so I searched www.iaopc.com/ for a good pet cemetery. When I came across one that was haunted, I stopped looking. I also wanted to include a racehorse cemetery since Ocala in the north central part of the state is so important in that industry. At least four Kentucky Derby winners trained there, as well as over half the 2009 field. I'd expected to find several horse cemeteries but in the end I found only the one I covered (Winding Oaks Farm).

Now, I'm well aware I may have left places off my list that you think deserved to be included. If you have your own favorites, I'd love to hear from you. Just drop me a line, care of the University Press of Florida, and tell me their names, their locations, and why you think they deserve attention. That way, if I ever decide to reprise this idea I'll know where to start.

I should probably warn you before you read even a page further, that some of the stories in this collection are wild—particularly the tale of a self-proclaimed count who dug up the woman he loved and lived with her for seven years. But they're all true, even the one I made up. And it's my dearest wish that you'll have as much fun visiting the cemeteries in this book (their addresses are in Appendix 1) as I did writing about them.

A number of fine people have helped me in this journey. First, I'd like to thank Gary Mormino of UCF for suggesting I look into this idea and Bill Dudley of the Florida Humanities Council for getting me oriented. I'm grateful as well to the following generous souls: John Thrasher and Diana Cohen (Micanopy); David Nolan, Charles and Mary Steadham, and The St. Augustine Historical Society (St. Augustine); Bill Jennewine and Robert Mueller (Jacksonville); Phil Hronek (Winding Oaks); Elmer Spear (Mt. Horeb); Bill Spohrer, Lynn Wilson, Dolores Roux, and Laura Moody (Apalachicola); John Wilkerson, Serena Padgett, and Mario Soto of Army Special Forces (Glendale); Margo Stringfield and Rhoda Warren (Pensacola); Carl Haskins and Christine Best (Upsala); Christine Rodriguez (http://www.ghostecho.com/) and Sandy Ketchum (Broward Pet Cemetery); Elmer Spear of Elmer's Genealogical Society (Madison); and Arthur Ivester of the city of Pahokee (Port Mayaca). I appreciate you all. Without you, this book wouldn't have been possible.

FIFTEEN FLORIDA CEMETERIES

PART I

TALLAHASSEE AND
THE PANHANDLE

THE OLD CITY CEMETERY, TALLAHASSEE

The Florida Spain ceded to the United States in an 1819 agreement (ratified by both countries in 1821) was divided into two administrative units: East Florida governed from St. Augustine, and West Florida governed from Pensacola. At first, the new legislature met alternately between those cities. But the travel involved proved to be both time-consuming and financially wasteful. It was also, given the rough state of Florida roads, highly uncomfortable. So in 1824, after its first two sessions, the legislators decided to scrap the two-city system in favor of a new, single capital. They chose Tallahassee in spite of the fact that it was mostly forest at the time because it came closest to meeting the geographical requirement they'd set themselves: that the capital city be located as close to midway between St. Augustine and Pensacola as possible.

In its early days as capital, Tallahassee was violent and lawless—memorialized by Ralph Waldo Emerson as "a grotesque place of land speculators and desperados." Though Tallahassee's bar-fight reputation softened considerably with the development of a plantation economy, living there still had its problems. In its first twenty years its citizens had to face Indian attacks (Henry Hutchinson, for instance, died in 1839 while trying to catch some Indians who had murdered a family at Chaires), yellow fever epidemics, bank failures, hurricanes, and a fire that devastated much of downtown. Still, by 1845, when Florida became a state, things had settled down enough that Tallahassee was allowed to continue in its role as the seat of government.

Tallahassee's Old City Cemetery, established in 1829, isn't the oldest cemetery in Florida—that honor belongs either to St. Michael's in Pensacola or to Tolomato in St. Augustine—but it does have the distinction of being the oldest public burial ground in Tallahassee. The Territorial Legislature managed it for its first eleven years then turned it over to the city, which still runs it.

Old City lies only a few blocks from the capitol in a pretty residential area of tree-lined streets today, but when it was founded it was so remote that it abutted the two hundred-foot perimeter area Tallahassee's settlers had cleared so they could see attacking Indians before they got too far. As you might expect given its location, in its early days Old City's premises were rather messy. Cattle and hogs ran freely over its graves, most of which had been allowed to overgrow. And what livestock didn't tear up, the jolting carts that brought bodies in for burial did. Burials too tended to be crude affairs, with coffins lowered into their resting places by ropes that often slipped, unceremoniously spilling the dead out onto the ground. Things got so bad that within five years of the cemetery's founding, at least one strongly worded letter arrived at the newspaper, complaining both of the general dishevelment of the grounds and of the carts that were making the situation worse. There's no record of an official response but since for many years no one complained as loudly as that first letter-writer, it's possible something was done.

After that shaky beginning, Old City operated in relative obscurity until the 1980s, when a series of brutal vandalisms galvanized the town that had taken it for granted. In the heat of the occasion, sufficient funds were raised not only to undo the damage the vandals had inflicted, but also to make other, overdue repairs, even improvements. In the early 1990s, skilled craftsmen finished the restoration process by installing the iron fence that surrounds the grounds, echoing the cast-iron fences within.

There are many of those fences within because in Old City—with the exception of war dead—most people are buried in family plots. Burials here were always segregated—white families in the east along what is now Martin Luther King Jr. Blvd, slaves and free men of color in the west. But the racial bifurcation wasn't made official until 1841, when a city ordinance institutionalized it. The ordinance, prompted by a particularly violent epidemic of yellow fever that year, consisted of a declaration that from henceforth "in the interests of sanitation" the cemetery supervisor would keep different books for white and black interments. In 1937, the city council took the final step and voted to close burial in Old City to any blacks who had not already purchased plots (I say "blacks" rather than "African Americans" because Tallahassee's population of color included a number of people who came not from Africa but from the Caribbean). In response to the council's move, the black community established its own burial ground, the very interesting Greenwood Cemetery.

From Martin Luther King Jr. Boulevard, Old City offers a peaceful vista, with many trees sheltering the graves. Some of the trees, especially the magnolias, are large enough to have been here for centuries. And though others—dogwoods, sycamores, cypress, and oaks—are clearly younger, a walk along the paths reveals stumps that testify that older trees once stood where these youngsters are now. The varying heights of the grave markers coupled with the fact that a number of them are very tall gives the impression of a skyline, so you feel that you're entering a city which, as in every cemetery, you are.

Now sheltering trees, skylines, and so on are fine conceits, but they evanesce before the sad fact that, especially in Tallahassee's early days, so many children died young. Just inside the gate I came upon the Andrews family plot that remembers two of these: Georgiana, who died in 1848 age 1 year, 6 months, and 4 days and her sister Mary Louisa, lost at 2 years, 4 months, and 18 days. Here where the sisters have come to stay, a new tree struggles up from the stump of the old. After the Andrews children, I passed in quick succession John Samuel Shine, 3 years, 9 months, and 11 days, "Little Fenton," the infant daughter of T.R. and E.G. Tatum, who lived two days in 1862, and Nonnie Hunter, another child of initialed parents, who lived 1 year, 10 months, and 27 days. The stone for Isaac

Flag, who died at only a month, heartbreakingly specified that he was "the only son of Francis and Nancy."

Many families here had to weather not one but multiple sorrows. The Perez Brokaw plot for example contains three stone lambs, all children of one mother, Cornelia, all dying young, in 1853, 1855, and 1858 respectively. How little all the Brokaw's money from their livery stable must have signified and how much Cornelia must have hoped each time she became pregnant. A few steps west, nearer the path than the Brokaws, is a large obelisk in memory of "My Grandchildren": Henry Clay (three months), William Adolphus Leonard (one year, nine months), and Henry Clay (who followed his namesake into death at fourteen). The inscription finishes: "The link is broken." On the top of the memorial an angel holds a large cross as if his upward glance alone could have saved the Clay line from extinction.

Henry Clay wasn't the only child to survive the early years only to falter before he reached maturity. Andrew Brevard, who died in 1848 at fifteen, earned a lengthy inscription. After many lines describing the brilliant future that had seemed to lie ahead, it went on to proclaim that "to the crushed spirits of his bereaved parents, there is no balm that is of earth." And though Andrew's parents did mention Heaven toward the end, I didn't catch much conviction in their words. Another failed young man was Alexander Jackson, born in Virginia March 18, 1815, who died "on his way home from the university of his native state to the residence of his father in the city of Tallahassee, Florida, on May 6, 1836."

That early Florida was pestilential and that many children didn't survive to adulthood wasn't new information to me, but the sorrow of all those losses settled into my chest anyhow. What I found particularly affecting was the specificity in the way a child's lifespan would be expressed on her stone, making it clear how valuable each day can be when there are so few. And because I have children of my own, I was sure that those children's burial days wouldn't have been the last time their parents thought of them. Not long ago I was walking back from the store with a neighbor who was ninety years old on her last birthday. We were talking of this and that when she suddenly stopped on the path and told me that almost twenty years ago she had lost a son to cancer—he had been in his fifties. "I cry every single day," she said, and fell into my arms.

Illness, of course, isn't the only reason a life can get cut off prematurely. Many people die from accidents for instance, or, more commonly, in war. On the left (east) side of the cemetery, toward the fence, and near the Martin Luther King Jr. Boulevard entrance, lie a number of Confederate soldiers, some of them casualties of the southern victory at the Battle of Olustee/Battle of Ocean Pond. I counted fifty-five markers in that area, but since an 1899 census of the cemetery reported 186, some of the original memorials must have been wood. This sort of discrepancy—between number of burials and number of markers—is common in Florida. Here in Tallahassee, because stone was expensive and because when the city was founded most people were just starting out, very few markers in Old City carry early dates. The earliest you'll find is 1829, the year the cemetery was founded. It's on a marble marker remembering a Daniel Lynes, "a merchant of the city of New York." Mr. Lynes, according to his inscription had, ironically, been visiting the city "for his health."

Most graves in Old City, including the ones that harbor Confederate soldiers, face east in accord with the Christian belief that on the Day of Judgment Jesus would appear from that direction. At one point the local religious climate was so intense in this respect that the fact that the inscription on Elizabeth Budd Graham's grave—east of the Confederate area (toward Martin Luther King Jr. Boulevard)—faced west led to whisperings that she had been a witch.

But back to the Confederates . . . The United Daughters of the Confederacy and the Sons of Confederate Veterans conduct services here on April 26, Confederate Memorial Day. In their early incarnation, the services honored only Confederate soldiers, but since the 1870s—at the behest of a Florida governor named W.D. Bloxham—they have involved strewing Union as well as Confederate graves with flowers. On the November day I visited here, a child-size flag was flying by one anonymous grave in each area, Confederate and Union. Both flags were equally faded.

Near the fence on the other side of the grounds are the graves of twenty-two of the twenty-nine black Union troops killed in 1865 during the Battle of Natural Bridge fought near Tallahassee. Thirty-nine soldiers went permanently missing after that battle. To this day, no one knows what happened to them. Perhaps they died in the woods. Perhaps they simply ran away.

The vast majority of the markers in the Union area say simply, "U.S. Soldier," but there are at least two exceptions: Edward Hays who died at Quincy when he was forty-six, whose company erected a memorial for him, and James Kelly, who fell at twenty-five, whose memorial was sponsored, it said simply, "by his sister." Looking at those inscriptions, I was struck by how important it is that we honor graves that aren't marked equally with those that are. How can we not, when we think how sad it is that so many who must have had parents, brothers, sisters, perhaps even wives and children, lie nameless here.

There are twenty-two fewer Union dead in this cemetery than there used to be. That's because in 1866 an entrepreneurial Union Colonel named J.P. Low—who charged $8 for each relocated body—moved the missing men from here to Beaufort, South Carolina. He had moved 128 bodies from various Florida cemeteries and would have moved more if the residents of Jacksonville hadn't taken advantage of a Florida law that made it illegal to open graves after May 20. The rationale underpinning that law, by the way, was that people were convinced that the miasma excavated bodies were thought to send into the air would be injurious to the public health. Though that belief turned out to be mistaken, it was responsible for the founding of many a rural cemetery.

In the black section of this one, the Proctor family is worth a visit. The paterfamilias (who isn't here) was a renowned builder, a free man of color who decided to try his luck in California. When he failed to come back, his wife and children were sold into slavery. His son John, who had been sold to a druggist, ended up serving in both the Florida House and Senate after the Civil War. He died in 1944, just shy of his 101st birthday. It's emblematic of the racial mélange Florida had become by John Proctor's lifetime that the Muskogee (Creek) community celebrates him as "a black Creek."

Another occupant of the "black" side of the cemetery is a physician named William Gunn. Gunn, like John Proctor, lived to a ripe old age (ninety-seven). Born in 1857, he was the first African American in Florida to graduate from medical school. In the 1880s, he started a practice in Tallahassee which he pursued honorably until he died.

The white (east) section of the cemetery contains an elaborate memorial to another prominent man born the same year as Dr. Gunn: a Professor John G. Riley. The Masonic symbol on his grave specifies that he was "A Grand High Priest, State of Florida, 33 degrees." The northeast quadrant holds two sites I thought were especially interesting. The first is a striking gravestone in the shape of a tree trunk, typical of the memorials an insurance company/service organization named Woodmen of the World provided to its members. The other point of attention, farther into the quadrant, is the Scott family plot, one of the few that is known to contain victims of the 1841 yellow fever epidemic.

You can pick up a brochure laying out a walking tour from a kiosk at the entrance to the cemetery on M.L. King Jr. Boulevard. But don't let that limit you. After all, it's not only the prominent who matter. If you walk slowly and stop here and there to remember someone who might otherwise be forgotten, you'll get the best possible benefit from your visit.

When you leave Old City, you may want to cross Call Street to another graveyard, established in 1840 and now attached to St. John's Episcopal Church. There, you can pay your respects to Prince Achille Murat, the son of the King of Naples and nephew of Napoleon Bonaparte and his wife, Catherine Gray, who was George Washington's great-grandniece. Their story, being the most compelling story on the block, follows this one.

Should you have been attending a ball or a performance of *Macbeth* in 1840s Tallahassee, you might have encountered a glittering couple: Prince Achille Murat, nephew of Napoleon Bonaparte, and his wife Catherine, great-grandniece of George Washington. Seeing them for the first time, you'd probably have assumed that Murat had spent his entire life amid carriages and diamonds. But you'd have assumed wrong, because though Murat was born to the aristocracy, he hadn't by any means always lived that way.

Murat—christened "Achille Charles Louis Napoleon" by his uncle—was born in 1800, soon after his mother narrowly missed being killed during an attempt on her brother's life. She, eight months pregnant, and her sister-in-law Josephine, had been riding in a carriage behind Napoleon's on their way to the opera from their home at the Tuilleries when, only seconds too late, someone detonated a wagon packed with explosives. The ladies' horses bolted for home, where they arrived with Caroline and Josephine shaken but unhurt. Murat entered the world a month later. Perhaps his childhood health problems were related to the trauma of what happened that day, perhaps not, but we do know that until he was seven, he was subject to fits and nearly died several times.

Murat's mother Caroline and his father Joaquim, a handsome and ambitious young man, had married for love. By the time Achille was four, Joaquim had been appointed governor of Paris, then after Napoleon became emperor, "Grand Admiral of France" and finally "Prince Imperial." Four years after that, he was crowned king of the two Sicilies, which made his son Prince of Naples, an identity the boy never relinquished. Even as an adult, he considered himself more Italian than French. A female relative explained this preference by saying that when Achille was a child, his uncle had pulled his ear so hard that he screamed at him and called him a villain, at which Napoleon slapped the boy's face and stomped out of the room. From that moment on, according to her, Achille wanted nothing to do with France.

Be that as it may, in both France and Italy Achille was educated by tutors who found him delightfully quick-minded but the kind of child who would pay attention only when he was interested. What interested him seems to have been words. He spoke several languages by the time he was eight, and in his middle years he would publish books and articles (mostly on political subjects though he did attempt a novel).

Outside of his formal education, Achille was given to wild enthusiasms, and not only for the obvious, a tendency that would continue throughout his life. Many years later for instance, his wife Catherine would return home from visiting a neighbor to find her house aglow. Terrified it was on fire, she rushed inside to find Achille tending huge vats of boiling dye into which he had thrown all her clothes. He had been experimenting with the potential of a certain rare wood and in the process had colored every stitch of apparel she owned bright pink.

One more point needs to be added to complete our portrait of the young Achille: that besides being highly intelligent he was a charmer, which meant that for most of his life, he could and often did get away with a good deal.

Achille's father Joaquim was also a charmer but his penchant for political intrigue caused the boy's childhood to run anything but smoothly. When it looked as if Napoleon could lose his empire to the Austrians, Joaquim signed a treaty with the latter in which he renounced France. But then, when Napoleon escaped from Elba, Joaquim repudiated the treaty and marched north to liberate Italy from his former allies. When the Austrians prevailed, Joaquim fled to an island off the coast where he spent the next year buying ships to try to retake his former kingdom. But since his former citizens didn't support his efforts, he didn't succeed. Instead, he was captured and, on the day Napoleon arrived at St. Helena, executed. Joaquim's last salvo was said to have been: "Aim at my heart but spare my face." Then: "Fire."

In the meantime, Caroline and fifteen-year-old Achille had taken refuge in Austria, where for people accustomed to living in the highest of luxury (Achille's birthdays had been national holidays) they were short of money. Their problems came from the fact that when the family had moved to Naples, Joaquim had renounced his properties in France in return for 500,000 francs a year from Napoleon's Sicilian holdings, an agreement which, when Austria won the war, it refused to recognize. Before returning to Italy, Joaquim had begun a lawsuit on the point but it wouldn't be settled until after Achille had died.

The family's straitened circumstances meant that in order to maintain a semblance of her previous lifestyle, Caroline had to sell some of the jewels and artwork she'd brought with her when she went into exile. With the proceeds, she bought an elegant but shabby castle called Frohsdorf with a staff of fifteen—luxurious to some, but for her a step down. In Frohsdorf, she and the children lived under the watchful eye of the Austrian secret police who reported everything they did to Metternich, who feared a Bonapartist return and in particular didn't trust Caroline, who had at one time been his lover.

The atmosphere in the Frohsdorf household was claustrophobic. Even if the French hadn't prohibited anyone related to the Bonapartes from returning to France, Caroline couldn't have gone there, nor anywhere else because the Austrians were keeping her and her family under house arrest. This confinement made for a dull life compared to what the Murats were used to, since it deprived them of the glittering social seasons taking place in tantalizingly close Vienna.

The teenage Achille responded to his changed circumstances by smoking up to twenty pipes of tobacco a day and drinking heavily. At the same time, he was more and more attracted to the idea of freedom, fed no doubt by what he was hearing from his Uncle Joseph, now living a life of luxury in America. When he was twenty-one, Achille professed a desire to emigrate, and when Caroline saw he was serious, she financed his passage by mortgaging her castle. At first the Austrians refused to let Achille leave, but changed their minds after Bonaparte's death in 1821. They did require, though, that Achille travel as "Mr. de Frohsdorf," and that he promise he wouldn't return to Europe without their consent.

On December 17, 1822, Achille left "my tearful family" in the middle of the night without saying goodbye. Ten days later, after a very cold journey, he reached Hamburg, and five months after that he arrived in New York, where he disported himself in society before settling at his Uncle Joseph's estate on the Delaware River. But when he'd been at his uncle's only a few months, news reached him of the Spanish Revolution and Achille, ever enthused, reneged on his promise to the Austrians and sailed to Spain to join the cause.

Though he returned to America after the revolution failed, Achille's precipitous return to Europe caused his mother a good deal of trouble. She wrote him that because he had endorsed this "most stupid of all undertakings," Metternich was now bound to suspect her of sympathy with that cause. And her concern turned out to be well-founded since because of Achille's involvement in the Spanish revolt, Metternich ordered her to leave Venice where she had settled, she'd thought, for good.

Back in America, Achille's love life was proceeding apace. When he had first arrived, his Uncle Joseph—overlooking the fact that Achille was one of the least financially appealing Bonapartes—had offered him the hand of his daughter Charlotte. Initially, Achille had said no, and in no uncertain terms. But after he returned from Spain, he softened, writing a friend that

> my family, except for Charlotte through sentiment and Joseph through generosity, has abandoned me. . . . That is what I have gained at the risk of my life, my liberty, and more than half of my fortune. . . . I find myself alone and ill and without future prospects. . . . You know that I am not lacking in energy. I will summon it to my aid and soon will have taken my calling. I would not stay in tow of my uncle. . . . Besides, my cousin Charles (a bird-stuffer and a true Roman prince, filled with all the prejudices . . . of the most detestable aristocracy in Europe) . . . poisoned my visit [to Joseph's estate] so that I would have left much sooner except for the consoling balm that Charlotte sprinkled on my wounds.

Soon after this letter, Achille declared himself in love with Charlotte (whom one uncharitable observer described as "a dwarf") and she, by all reports, returned his affection. Soon after that, with Charlotte's blessing, Achille went to Washington and from there to Florida, to find them a home.

Achille had been attracted to Florida for some time in spite of what a Roanoke booster had thundered: "A man, sir, would not emigrate to Florida . . . not from hell itself!" Achille had his reasons. First of all, he had always admired a Southerner as opposed to a Yankee who, Achille said, may be recognized by "the evasive manner in which he answers questions addressed to himself . . . and particularly by the rapidity with which he manages to eclipse himself when there is something for him to pay." Furthermore, his good friend Robert Keith Call who preceded Achille to Florida, had already acquired a position in Washington, an outcome Achille, who had decided to enter politics himself, hoped to replicate.

Achille's first destination in Florida was St. Augustine, a city which, he said, reminded him of Italy. There, he was immediately welcomed into society. His initial plan had been to rent lodgings until he felt himself well-oriented. Instead, being an impulsive twenty-three, within two months he was seduced into purchasing a pretty but barren estate of 1,200 acres for which he paid $1,960, far above the going price at the time. He named his new home "Parthenope" after a Greek siren and fifteen minutes after acquiring it rushed back north to secure Charlotte's hand, only to find that his uncle had turned against him. Angry at Achille's having squandered in his ill-advised Spanish venture not only the family's prestige but also Caroline's hard-won financing, Joseph had decided to send Charlotte to Europe to make a more suitable match. And when the lovers approached him with their proposition he was in no mood to change his mind. Charlotte and Achille agreed to bide their time and Achille returned to Florida and Charlotte went to Europe. At first she wrote Achille passionately, then less passionately, and finally, after a long hiatus, she wrote to say she was betrothed elsewhere and to ask him to return her letters.

Instead of complying with Charlotte's request, Achille wrote his uncle to the effect that he scoffed at his wrath and expected never to see him again. What he got in return was what he had probably expected: silence. Charlotte, said her disaffected lover in a letter to someone else, "has preferred a white-nosed master, a pale youngster with a tutor at his heels to a man tested in a storm . . . has preferred the luxury . . . of the papal court to republican virtue. . . . May she enjoy her choice. . . . This is not the Charlotte I loved. . . . I'd rather live a bachelor."

Achille's first post-Charlotte move was to sell Parthenope, having belatedly realized its soil was too poor to make him a living. To replace it, he purchased a large tract of fertile land near Tallahassee in partnership with a friend, a surveyor named James Gadsden, and proposed to move there.

In 1826 in basically roadless Florida, a move of this distance was no small undertaking. For Achille it involved thirty-one days of driving a wagon through thick forest, accompanied only by some negroes (slaves), a pet owl, a hundred head of cattle, and a compass. Since there were no inns along the way, the trip also involved sleeping rough every night.

For some time after his arrival at what he would eventually call "Lipona" (an anagram for Napoli), Achille and Gadsden lived simply in a two-room cabin in the woods while they worked at clearing their land. But they weren't as isolated as you might think. Achille wrote not long after his arrival that "we are receiving fifteen newspapers and we have some books [and] are in correspondence with all the important people of the union &c."

Here's how he describes his commerce with those important people: "The contrast is . . . comical . . . me . . . in a straw hat, tattered dress coat, trousers, blue stockings and muddy shoes coming to consult others dressed in about the same manner on the construction to be given a treaty made with the Indians. Yet these are the governor and the commissioner of the state. . . . They seat themselves at table around a piece of salt pork, and there questions of profound public interest . . . are dealt with."

Murat's interactions in those days involved all comers. On the 4th of July, 1825, he wrote that "often a planter with whom I am not acquainted . . . sprawls out on the sofa, tosses off a glass of grog, thrusts a piece of tobacco into his mouth then says . . . Neighbor I have come to talk to you on such and such a matter; one must be ready to . . . uphold his opinion before a consummate boor with as much care as he would exercise before an assembly. . . . I am . . . delighted with all these opportunities and my role in my territory is illustrious and above all very happy."

Murat's happiness had a routine. Every day he'd rise with the sun, give the overseer his orders, shave, then get on his horse to make his rounds. He'd breakfast around eight or nine then write until around noon. Then, after a pause for lunch and a stroll around his orange groves, he'd ride out to check on the day's work. At dusk, his overseer would report to him. After that, he'd have supper, enjoy a few cigars, and finally fall asleep, usually, he said, to *Blackstone's Commentaries on the Law* (well known to today's law students). In the morning, he'd get up and do it all again.

On January 7, 1826, Achille attended a ceremony in which a cornerstone was laid for the city of Tallahassee, forest only eighteen months before but now boasting more than 100 houses. The ceremony involved a dinner and a speech and was attended by Governor Duval's cabinet in full dress.

In July of that year, Achille married Catherine, the great-grandniece of George Washington. Catherine's nature was said to have been the perfect counterbalance to Achille's: calm to his impulsiveness, water to his fire. They were said to be alike in only one way: they were both kind. Like his parents', Achille's was a love match, since Catherine's dowry consisted of ten negroes—seven of whom were children—and an old house in Virginia the only value of which, her husband-to-be pointed out, was the $300 in insurance he'd collect if it were to burn down.

By the time Achille married Catherine, he had spent most of the money he had brought to America, so the couple started married life by making do with the proceeds of cotton crops, proceeds which barely covered expenses. At this point, Achille professed two goals: to establish himself as a man of substance, and, eventually, to go into politics. By 1833, seven years later, he had achieved the first. His lands were four miles long by a half a mile to two miles wide. He owned ninety-seven slaves and one white workman. He wrote that "I kill an ox every Sunday to feed my black and white family. My mill is in operation. I make 100,000 bricks, half for my home, half to sell." His cotton harvest too was thriving: "about 100 bales which will be worth from 7 to 9,000 pounds."

Achille's second goal—going into politics—would be achieved only after some peregrinations. Following a trip to New York, he went to New Orleans where he pursued a legal career. In those years, he wrote several books and articles in support of America. In an article published in France, he defended decentralized federalism by asserting that "They govern well here and badly in Europe."

In 1829, Achille declined the offer of a judgeship in favor of returning to Europe in the hope that after the Bourbons' fall, he could win his family's long-running suit against the French government. He also thought that Italy and Spain might revolt and that his lifelong dream of a united Italy might be realized. When none of this materialized, he came back to Lipona only to decamp again two years later, this time to London with Catherine.

While Achille was in London, the idea of his becoming regent of France came up in Paris but was dismissed, reportedly because people were troubled by his physical resemblance to Napoleon. Achille himself confirmed this, writing around that time that "I have become short and fat like my uncle. . . . I am even getting bald. I hope this is a prognosis of wisdom." In any case, he must not have been too deeply disappointed since by now he considered himself to be neither French nor Italian, but, as witness his writings, thoroughly American. The couple returned home. Achille would see Europe only once more, and briefly, to settle his finances after his mother died.

On his return from Europe, Achille accepted the rank of colonel in the U.S. militia and was appointed postmaster of Wacissa. Before he died, he would be a judge, an unsuccessful candidate for office, a bank manager, an inspector for West

Point, the president of a company purchasing land in Texas, and a member of the Anti-Abolitionist Vigilance Committee. As he wrote his sister in 1835, "You want to withdraw from the bustle of affairs. I am just the opposite. It is only in the midst of whirlpools that I am happy."

Achille's eventful life ended on April 16, 1847. On his deathbed he was said to have told Catherine, who would outlive him by twenty years, "Kate, you have been the light of my life." When Achille's cousin Louis became Napoleon III, he granted Catherine a pension of 40,000 pounds for her immediate needs and added to that an 80,000 pound per year living allowance. In gratitude she later traveled briefly to France. Soon after returning home, she died of typhoid and was buried beside her husband. Achille's life wouldn't be a poor model to follow. Though his passions may have led him on many chases, and may sometimes even have been foolish, at least he never shrank from them. As a result he lived fully, something any of us, when it comes our time, would be glad to say.

2

MOUNT HOREB CEMETERY, PINETTA

The Mount Horeb Cemetery lies behind the church of the same name just past the "Pavement Ends" sign on a spur off a rural road near the community of Pinetta, Florida. The church and cemetery take their name from the holy mountain of Exodus, called Meribah by Moses. The church, the Mount Horeb Primitive Baptist Church, was founded in 1857. By 1890, attendance had slid to the point where it closed its doors and over the next decade or so, though the community kept an eye on it to make sure it wouldn't be vandalized, both it and the cemetery fell into disrepair. Finally, in the 1990s the people of Pinetta, some of whose great-greats had worshipped here, came together to restore the building and clean the stones of those who lie in its yard. Now the church is back to its authentic self and the cemetery is kept with care.

Since the point of view of Mount Horeb's denomination, Primitive Baptist, informs every physical detail of the church and at least one feature of the inscriptions in its cemetery, some background information may be helpful. To begin with, the word "primitive" in this context doesn't mean "behind the times" but rather "original" or "authentic." The term is used because white Primitive Baptists (the beliefs of African American Primitive Baptists are somewhat different) subscribe only to what is directly in the Bible. This means they reject such traditional Christian institutions as seminaries—P.B. ministers are laypeople and are not salaried—and Sunday schools. And since the Bible doesn't refer to musical instruments in the context of worship, Primitive Baptists sing only a cappella. White Primitive Baptists are also sometimes called "foot-washing Baptists" because their congregations typically symbolize their mission of service by washing each others' feet.

Though only a minority of Primitive Baptists believes that *every* event that has taken place and will take place is predestined, all members of the sect think that God chose His Elect before the world began. So rather than teaching, the way most Christian sects do, that God loves everyone, Primitive Baptists teach that God loves only the Elect. And though they do subscribe to the idea that Jesus died for our sins, the "our" in question also refers only to the Elect. Primitive Baptists counter the objection that these ideas can't be true because they're unfair by saying that predestination is a joyous thing when one considers that without it, the whole human family would have been lost.

It was predestination that split Primitive Baptists from the mainstream church in 1841, the year the Baptist Board of Foreign Missions was organized. The Primitives-to-be argued that since preaching cannot bring anyone not already Elect to Heaven, sending ministers overseas to "save souls" didn't make sense. When their point of view was rejected, the Primitive Baptists responded by leaving the church.

Things have changed somewhat since 1841 but not entirely. Today's Primitive Baptists run missions in Mexico and other parts of the world but they still reject the Mission Board, arguing that when the Spirit moves a minister to preach abroad, he (there are no female ministers) should answer the call at once and pay his own way rather than depending on the Board to pay it for him.

The original Primitive Baptists were highly conservative when it came to the lifestyles of their members. Early communicants of Mount Horeb, for instance, set up committees to investigate reports of non-attendance, failure to support the church financially, denying the faith, swearing, dancing, lying, drinking alcohol, or playing cards. If accused church members repented, they were allowed to remain in good standing but if not, they were stricken from the roster.

Though its absolutes have modulated somewhat over the years, the church's basic understanding of morality has remained consistent enough that it's easy to see how its pronouncements might have unsettled some of its younger members. What if they were caught dancing to rock music? Or playing cards? Or worse, as most teenagers do at one time or other, experimenting with alcohol? And though it's true that Primitive Baptists believe that if someone is born to the Elect his eventual ascension to Heaven is certain regardless of what he does, transgressions, even small ones, can still result in disgrace in this life. And being marooned in the land of guilt until you die is, Heaven notwithstanding, no pleasant prospect.

None of that may have caused the decline in Mount Horeb's membership but decline it did—from a peak of about 140 in the 1860s to single digits by the 1980s. By the mid-1990s there were only two active members left: a Mrs. Callie Crews and her daughter, Jessie. Still, though the number of its congregants declined, those who remained even loosely associated with the church kept fellowship alive by inviting the entire Pinetta community to "Big Meeting," every third weekend of July.

But Big Meetings, in spite of the spirit they represented, didn't rescue the church and cemetery from the disrepair they'd fallen into over the years. Finally though, in 1995, a group of fifteen or so local residents decided it was time to do something. They started by repainting the church, replacing its doors and windows, and generally doing all they could to turn it into, as they put it, "a beautiful antique." They then moved on to the cemetery, chopping out brush, mowing, even getting down on their hands and knees to scrub the gravestones with bleach. While this work was going on, Pinettans outside the core group would drop by to encourage, to help, or just to leave the workers some cold drinks or a watermelon. Two years later, on Big Meeting day 1997, the church was reopened with services held to celebrate its new life.

The care put into the restoration of both church and cemetery is obvious today. A direct descendent of the rough-hewn cabins erected by pioneers, the church is architecturally typical of Primitive Baptist houses of worship: a white, steepleless, rectangular building with its name painted in plain letters over the small front porch that leads inside. Inside, instead of a formal altar there's a wide table for readings from the Bible. Behind the table is no cross or crucifix, only a bare wall. The simple wooden pews lack cushioning. There are no kneelers, no icons of any kind, and no stained glass.

The simplicity inside the church mirrors its pastoral setting, which, if it had looked like this in 1858, would surely have brought God to mind. Both the church and the cemetery behind it are set back from the road, and flanked on one side by woods (across the sand track that continues what the paved road began), and on the other by pasture. The only sign of human habitation visible from either is a farmhouse at the far side of a field on which some Angus cattle graze, near the fence and down a slow hill toward an oval pond. The only sound that touches the ears is bird song and, in the far distance, the roar of traffic, that echoes as if the sea were nearby.

The cemetery behind the church is newly fenced. Just to the right of the gate is a post on which is affixed the kind of red information tube realtors use. The paper inside lists the families who tend the graves, together with their phone numbers, and asks that visitors please contact one of them should something be found amiss.

The first object that caught my eye across the vista of stones and flowers was a fading yellow plastic bulldozer. The bulldozer is guarded by an action figure whose pop eyes suggest some kind of alien. When I knelt to get a closer look, I saw that the toys were intended for Richard Keeling, who lived a single day in 1965. The most poignant thing to me about these objects was that Richard's parents left him not the rattle or plastic keys he'd have been attracted to as a newborn, but boy toys he might have played with if he'd lived five years instead of one day. In comparison with the toys, the small bunch of artificial flowers stuck at the foot of Richard's stone felt unimportant.

Farther into the cemetery, by the graves of not one but two children, stands a miniature American Flyer, the bright red wagon every child has sooner or later. This one is set in concrete and occupied by two laughing stone children, a girl in the wagon and a boy pushing her. Toward the back of the grounds I saw a heart-shaped stone remembering Jason Asbury, who died in 1986 when he was three. The stone carries an oval photo of the kind of smiling blonde boy who surely would have grown up to be a magnet for the girls.

There are also, from earlier times, a number of traditional stone lambs memorializing children. One family lost two sons, one in 1868 at five days old, the other in 1871 at six months. Another little girl, Nancy Jane, was born on my own son's birthday, November 19, in 1883, only to die six years later. There were outbreaks of scarlet fever in this area around those years. Perhaps it was one of them that took these little ones away.

It seems consistent with the Primitive Baptists' emphasis on *family* worship (children stay with their parents throughout the service) and also, no doubt, the central importance of family relationships in the surrounding community—that so many of the grave markers here bold-face the roles of those who lie under them. "Father," they proclaim. And "Mother." In contrast with most cemeteries, in which people are mourned first for themselves (name) *then* by relationship or at least by a democratic conflation of the two, the norm here is the other way around (first family role *then* name), the roles being typically above and in larger letters than what follows.

I don't think the relatives who commissioned those inscriptions consciously meant to stress position over person; that things turned out that way was just the natural outcome of their world view. Nor did following the pattern necessitate the loss of individuality. I noticed, for instance, markers that carried rather than "Father" and "Mother," the less formal "Dad" and "Mom" or the sweeter "Daddy" and "Mama."

The several Woodmen of the World grave markers here piqued my interest enough that when I got home I investigated their source. Here's what I found out: The Woodmen is a fraternal benefit society (with an auxiliary for women) founded in 1890 by Joseph Cullen Root of Omaha, Nebraska. The story goes that Root was inspired not by loggers but by a phrase from a sermon he heard at his church: "woodmen clearing away the forest to provide for their families." Originally, the only benefits the society offered were life insurance and a gravestone. Eventually, though, it evolved into a full financial services organization offering, besides life insurance and annuities, cancer insurance, mutual funds, prescription benefits, and college savings plans. Besides this, like the Elks or Moose, the Woodmen of the World give back. Today, more than 810,000 Woodmen in 2,000 lodges celebrate "Woodman Day" every June 6, and perform community service both locally and, in partnership with the Red Cross, nationally.

Since the Woodmen's first motto was "No member shall lie in an unmarked grave," early Woodmen certificates provided gravestones free of charge. The look of these was supposed to conform to a design sent by the Home Office to local stone-cutters, typically stubs of branches symbolizing a life cut off. Some of the more elaborate prototypes included vines running up the sides and backs to represent the life that continues after death. But since local cutters had their own ideas, many Woodman memorials ended up idiosyncratic. They tend to have certain aspects in common, though. They're above-average in height—four or five feet—and nearly all of them include either a tree stump or a stack of wood.

The Woodmen offered free markers for only about thirty years. As the cost of stone rose, the markers became subject to a $100 rider. Finally, sometime in the 1920s, the Woodmen stopped providing markers altogether, partly because of the expense and partly because around this time cemeteries had begun prohibiting above-ground memorials because they interfered with mowing. Recent graves of Woodmen are still marked, but only with a logo or a plaque.

The Cowart graves by the back fence, husband, wife, and son are good examples of elaborate Woodman markers. You can see the parents' memorials from across the cemetery, two interrupted trees, side by side. Their son, who died when he was only two, is remembered by a smaller tree topped with a stone lamb.

Although poems were common on nineteenth-century markers, only one family opted for that here: a father and mother, with a poem on the reverse of each stone. A number of the graves do make short comments. On the grave of an infant who died the day he was born, it is written: "Weep not he is at rest." You may be sure they wept. There are, as you'd expect in a cemetery associated with a church, inscriptions turning on faith: "Asleep in Jesus," "We shall meet again," "Gone to a higher home." And at the base of two large stones for "Dad" and "Mom," both of whom died of scarlet fever in 1922, you'll find, touchingly, "Gone with a friend." A few families pay tribute to the lost: "She was too gentle and fair to dwell in this world." Other graves—and I hadn't seen this elsewhere—offered slogans: "A good name is rather to be chosen than riches," "Be sure you're right then go ahead," "One day at a time."

One remembrance that touched my heart was a simple marker beside which sits an angel, weeping. It reminded me of an editorial cartoon after Jackie Gleason died, which depicted not him but a grieving Alice, her face buried in her apron. Another made me wonder. That one, belonging to a Jesse James Bullock, 1929–1995, sports a plastic squirrel. Why? Did he enjoy squirrel stew? Did he adopt squirrels? Probably the most unusual grave in Mount Horeb belongs to "Milton," who died on September 29, 2005. Under Milton's name and dates is written "Little Buddy" and beside his stone sits a brown and white plaster dog staring up at the enormous red fire hydrant with which, his family clearly hoped, he will have met in Heaven.

While hickory nuts have fallen aromatically from overhanging branches beyond the cemetery, only a few small trees grow within it—a palm, a cypress, and some scattered oaks. But even without shade, the place in its peaceful surroundings is clean and welcoming and everything about it says that Pinetta was and is a nice place to live. Perhaps you can come to Big Meeting some day and tell the fine people that yourself.

SPOTLIGHT: THE CASE OF THE MISFORTUNATE MAIL CARRIER

Imogene Rogers was eight and a half months pregnant on August 3, 1973, the day she started home toward Pinetta from the beauty parlor in Clyattville, a small town across the Georgia line. As she navigated the two-lane road, she may have been thinking about the baby who'd be her and Franklin's first son. Having grown up in a family of eleven, Imogene wouldn't have worried that she wouldn't know what to do when he was born. Maybe she was basking though, in how fine it would be to smell his baby odor or to reach over and pick him up from the cradle Franklin had installed by their bed.

But all that's speculation. What we know for sure, from her testimony at trial, is that she was almost home when she saw a green car, coming up on her fast. At first she took the driver for a high school student, since kids often drove too fast along that road. But, as she testified, she soon learned it wasn't anyone like that. Adrenaline must have turned her cold and the baby cold inside her, as the green car followed her when she turned off the state road onto the dirt one that led toward her house. The car—by this time Imogene had noticed that its driver had bright red hair—pulled up alongside her and forced her onto the littered shoulder. Imogene was suddenly afraid she might hit broken glass. And she knew that if she did, and got a flat tire, she wouldn't be able to get away. So she panicked and jerked the wheel and in that split second she lost control. She overcompensated and slid. The redheaded man cut onto the ragged grass in front of her and stopped. Imogene slammed on her brakes just in time to avoid hitting him. He got out and walked toward her window. She had just enough time to see the gun in his hand before he shot her six times. Then he leaned into her car, smiled (in the trial she described it as an evil smile, born of his conviction that she wouldn't survive to tell the tale), and took her purse off the seat. Then he drove away.

When the puffs of his dust had settled back on the road, Imogene dragged herself out of the car. She was close enough to home that a neighbor heard her calls for help and sent for the police. She was rushed to Jacksonville by ambulance and there, almost a week later, her baby was born. The doctors said afterward that given the trauma that preceded his birth, the baby shouldn't have lived. When he did, Imogene and her husband Franklin scrapped the baby name they'd had in mind and called him "Lucky."

The page of the local paper that reported Lucky's birth is a perfect window into what the Madison area was like in 1973. The small paragraph that mentions the attack lies in the undifferentiated middle of a list of local events that includes the fact that a Mrs. S.K. Driggers continues ill, that Linda Carol Reeder was one of fifty-three students to receive a degree from Andre College, Georgia, that the County Commission will be holding a special meeting to discuss the garbage franchise, that hogs hit a high of 60 cents at market, that there were no slaughter steers offered for sale, that Airman George A. Brooks, son of Mrs. Phyllis Butler, graduated from the U.S. Air Force security policeman course in Russell, Texas, and that Van Russell, having shown his slides of the Keys to the Rotary Club, recommends scuba diving for elderly Rotarians.

Within a couple of weeks of the day Lucky's birth notice was published, the police located the perpetrator of the crime. The man who'd shot Imogene (ejected shells from the .22 automatic he'd used in the crime were found in his car when he was arrested) turned out to be a habitual offender named Earl Daughtrey whose three-page arrest record consisted mostly of assaults on women. It came out at Daughtrey's trial, which resulted in his conviction for attempted murder, that he'd chosen Imogene at random. He was sent to prison for life plus fifteen years but in 1983, after serving ten years, he was released. Soon after his release, he violated parole and was sent back to prison. Two years after that, he was let out for good and, ironically for Imogene, went to work for the Georgia Department of Transportation.

In 1988, fifteen years after Daughtrey's assault on her, Imogene and Franklin were still living in Pinetta, with Lucky and his little sister, Cindy Darlene, and Imogene, completely recovered, was carrying the mail. Among the rural carriers in her area, Imogene was famous for her consistency. Every morning she would have loaded the day's mail into her car by 10:30 and every day by noon she would have arrived back at the post office to clock out.

On June 20, 1988, when half the mail on Imogene's route didn't get delivered, several of Imogene's customers, knowing how reliable she was, called the post office to find out if she was sick. When there was no sign of her by mid-afternoon, the postmaster was worried enough to talk to the Madison County sheriff.

It took deputies only a few hours to find Imogene's battered Datsun pulled off into the woods with her body spread-eagled inside. She'd been strangled from behind with the straps of her own mail bag which had, it came out later, been wrapped twenty-four times around her neck. Mail usually rubber-banded in Imogene's mail bag or on the passenger seat beside her was scattered everywhere. At some time during the assault she had pressed her foot into the brake pedal so desperately that her shoe had left a mark.

The people of Pinetta—not so much a town as a loose association of rural houses—rallied around Imogene's family. They were also stunned that something like this had happened in their community. From time to time, sure, a man might go after his ex-wife or someone might get drunk and stab someone else but everyone had thought the Daughtrey affair had been a one-off. But twice now, a stranger had attacked. Pinettans were checking their locks at night and no one was sleeping well. For this and many other reasons, the crime had to be solved fast.

Daughtrey was the obvious suspect. Like everyone else in Pinetta, the sheriff knew he had been released from prison, and the more the lawman thought back on how calmly Imogene had testified at trial, the more convinced he was that Daughtrey must have come back to finish the job. He sent Postal Service inspectors to Georgia to track Daughtrey down (the Postal Service had gotten involved because Imogene had been working for them when she'd been killed). The inspectors found their man, working on a bridge in Albany.

But when they brought him in for questioning, it was clear that though Daughtrey was a career criminal—besides the string of offenses against women for which he'd been convicted, he'd been charged with three other murders—he hadn't killed Imogene. Several witnesses placed him miles away from Pinetta at the time she was strangled.

At this point, the sheriff called in a profiler named Dayle Hinman. Hinman told him that in her opinion Daughtrey had never been the logical perpetrator. If he'd spent twelve years in prison thinking about revenge, he'd have made a plan, probably one involving a weapon. Besides, the way Imogene had been killed clearly suggested that her murder had been a crime of opportunity. Beyond that, Hinman concluded, the odds were that Imogene had been killed by someone she knew because in order to strangle someone, that someone has to have allowed you within arm's reach. And given Imogene's history, she would never have let a stranger approach her that closely.

Armed with this theory, Hinman and Sheriff Bunting set out to reconstruct the crime. Since Imogene's car had been found not far from Box 41 and no mail had been delivered past that box, Hinman hypothesized that Imogene had been killed by someone connected either with that box or with the one following it. They eliminated Box 41 because everyone living at that address had a checkable alibi for the time Imogene was murdered. But this wasn't true of several members of the African American family at Box 42. Specifically it wasn't true of Joseph Williams, one of Sheriff Bunting's poker buddies who, when questioned, denied he'd seen Imogene that day then refused to say anything else.

Looking for evidence that might connect Williams with the scene, investigators decided to see if the mail that had been found in Imogene's van had any relevant fingerprints. It was a complicated process since before checking could start, the team would have to accumulate the prints of the hundreds of people who might legitimately have handled those letters, but the team investigating Imogene's death didn't have a choice. There were no prints in the car or on the bag, so the mail was the only tangible evidence possibility left. The Florida Department of Law Enforcement assumed responsibility for the twenty to thirty pieces of mail that had been on top of the scatter and the Postal Service took charge of the rest—some eight hundred pieces. The sheriff got the process started and settled back to wait.

A phone call to the sheriff's office cut the wait short. It was Williams, volunteering to take a lie detector test. Later, investigators would say that when Williams arrived to take the test he came across as almost shockingly calm. On the kind of summer day when most foreheads are dotted with perspiration and most hands are damp, Williams's arm, when he laid it down to have the sensors applied, was cool to the touch. And when he lifted his hand off the table, it left no outline. This wasn't normal.

Williams's response to the first few questions elicited exactly the patterns one might expect of an innocent man. But when the administrator asked him "Did you cause the death of Imogene Rogers," the response was anything but normal. The needle leaped off the chart. After that, Williams clammed up. The team was now sure he had killed Imogene but in the absence of any other evidence, they had to let him go.

A few days later the results of the fingerprint scans came in. Williams's prints had been found on a piece of mail. That afternoon, he was arrested for the murder of Imogene Rogers. At the trial he pled guilty and was sentenced to life in prison.

After the fact, people have put forward many theories about what might have happened to cause Williams to strangle Imogene with her own mail bag. Maybe, for instance, she wouldn't hand him a letter. Williams has always refused to say why he killed her so unless he changes his mind, we'll never know. And maybe it doesn't matter, because whatever his reasons what we're left with is Imogene the misfortunate carrier, a woman by all accounts happy in her life, a woman who never did anything to deserve what happened to her, lying beside her widowed husband at Mount Horeb where the wind in summer blows softly and in the winter birds sing, then fly to the pasture beyond.

3

CHESTNUT CEMETERY, APALACHICOLA

Apalachicola's name is a combination of two Hitchiti words: "apalahchi," meaning "on the other side," and "okli" meaning "people." Some parse this as "the people on the other side of the river," while others say it means a ridge of earth where the ground has been swept for a council. Modern Apalachicola bypasses the controversy by calling itself "a town of friendly people." It's home to just over 3,500 of those friendly people, about the same number as at the turn of the twentieth century. Earlier in the nineteenth century the population would have been greater than that, but only in cotton season, since once the crop was in, people decamped in droves out of fear of catching yellow fever or malaria. Yellow fever in particular was so rampant in those days that in nearby Port St. Joe, there's an entire cemetery devoted to its victims.

It was yellow fever that precipitated Apalachicola's most famous scientific advance. Here's what happened. In the 1840s, a local doctor named John Gorrie began hanging buckets of ice under vents in the ceiling of his hospital because he'd noticed his patients seemed more comfortable when they were cool. Eventually he theorized that since yellow fever outbreaks tended to coincide with the onset of hot weather, heat itself might be causing them. If he was right, then keeping his patients consistently cool might turn out to be not just cosmetically but medically important.

But Gorrie had a problem. To test his hypothesis he needed a consistent source of ice. But he didn't have one, because the ships that carried the cold stuff south from New England tended to sell out before they reached Apalachicola. So he set out to find a way to make his own. The result, in 1851, was the first U.S. patent ever issued for a refrigeration machine.

Once he'd protected his invention, rather than pursue his research, Gorrie took a prototype to New Orleans, thinking it would make his fortune. Unfortunately, it didn't, and he died four years later without having sold a single machine. It turned out that his contraption, which worked by running compressed air over water, had a couple of flaws from a sales point of view. First, the amount of ice it could produce was tiny compared to what ships could bring in. Second, and worse, it turned out to be unreliable. Still, Gorrie's invention (which led to the air conditioning that would change Florida forever) earned him such fame that when the federal government allowed each state to put two statues in the Capitol Building, Florida chose Edmund Kirby Smith (a general in the Civil War) and Gorrie.

Now what Gorrie did was relatively recent. Here's a quick storyboard for what happened before his time. Shell mounds found in the area go back ten thousand years and prove that even then, people were eating oysters. In 1528, some Spaniards tried to found a settlement west of where Apalachicola is now, but things went so poorly that they killed their horses, made the hides into water carriers, and left in small boats. Later in the sixteenth century, other Spaniards would claim and keep this whole part of Florida. The English had designs on it for awhile but after 1815, when Andrew Jackson defeated them at New Orleans, they contented themselves with fighting what turned out to be an abortive proxy war, using Indians and runaway slaves.

In 1819, Spain ceded Florida to the United States and Apalachicola changed hands for the last time. Three years later, President Monroe officially recognized the city's potential by appointing a port collector. A year after that, the new port was doing so much business that the government moved its customs house here from St. Marks. In 1828, the town, which had been known as Cottonton (even then, cotton was king), incorporated as West Point. Finally, in 1832, the Legislative Council of the Territory of Florida renamed it Apalachicola.

On the eve of the Civil War, Apalachicola was the third busiest port in the Gulf of Mexico. But after that war, when moving goods by rail became cheaper than moving them by river and sea, the city's economy went into a slump which lasted until late in the nineteenth century, when two industries reinvigorated it. The first was timbering. From the 1880s until the 1920s when the cypress was finished, the river was awash with logs and the port full of ships sending them north to be made into timber and shingles. The other important industry was sponge fishing. It peaked in 1895 when Apalachicola's harvest ranked third in the state, then evanesced from there when the sponge population inexplicably declined to the point where it was no longer commercial.

The one constant that runs through the city's history from its earliest days has been seafood. Though Apalachicola has fine fresh fish and shellfish, what it's famous for is the oyster: a delicacy so slimy when raw that one wonders at the courage of the first person who decided to try it. Apalachicola accounts for 90 percent of Florida's oysters and 10 percent of all the oysters in the United States. If you come into town from the east, you may see harvesters working below the bridge. They're still using two forks to bring up the oysters, not because they're nostalgic but because the more modern approach—dredging—would destroy the grasses sprat need to survive.

These days, I think it's fair to say, Apalachicola is famous for another reason besides oysters, and that's its small-town charm. And yet, in spite of the fact that the oldest cemetery here lies on a main road within walking distance of most hotels and B-and-Bs, very few visitors seem to find it. That's a pity because the place is more than worth the time.

The cemetery in question, Chestnut Street, was established in 1831. It's interdenominational but for most of its existence has been managed by the nearby Episcopal church, which dates back to 1837 and is one of the earliest prefabricated buildings in the country. Besides that claim to fame, the church boasts a functioning organ that goes back to the 1840s.

Chestnut Street Cemetery takes up several mid-city blocks

along Highway 98—a lot of land for a town this size. In contrast with the intentions of Apalachicola's founders, who laid their town out in a grid based on Philadelphia, Chestnut Street has no discernible organization and not a single obvious path. The only exception to the disorder (even the lovely oaks and palms seem to have been placed randomly) is that nearly all its memorials face east so that, as you may know, when Jesus comes down on the Day of Judgment, the resurrected population won't have to turn around.

There are several barren-looking stretches in the back corner of the grounds. That they aren't empty I have on good authority since Dolores Roux, the captivating folklorist who runs a sweet-shop-cum-diner downtown, explained on my first visit here that for many years Chestnut Street has been so full that the only way you can be buried in it is if there happens to be room in your family plot. The explanation for those apparently untenanted stretches is the one that repeats itself in older cemeteries throughout Florida: that the original markers were wooden. You can see one surviving wooden marker, a seventy-five-year-old cypress cross that's already fraying at the edges and will probably be gone a hundred years from now.

Besides being randomly arranged, Chestnut Street is disheveled. Fitful grass struggles for a foothold in patches of exposed sand. The locally made wrought-iron borders that mark family plots are ragged with rust. And though the grounds contain many beautifully carved gravestones, some of them are broken, others are leaning.

And yet, with all its disarray, the place captivates. In fact, for those who enjoy surprises, Chestnut Street may be even more appealing than its done-up cousins. Think of the fun you may have had prospecting through clothes or any other wild assortment of objects heaped on tables. In other words, Chestnut Street's wander-y layout and tousled state may well trigger your inner treasure hunter. There's plenty of unexpected beauty here—some lovely late Victorian carved stones for instance, and a particularly spectacular Woodman of the World memorial, not to mention several interesting and unusual inscriptions. And concealed in the disorder, if you're perceptive, you'll come across dozens, even hundreds, of stories.

Here's one of Dolores's. On a sunny afternoon early in the twentieth century, some families were having a meal at a social club on the river. As the grownups drank and talked, the children were running around playing. Somehow, a little girl named Louisa Brunie fell off the dock. Her cousin and best friend Frank Messina, who lived across the street from her, jumped in to save her. By the time the adults noticed the children were gone, it was too late. When their grieving families pulled them from the bottom of the river, the cousins' arms were still wrapped around each other. You can find Louisa and Frank side by side in Chestnut Street under a double tombstone as small as they were.

There may be even more children's graves here than usual because Apalachicola, being surrounded by water, was particularly a-whine with disease-carrying mosquitoes in the warmer months. For me, the saddest markers in the cemetery other than Louisa's and Frank's lie side by side: "Our Little Son Francis" (another Frank) who was born in 1884 and died in July of 1886, too soon to meet his sister "Little Nell," who lived for six days, six months later. I ache for their mother, losing two children within six months. She must have woken often, longing for even a dead child to hold. The tallest monument in the cemetery—his family must have wanted to lift him as far toward heaven as they could—is for a child: an obelisk dedicated to a little boy named Cornelius, who was born in 1851 and died in 1853.

Though Chestnut Street was officially founded in 1831, I came across one grave older than that. Its stone reads "James Ruan, W.I., d. 1818." I tried to find out how James died but no one knew. The best guess I elicited was that since he identifies himself as West Indian, he probably perished at sea or in one of the shipwrecks that were common on the shallow shoals offshore.

Many of the graves bear locally important names. One of them is "Coombs." James Coombs was a lumber baron who was at one point the richest man in town. In 1905, he built a magnificent house across the street. Five years later, the house caught fire. Because the blaze started in the attic, firefighters managed to put it out before the house was destroyed, but the smoke and heat did so much damage that the next day all Maria Coombs's fine furniture was seen piled, blackened and wet, on the street. She died soon after; it was rumored that the cause was grief. Her husband outlived her by only ten days, struck down, said the whispers, by his broken heart. The Coombs's son William Percy, whose grave is close by his parents', is of interest for his own reason: he used to carry money with his picture on it. The money was perfectly legal tender at the time because in those days, if you had enough gold on deposit with the U.S. Treasury, you could have your bills printed any way you wanted.

Eventually the last Coombs descendent moved away and their ancestral house fell into disrepair. In the 1970s, Bill Spohrer and his wife Lynn Wilson bought and lovingly restored it. Painted a warm yellow, it is now a bed and breakfast.

Around the turn of the twentieth century, probably the most prominent family in town after the Coombs was called Ruge. Herman Ruge was a German immigrant who operated a lumber/seafood-canning business with his sons, George and John. Dolores Roux's mother worked for John's wife Fannie as a social secretary. Her mother's job, Dolores told me, was to write and answer invitations and to listen to Fannie complain about her husband who kept her on such a strict budget that, rich as they were, she was seldom possessed of a pair of drawers. The truth of Fannie's complaint was laid bare for all to see one day, when she fell in the street and her skirt upended. But Fannie got her revenge. After John died, she went out and bought herself a dozen pair of drawers, all at once. She also, Dolores says, availed herself of the charms of two or three further husbands.

Grady is another locally well-known name. Mr. Grady ran a chandler/general store. If Grady doesn't have it, the saying went, you don't need it. One day, the story goes, Grady left his shop in the hands of a clerk. That the clerk couldn't read or write shouldn't have been a problem because Grady's custom was to mark the price of everything on sale at one dot per dollar. When Grady came back, the clerk said he'd sold a particular article for $10. When Grady protested that it should have gone for two, the clerk said, "Well, there were ten dots."

To which, according to legend, Grady rolled his eyes and responded, "God bless the flies."

The inscriptions in the Orman plot are worth looking for. If you know that the Ormans owned the first telephone office in town, and were also associated with the electricity business, you'll appreciate how beautiful it is that so many of their inscriptions reference light.

Groups of local little girls used to be asked to tea at the Orman's. Afterwards, they were allowed to dress up in clothes kept in trunks in the attic and parade downstairs, one by one, for a fashion show. During the Civil War, it's said, the Ormans used to signal the Confederates when it was safe to come into town by putting a barrel on their roof.

The four Hule brothers' graves testify to what that war must have been like for those who fought in it. Two of the brothers fought for the Confederacy, two for the Union. You're advancing across a field. It's hot, it's loud. Your throat burns. Your heart is trying to jump out of your chest. You've just stepped over a body when through the haze you see an enemy soldier, gun at the ready, advancing toward you. Suddenly you can't breathe. The soldier is your brother. Your *brother*.

Chestnut Street doesn't segregate by race, which is why somewhere in the middle of things, you'll find the Fullers, she a freed slave, he a light-skinned black man. The Fullers owned the most prominent hotel in town. For awhile that was because it was the only hotel in town but even after competition arrived, Fuller's was still the traditional destination of choice. The Fullers had no children, so when they died they left the hotel to another couple, a Mr. and Mrs. Jinkins, also African American, who'd worked for them. Dolores, who lived next door to the Jinkinses at the time, remembers the day in 1937 that their house caught fire and her father pulled Bella Jinkins to safety. Unfortunately, he couldn't save her. She died of her burns three days later.

Military graves aren't segregated either nor are all of them associated with family plots. Scattered about the cemetery you'll find both Union (several) and Confederate (some seventy-five) graves. All of them are marked by fading miniature flags stuck into the ground. Some of the graves carry

Confederate flags, some American (not Union); some carry both. A few Confederate graves also display bronze plaques, installed by an organization called Sons of the Confederacy, one of whose missions is to supplement crumbling Confederate memorials with permanent metal ones.

Some of the burials here are identifiably water-related, being decorated with loose conch shells for instance, or carrying inscriptions mentioning ships. One of these is a memorial erected by his crew for a young steamboat captain who died when his ship exploded around him. The explosion wasn't an isolated incident. Steam was dangerous enough that many captains died early. The ones who survived long enough tended to be appointed inspectors when they retired. I noticed at least one inspector; you may find more.

Two facts—that the gates to Chestnut Street are never locked and that it's right in the middle of town—have made it a living part of the community in a way not all cemeteries are. According to Dolores, no one would play with any child who'd just come to town until he or she had climbed the chimney that stands alone in the middle of the cemetery (no one knows where it came from) and hollered down it. Dolores and her friends also used to make up games that involved pretending to be two little girls buried here, twins named Catherina Sofia and Sofia Catherina.

I'll leave you with a pair of inscriptions I found especially intriguing. The first is the tribute paid to a James McKinney who died in 1849, having achieved the same age as the century. No one seems to know who he was and if his burial is any indication, he seems to have had no local family. And yet he must have lived here long enough to establish a reputation because his stone reads: "A good citizen/ A firm friend/ An honest man." Don't you wonder who put those words on his grave, and what James had done to earn them?

Last but far from least, be sure to have a look at the Zingarelli family plot. The Zingarellis emigrated from Italy in the middle of the nineteenth century and set deep enough roots here that you can still find their descendents in the phone book. Their plot struck me for a couple of reasons. The first is that one of the graves has what may be the most beautifully carved vines and flowers in a cemetery that offers many lovely stones. The second is more personal. It has to do with Joseph Zingarelli, who died in 1907 aged thirty years, five months, and ten days—precisely five years younger than my son is now. Even knowing that life spans were shorter then, I felt a stab of grief for Joseph as if he had been mine. Then I read his inscription: "All that which pleases is only for a moment. All that which troubles is only for a moment. That only is important which is eternal" and the words rode quietly beside me all the way home.

SPOTLIGHT: THE RHODODENDRON

It's April 4, 1899, and a tall, handsome white-haired man carrying a lacquered box is walking through the woods near Apalachicola. He's dressed in the dark blue suit he always wears, even at the height of summer. He moves slowly, not because of his age but because he's looking for something: the blossoms of a rare species of ash. His name is Alvan Chapman. He is eighty-nine years old. In three days, at the end of another productive and busy afternoon, he will be dead.

Two years earlier, in an address to the Philaco Women's Club, he had described his life as having been "uneventful," a description that speaks considerably more to his modesty than to the truth. Here are the bare limbs of a tree to which we'll soon add leaves: Dr. Chapman (he was a medical doctor) was the author of *Flora of the Southern United States*, which for more than half a century was the only work on the subject and was, with Asa Gray's treatise on northern botany, the Bible for scientists all over the world who wanted to study American plants. Chapman identified nearly 100 new species, probably a record in the northern hemisphere. Furthermore, a genus of rhododendron and a dozen other plant species are named for him. Besides his many contributions to botany, Chapman was interested in entomology, and generated a good deal of information about southern insects. And he accomplished all this in spite of having had no formal botanical or entomological training whatsoever.

Alvan Chapman was the youngest of five siblings. He was

born in 1809, in Southampton, Massachusetts. His mother was descended from the Ponsonbys, a Devonshire family with claims to aristocracy. His father's family was identified only as from "The North," a designation that in England, in the absence of evidence to the contrary, implies working class.

Chapman was given a classical education, and it stuck. To the end of his life he enjoyed reading Greek, Latin, and French. He even learned German when he was eighty years old, in order to correspond with a scientist in Germany who had expressed interest in his work. In 1830, when he was twenty-one, he graduated from Amherst and the following May went south to tutor the children of a family living on an island off Savannah. After a little time, he left them to become principal of a school on the mainland and to study medicine. In the winter of 1835, a Dr. Nicholson persuaded him to come to Florida, where doctors were in short supply. Dr. Chapman practiced first in Quincy, then in Marianna (where he met his wife Mary Ann), and finally in Apalachicola, where he lived for more than sixty years.

As a boy, other than enjoying the occasional tramp in the woods, the doctor hadn't shown any particular bent for botany. After he moved to Florida though, he grew more and more intrigued with the unfamiliar plants he saw on his frequent walks. At that time, the Florida panhandle was a botanical terra incognita. And since hundreds of species of plants grew there that could be found nowhere else, once Chapman started looking he made discovery after discovery. As his interest in local botany deepened, so did his attraction to parts of Florida well beyond the panhandle. In 1843, for instance, his work led him all the way to Key West, a distance of over eight hundred miles and a punishing drive even now.

From early in his explorations, Dr. Chapman had been mailing specimens to John Torrey, a famous botanist in New York, who in turn passed them on to one of his students: the young and soon to be famous Asa Gray. Eventually, Chapman had sent so many previously unknown plants north that Gray suggested his friend publish a manual of them. When he found his advice ignored, Gray decided to go to Apalachicola in person, his official excuse being to see a new rhododendron

Chapman had told him about. It didn't bother Gray—or maybe it appealed to him—that Apalachicola was so remote back then that the only way to get there was via the river steamer that called in once a week. Here's how Dr. Chapman describes their meeting: "Fortunately he came early enough to catch the pretty witch in bloom. I took him to the reaches where the flower grew. It always looked white to me, but Gray said 'it blushes pink.' He knelt down and studied it. . . . When he arose he came and offered me his hand. 'You are right' he said. 'I never saw this species. I congratulate you on *rhododendron chapmanii*.'"

As you may have gathered from what you've just read, Dr. Chapman had an odd affliction for a botanist: he was colorblind. But not in the traditional red-green way: his problem was that he couldn't distinguish red in any of its shades. This meant that he could accurately describe the color of a red or pink plant only by asking someone else what it looked like. In his later years, he was also deaf, a condition he sometimes downplayed (to the end of his life he was a dapper man, particular as to his aspect and appearance) and sometimes enjoyed because, as he told a young lady friend of his, "if I can't hear people's groans, they won't send for me." He went on to make a prescient statement: "If people did but know it, fresh air and sunshine, just what keeps the plants growing, will keep most of us well. Why, unless it was a case of easing a soul in or out of the world, I did my best practice with hot baths and bread pills."

Asa Gray's trip achieved its goal. After he departed, Dr. Chapman started work on a compendium, and in 1860—he was still in his thirties—the six-hundred-page first edition of *Flora of the Southern United States* was published. The book would see three more editions—the last in the doctor's eighty-eighth year—and be the gold standard of southern botany for generations. Its introduction, explaining to the novice botanist what to look for, is crystal-clear, a fitting testament to the brilliant teacher Dr. Chapman must have been.

In the year of the first edition of *Flora*, the doctor and Mary Ann were living quietly in their big white house next to the cemetery, he botanizing and practicing medicine, she performing her domestic chores. The only shadow on their life together had been the baby they'd lost. But since the doctor considered the two daughters Mary Ann had brought to their marriage his own, the couple wasn't even really without issue.

In January of the following year, Florida seceded from the Union. Six months later the Union blockaded the port of Apalachicola to stop its facilities from being used by the Confederacy. The following April, Union soldiers peacefully took the town. It would change hands several times before the war was over, but always quietly.

Rarely did the war directly impact the doctor. The exceptions were two. At one point, the Yankees threatened to destroy Chapman's papers because he was treating enemy soldiers. They backed down when Asa Gray intervened on his behalf. And once, when the Yankees were considering burning the town, Dr. Chapman persuaded them otherwise.

In spite of its lack of direct drama, the war came close to breaking up the Chapmans' marriage since Mary Ann was a staunch supporter of the Confederacy but her husband, in spite of the years he'd spent in the South, was a confirmed Yankee. Neither would concede anything to the other and soon after the fighting began, Mary Ann moved back to Marianna and stayed there until the war was over.

The doctor did very little botanizing during this period. As the only medical man in town he was often called upon to treat a wounded soldier of one side or the other. And in the scant free time he did have in those days, he was doing everything he could to honor what his father had told him: that if the Constitution were ever attacked, it would be his duty to defend it. Chapman's defense consisted in this case of helping Yankee soldiers who'd escaped the Confederate prison at Andersonville. Typically, escapees would follow the river south until they reached Apalachicola. Then they'd hide in the marsh. That's where the doctor came in. His slaves would tell him where the Yankees were. Then the doctor would wait for dark, borrow a friend's boat—his own had been destroyed—and row the ex-prisoners out to one of their ships.

The war had been over for some time—in fact it was 1887 and the doctor was seventy-six—when Winifred Kimball arrived in town. Her father, who was doing government work in the harbor, had brought his family because he thought Apalachicola would interest Winifred's mother. The Kimballs stayed in the Fuller House which, according to Winifred, was where the locals gathered. Yankee tourists, she said, patronized another hotel, reputedly run (Winifred had probably heard this on the front porch) by "poor white trash."

Winifred's mother, who needed something to do, decided to make a project of the Fuller's neglected garden. One afternoon she was working at the flowerbeds—no doubt with a comet or two of dirt on her cheek where she'd pushed back her hair—when Dr. Chapman, who took his meals there (Mary Ann had died in 1879), approached her, doffed at least his metaphorical hat, and said, "Madam, I see you love flowers." This was the beginning of Mrs. Kimball's, and through her, Winifred's, long friendship with this man who also loved flowers.

When the Kimballs moved to Apalachicola for good (even today, the town is full of people who came on vacation and ended up staying), Winifred began to study botany with Dr. Chapman. She said that whenever they went on collecting expeditions, the doctor would insist on walking ahead with his specimen box because, he said, ladies don't carry.

Winifred must have been a good student. She was certainly a good observer. She described, for instance, in a reminiscence she delivered to the New York Botanical Society, how the doctor always walked with his head slightly down, a habit acquired from years of looking for specimens, and how, when he didn't have his box, he'd walk with his hands behind his back as if he were thinking. She also said that to her his white hair had no taste of snow but was instead "the kind of white hair that age and clean thought give to a man." His eyes were blue, she remembered, and always glittery.

Dr. Chapman and Winifred had many conversations on subjects other than botany. Once, when she asked him about the war, the doctor told her that after Mary Ann left for Marianna, he didn't see her for the next four years though "she sent me four shirts. They were very good shirts and I thanked her for them." "Didn't you miss her?" asked Winifred. "Some," said the doctor, "but those were stirring times."

One day, Winifred told the Botanical Society, she came in when Dr. Chapman was looking at some ferns under his microscope. When he motioned her to the lens, she didn't at first see the appeal of the brown dots he pointed out. She doesn't say whether she told the doctor this or not, but she does remember what he said next which was, according to her, "Behold the hand of the Almighty! The spores of these particular ferns are all coordinated in multiples of four. Never an exception."

When it came to the Almighty, though, the doctor wasn't a conventional Christian. Religion, he once said, wasn't God but rather the perfect love of nature. And for his luck in that respect, we know he was grateful. The year before he died, he took a trip into the countryside to see if he could find a certain species of violet that Asa Gray didn't have in his collection. If he'd come earlier in the season, there would have been plenty, but he'd come late, and most of the violets had dropped their blooms. He searched and searched. He'd given up and was returning to catch his train when just before the station, nestled in a corner of the fence, he found the perfect specimen. He plucked it, took off his hat, and said, "I thank you!" If Dr. Chapman had told me this story, I think he would have looked straight at me, his eyes as blue as a summer sky between clouds, and ended it, verbally or not: "And now do you see what I've been trying to tell you?" And I'd have answered, verbally or not, "Oh yes, yes I do."

4

GLENDALE NATURE PRESERVE AND CEMETERY, GLENDALE

Many of us in the United States will never see a loved one die. But if we do, we tend not to bear our witness at home but in a professional setting, at best a hospice room, at worst a sterile chamber smelling of antiseptic. And we tend to leave what happens after death to the professionals, too. We don't wash our mothers' bodies; we don't dress them. And if we do sit with them, it's only after they've been prettied up by someone else. Maybe it's because so few of us experience death in a natural way that so many of us are so terrified of our own. It's worth thinking about that in the Hindu faith, the drawing of the final breath is seen not only as the culmination of life, but as its happiest moment.

We don't bury our dead naturally either. Instead of simply laying them into the earth, we have them embalmed (to the tune of 827,060 gallons of fluid a year). And it's no coincidence, since embalming fluid is laced with formaldehyde, a substance known to be dangerous, that undertakers die of arteriosclerosis, leukemia, and colon and prostate cancer at far higher rates than the general population.

And after embalming, what do we do? We put our altered loved ones into a non-biodegradable casket (90,272 tons of steel and 2,700 tons of copper and bronze a year) and bury them in a faux park that has to be kept up forever.

The goal of the green cemetery movement is to change all this by returning burial to its preindustrial roots. The concept is well-established in Britain but is just beginning to catch on in the United States, which makes the Glendale Nature Preserve—a 350-acre family farm/green cemetery in the Florida Panhandle—a pioneer in the (pardon the pun) field.

Green cemeteries like Glendale don't look like cemeteries. Instead, they look like undisturbed land. That's because they typically allow only flat markers, and require the area the markers stand in to be left in at least a seminatural state. Some green burial grounds also require that their markers be indigenous stone but since almost the only rock in Florida is limestone and that erodes, Glendale uses round metal disks.

I said "seminatural" state just now because many green cemeteries do permit families to plant (preferably native) flowers, trees, or shrubs. Glendale allows that too but in its case only a few choices will work because the owners maintain the land by fire.

Unsurprisingly, only under very exceptional circumstances can someone who's been artificially preserved be buried in a green cemetery. In other words, cremains (a corporate term, but descriptive) are okay but not embalmed corpses. And they limit burial accoutrements to biodegradables such as wooden boxes or shrouds. Burying people this way, in case you were wondering, doesn't pollute the groundwater since green cemeteries, like all cemeteries, are subject to laws about minimum distances between corpses and water.

Untreated corpses won't cause disease either. In the past, people thought they could, which is why in the nineteenth century so many cemeteries were moved out of cities. But it wasn't true then, and it's not true now. Direct disinfection of corpses, by embalmment or otherwise, is also a nonissue. Since most lethal viruses, even AIDS and Ebola, die naturally within forty-eight hours of the deaths of their hosts, all you have to do to avoid infection is isolate the body for that long.

Before I leave the subject of who can be buried in a green cemetery, I need to add that most of them allow pets. At the time of this writing, for instance, Glendale was home to one cat, eight dogs, and one guinea pig.

Green burial is legal in most states. The only caveat in Florida is that if you decide to handle every step of the process personally then you have to follow a few simple procedures, the main one being getting a death certificate because you can't legally bury someone without it. You're not required to hire a funeral director, though, and as long as a decedent is buried or refrigerated within twenty-four hours of death you don't have to hire an undertaker either.

In other words, if you live in Florida, you can wrap your mother in her favorite blanket, you can write her service, you can dig her grave, and you can lay her into it. You may find taking control of the process a comfort, and the idea of your mother nourishing the earth beautiful. And when it comes your time, you may want it too. On the other hand, you may prefer another way. Maybe you dream of being scattered in the mountains, or on the sea, or under your big brother's truck. Or maybe you want to join the community of believers in a churchyard, or to rest beside your neighbors in your home town, or to pass eternity in the company of your fellow soldiers. But if your deepest desire happens to be to become part of a landscape, then a preserve like Glendale may be what you've been looking for.

Because green cemeteries are kept natural, which usually means they're allowed to overgrow, their managers have had to work out a way for visitors to find their relatives' burial sites. The method they use varies from place to place. Glendale maps its graves using a grid of concrete posts, most of which have bluebird houses on them. John Wilkerson, who with his brother and Wilkerson's partner Barbara, manages the cemetery, says that they decided on hand-mapping using the posts partly because affordable versions of GPS aren't accurate enough but mostly because they think green cemeteries should go back, not forward, in time.

John and his brother Bill reinvented their 350-acre family farm as Glendale Nature Preserve and Cemetery in 2002. Their parents, who'd settled in the area after World War II, had produced besides soybeans, cotton, and cattle, a less familiar product: pine resin, taken from native longleafs. Pine resin, originally called "naval stores" because it was mixed with fiber and used to caulk ships, was the first export of value from this part of the world and was in great demand in Europe starting in the 1700s. When the age of wooden ships passed and with it most of the market for resin, longleafs were logged so brutally that of their original 93 million acres only 2 million remain, most of those planted.

A few first-growth longleafs in Glendale were spared the saw because they shaded a school. John has supplemented these with others, and uses the original trees only if they fall naturally. The originals are so large that after one winter storm, John milled enough lumber from one downed tree to build the workshop/sawmill that stands by the house. Today, he makes caskets of the planted longleafs, inserts shelves in them, and sells them to be stood on their sides. The plan is that when the buyers die, the shelves will be removed so the body of the person who used them can be laid in the resulting casket. Finally, the casket will come home, to be buried near the trees from which it was made.

The cabinet to coffin scheme is ingenious for sure, but what really sets Glendale apart from other cemeteries is its funk art. A pair of missile cones flanking the entrance drive sets the tone, and junk sculptures around the grounds complete it. These offerings come from all walks of life and include *Rustasaurus*, *Three Musicians*, *The Cole Sisters* (who began life as Cole fertilizer machine parts), and *Panda*, who spreads his paws from a bamboo grove so invitingly that someone's decided to be buried behind him.

According to John, the sculptures belong to a sect called the "Rustafarians," whose rituals consist of smoking and watching iron oxidize. Their leader is a "Miss Nessie," who died as ductwork from a factory that made cotton thread and has risen again, this time sporting a mop-bucket head.

My visit here was full of surprises like those. As I got out of the car, John came toward me, shooing off a friendly but noisy crowd of dogs. After we shook hands, he motioned me up a path lined with bowling balls to the steps of the owner-built house where he and his partner Barbara Chudzinski live. The house's inside walls are a crazy quilt of the wood samples that John nailed up for his sawmill customers. The sample display may have been commercially motivated but its effect is definitely art. Sunlight streamed in the high windows behind us as Barbara, a small woman with a big smile, passed us mugs of warm cider punctuated by cinnamon sticks. We wrapped our hands around them and settled in at the kitchen island.

John told me he has always seen himself on a farm. When he went to college he majored in agriculture and in the mid-1970s after a stint in the army, he came home, determined to stay. But the farm wasn't profitable enough to support the family, which then consisted of his parents, himself, and his brother Bill. John's first idea, chufa seed, a bunch grass with an underground nut planted for game like deer and turkeys, did well for a couple of years, then failed. Though the crop subsequently rebounded, it was clear that it wouldn't be enough to sustain the farm permanently. So for supplemental income, John began timbering, cutting first his own trees then other people's.

Before John had come home, his parents had donated land for a cemetery to the Presbyterian church that adjoined their farm. The church immediately fenced the grounds and banned live flowers, prompting John's daddy to describe the place as "a stone orchard; nothing out there you can eat." But in 1997, when the elder Wilkerson died, John and Bill buried him there anyway in a plain (and by the church's bylaws, illegal) wooden coffin. Two years later, when John's mother passed away, they buried her there too.

With both parents gone, John began casting around for ways to save the farm from eventual development. His first idea was to declare it a nature preserve so he offered it to the Nature Conservancy. But the Conservancy didn't think the land was environmentally important enough to keep. They'd buy it, they told him, but then they'd resell it and use the proceeds to save something higher on their list.

So the preserve idea wouldn't work. What would, John didn't know until two things happened. First, a friend decided she wanted to bury her mother on John's land. Then, at about the same time, someone else sent John the URL of Ramsay Creek, a green cemetery in South Carolina. John got in touch with Billy Campbell who owned Ramsay Creek and events proceeded from there. In 2002, the Glendale Nature Preserve and Cemetery opened for business.

We handed Barbara our empty cider mugs and went

outside. After John showed me around his workshop-cum-sawmill and the fifty-year-old bamboo grove his mother planted near the house, he said we'd drive to the rest.

John's runabout is, like everything else he's involved in, quirky, being 30 percent water-powered, a technology that John said was invented in the early 1800s. As we bumped along the road that leads to the cemetery (the road is paved with carpet scraps to keep the dust down), John explained that he picked its location and a couple of other projected burial spots because those were the places he'd never, even in wet weather, gotten stuck.

Past the churchyard where John's parents are buried and past the old growth pines, we pulled up to a hundred-foot fire tower John had moved to the property to act as a landmark. When he asked me if I'd like to climb it, I being the sort of girl who's always loved to climb anything, jumped (almost literally) at the chance. It was a long, and gratifying, way up. When we pushed through the trapdoor that leads into the top, John opened the windows to release the clouds of nonstinging wasps that congregate here every winter. The view was a dazzling mélange of cerulean and green and I wondered how it might change someone who sees it every day.

After a few minutes we climbed down and back into John's rover, then a few hundred feet after the tower we turned left and arrived at the cemetery. I'd have taken it for a straight pine plantation if I hadn't seen the chapel—an open air tin-roofed structure supported by massive power poles. Because the poles are deeply angled, the chapel has an upswept feeling, almost as if it was meant to fly. The altar inside is a salvaged marble counter top. The seating consists of benches, porch swings, and some folding chairs hung in the rafters.

I asked John what kinds of services he'd seen here. Not many, he said, because he tries to give the families privacy. But he did offer a couple of examples. The first was a woman who'd asked for (1) no tears and (2) to be ushered out by the Rolling Stones ("You can't always get what you want") and the Beatles ("Lucy in the Sky with Diamonds"). The other service he mentioned was performed by people who didn't use the chapel at all but ringed the grave with lit candles, then held hands in their flickering light and swayed in unison, an effect John described as eerie.

The chapel stands in the middle of some planted longleaf that John said he'd harvest, if ever, only one at a time and only for coffins. The graves are simple mounds softened by pine needles. At the head and foot of each is a metal disk, hand-engraved with a name and two dates. I noticed that some of the disks' names are endearingly off-center and that a couple of the dates on them had to be minimized to fit them in.

When I visited the cemetery, its population was twenty-eight. Though the first person to be buried here was local—a neighbor of John's named Robert Pridgeon, who died of cancer at forty-six—most of the graves belong to people who lived and died some distance away. One of those people is a lady from Sanford, in central Florida. Two or three years after she died, her family came back with her dog and buried it beside her.

Beside one of the graves was a freshly dug gopher tortoise burrow. Checking its angle, John said he wasn't worried it would be a problem, especially considering the coffin that's in that grave. A man from Deland had built it for his mother, who'd passed away at the ripe old age of 100. To be sure it was waterproof, when he finished building the coffin he'd put fifty pounds of ice in it, loaded it into the bed of his pickup, and driven to Glendale. He arrived dry-bedded and triumphant six hours later.

Eventually, John and Barbara plan to lay out a network of hiking trails through their property but when I visited, all they'd built so far was a boardwalk near the chapel. The boardwalk is made of cobbled-together sections of beach house decks the two of them salvaged after hurricanes. Perhaps the boards remember the darkening sky that sent them soaring. Perhaps they're grateful to have landed here, crossing marshy ground to a little gazebo that overlooks a water scene worthy of a Japanese brush painting. You could lean over the edge and contemplate the birds and that plant whose name you don't know. You could stay for hours.

When Tim Padgett was a baby, his sister Serena, who was five when he was born, treated him as if he were one of her dolls. She lugged him around on her hip long after he got big, and put him down only when the family told her that if she didn't, he'd never learn to walk. She helped him get potty-trained. She taught him to tie his shoes. And when he was killed in Afghanistan, she and his fiancée Stacy picked out his grave.

That the grave would be in Glendale was a given. When Tim had worked on the Wilkerson's farm for several summers when he was in his teens, he and John had become close friends. So when Tim found out he was going to be deployed to Afghanistan he asked John whether he could be buried in Glendale. He was afraid John would say no because, as they both knew, if Tim died in action, the military would embalm him. When John told Tim that they'd make an exception in his case, Tim asked to choose a site. But John wouldn't let him. "There's plenty of time for that when you come home," said John. "Besides," he added, "you'll be burying me, not the other way around."

When Serena and Stacy came to Glendale to pick Tim's grave site, they decided to walk among the longleafs until they came to the place where Tim would be most at peace. They were sure that when they found the place, they'd know it. When nothing happened on their first circuit, Stacy decided to ask Tim what *he* wanted. She told Serena afterwards that right after she'd put the question to him, something told her to look up. When she did, she saw a wild persimmon, standing by itself. And she knew that under that persimmon was where Tim wanted to be.

When Serena called her brother afterwards to tell him what she and Stacy had decided, his voice (if she'd been there she'd have said "he got a funny look on his face") changed, and he told Serena that when they went out hunting, Tim had always looked for persimmon trees because if the fruits were being eaten, it meant there were deer around. Neither Stacy nor Serena had heard that before, so there was no question that

Tim had been helping them. So there he lies, forever, under a persimmon in a sea of pines.

Lying quietly was the last thing you'd have caught Tim doing when he was alive. It was only because energy like his wasn't as rare in the Special Forces as it was in the outside world that his friends didn't focus on that but called him "Hee-Haw" because of his accent. His colleagues at the Fort Walton Fire District had called him "Rubber Band" because he was so quick to react, even when he was off duty, that they had to keep an eye on him or he'd get into trouble. With all that, he was so popular with his fellow firefighters that after he died, they named a road after him: Tim Padgett Way. They chose the name because if a fireman working under Tim questioned his judgment, he'd say: "Listen, I don't know how they do things anywhere else, but around here, we do them the Tim Padgett Way."

Tim had been a daring sort of person ever since Serena put him down. His adventurous spirit as a child led him to spend more than his share of time in emergency rooms. The first episode wasn't entirely his fault. It happened when all three kids were leaning backwards out the car window to watch their mother order food at the Tastee Freeze and Tim lost his balance. He landed so hard he severed an artery. Serena held him in her lap all the way to the hospital, keeping pressure on his head so he wouldn't spurt blood.

The rest of the visits, however, were all down to Tim. When he was three or four and got a Superman cape, he was so sure he could fly he jumped off the top of the recliner and knocked out two front teeth. They were baby teeth but because he lost them prematurely, they didn't grow back in until he was eight.

When he was six, Tim managed to lock himself inside the refrigerator his mother was defrosting. That incident featured his mother and the other kids running wildly around the trailer trying to figure out where those calls of *Mama! Mama!* were coming from. By the time they noticed the refrigerator door was closed, Tim was head to foot blue.

Tim's most spectacular accident happened when he was on a solo hunting trip and fell asleep in a tree stand. When he relaxed, his dead weight broke the strap that held him to the tree. It was a worst case scenario because instead of hitting the ground, he landed hard astraddle the bare branch below him. When he finally did manage to get down, he realized he had no feeling below the waist. He dragged himself to his truck and called for help. At the emergency room, he found out to his great relief that he wasn't paralyzed after all, only in shock because he'd ruptured his urethra.

Later, as an adult, sort of, Tim almost bought the farm. He had driven his pickup to the edge of the water to get as close as possible to a huge gator he'd decided to photograph. He wanted the gator's mouth to be open in the picture, so he poked at it with a hoe. But instead of opening its mouth, the gator took offense and launched itself at the truck with Tim just ahead of him. The gator rocked the truck bed so violently that Tim had to hold on to the sides to keep from falling out. And that wasn't all. He was lucky he didn't fall out since the gator was so angry at being manhandled that it chomped on the tailgate hard enough to leave tooth marks.

When I asked Serena if that last story was pretty much representative of the way Tim was, her face lit up. Oh, yes, she said, he did things like that all the time. She went on to tell me how he used to light firecrackers in his mouth and how once he and his best friend Kevin jumped without warning onto the back of a bull on Kevin's farm. And how one day he'd gotten so bored in class that he stuck a paper clip into an electrical outlet just to see what would happen.

Tim's love for the edge turned out to be vocational. Before he was old enough to drive, his mother would take him to fires so he could offer to help. Also, because the military appealed to him, he joined the National Guard in high school. After he graduated, besides being in the Guard (whose training course he'd finished by then), Tim went to fire college, got licensed as a paramedic, and started work as a firefighter in the same South Walton fire station where he'd volunteered.

When he was nineteen, Tim married his sweetheart Amy. Soon after they got married, under pressure from Amy, he resigned from the National Guard. He and Amy had a daughter, Summer, but not long after she was born, their marriage floundered, and they divorced. Amy is a teacher now, and she and Summer live a few miles down the road from where Tim is buried.

After a year or so as a fireman and emergency room EMT, Tim began to feel that his work wasn't challenging enough, so he volunteered for the Army Special Forces. At twenty-six, he was much older than the average recruit, but he was so outstanding they accepted him anyhow and sent him to Key West for training.

Now, since Special Forces is the elite arm of the army, its basic training is particularly demanding, so much so that Tim was lucky to escape with only a couple of chipped teeth and a busted ear drum. The day he graduated, he called his mother at work. She told Serena he was so weak he couldn't stay focused but every couple of sentences he'd stop and tell her he loved her. Tim also told his mother that his trainers had locked him in a concrete box in freezing weather for so many days he'd lost count, and that every hour they'd come back and hose him down. He added that several times they'd covered his head with a sack while other soldiers beat him, and that when the beating was over they'd march him and other recruits blindfolded into a courtyard then take their blindfolds off and make the group of them salute whatever flag was raised there. On the last day, it was the American flag, and Tim told his mother that that one salute was worth everything he'd been through.

Besides receiving general Special Forces training, Tim left Key West certified as a parachutist, though according to his mother, he didn't like parachuting. What was the point, he said, of jumping out of a perfectly good airplane? He also earned certification as a combat diver and a dive medical technician. As soon as his training was finished, Tim asked to be deployed. When his orders came and he told his family and friends where he was going (Afghanistan), they begged him not to volunteer for dangerous assignments knowing he would anyway because passion was so much a part of who Tim was that nothing—not even death—would take it away from him. Besides, he had a sense of mission. A photo he e-mailed from Afghanistan features a quote from Isaiah that says it all:

Whom shall I send? And who will go for us? And I said, "Here I am! Send me."

When Tim arrived in Afghanistan, he found himself in a setting featuring camels and people dressed like pictures in *National Geographic.* "I see things every day that I've never seen before...." he e-mailed Serena. But, he said, "The food is good, steak and lobster the other night. It's like they try to make up for everything else." In another e-mail, he added, chillingly: "Don't get used to hearing from me so often. I don't think it's going to last."

In spite of the army's best efforts, Tim, like most new arrivals, got sick. The fever and diarrhea subsided in a few days. The dust never did. It coated Tim's tongue and his boots and the weapons he depended on to keep him alive. Tim worried about those weapons along with everything else. Listen to him as he waits to go on a mission:

> I listen to the music playing on my ipod. I close my eyes.... Three hours until we have to go. I try to let my mind wander and relax, but it keeps circling back.... I need to oil my guns again.... We always wipe them down, slather on more oil before we roll. I've already replaced the batteries in my optics. I review the location of all the ammo in my vehicle.... I can feel my heart beating a little faster than usual. It's a simple plan, we just received the op-order about 30 minutes ago. But I know inside that things aren't always simple.... I keep running through the radio frequencies, grids, and routes in my head.... I finally drift off, my eyes blink and it's time to get up. The light is on and I throw the blanket off and step down onto the cold concrete floor. It's night, and it's time to go.

The Green Berets' mission in Afghanistan wasn't only military. It was also to help with building infrastructure like roads and schools and to have hearts-and-minds personal contacts with civilians. Mario Soto, Tim's commander there, remembers him as great at that—a happy-go-lucky guy with a big grin (from childhood, every picture of him featured it; it was, Serena said, how you could pick him out of group shots). Tim,

Soto said, projected his good heart everywhere he went. He told me that Tim not only gave toys to kids but also made a point of doctoring the locals, and not just for war injuries.

One of Tim's e-mails to Serena concerned one of those locals, a boy he'd been seeing for a severe fungus. The end of the story, Tim said, would be sad because unless the boy could wash his clothes and hat every day—impossible in a war zone—the fungus would kill him.

The last phone conversation Tim and Serena had was about another local patient whose tooth Tim had been trying to pull. The valium Tim had administered in lieu of anesthetic wasn't working and in spite of twisting and tugging, he and his assistant were having so much trouble that their patient looked about to pass out every time they helped him up to spit into the bucket that played the role of suction tube in their desert surgery. They were about to give up when the tooth suddenly popped out to the accompaniment of a loud sucking noise. Tim asked Serena, who was working as a dental assistant, if pulling teeth was always this hard. By his description Serena had figured out that the tooth had to have been a wisdom tooth, and she told him it was, but the whole situation struck them both as so comic that they couldn't stop laughing.

Tim had been stationed in Helmand, a southern province that's one of the most dangerous in Afghanistan for several reasons. First, it's home to the Pashtu, who though they've historically been independent-minded when it comes to Kabul, are highly susceptible to manipulation by the Taliban. Second, the majority of Afghanistan's opium comes from here. And third—as if the first two reasons weren't enough—Helmand shares vast desert borders, ideal for smuggling, with both Iran and Pakistan.

Soto remembers something that happened on May 8, 2007, as Tim's last mission was about to set out. After preparing the trucks and equipment, everyone but Tim had mounted up and was ready to leave. When Soto's team sergeant went looking, he found Tim in his tent reading the Bible. When the sergeant told him it was time to go, Tim marked the place and set the Bible back on his bed.

The patrol Tim was on that day was nearing the town of

Kajaki when Tim, who was manning the guns, felt something sudden enter his right shoulder. He said, "I'm hit," and fell. Because he was the only medic on his patrol, he had to coach the others as to how to patch his shoulder. By the time he passed out, the patrol was taking constant fire. Under those circumstances, a shoulder injury would usually have been left for later, but when Soto looked at Tim, he was worried enough to call in a medevac flight. The shooting kept the helicopter from landing for some time but when it finally did, medics strapped Tim to a stretcher and started for a field hospital in Tarin Kowt. But they were too late. By the time they got to Tarin Kowt, Tim was dead. What he hadn't known was that the bullet had passed through the shoulder and severed his aorta. Soto told his family afterward that Tim had been in no pain. He also said that the delay hadn't mattered, that an injury like that would have been lethal even in civilian circumstances.

Tim came home to a hero's welcome, first to Hurlburt Field where eight hundred airmen stood at attention, then to DeFuniak Springs where a crowd of friends and family awaited him, among them his daughter Summer, who had received the presents he'd ordered for her eighth birthday the same day as she learned he'd been killed.

At Glendale, an honor guard of firefighters and Green Berets lowered Tim's casket into the earth. Afterward came a twenty-one gun salute followed by a lone soldier playing taps. Finally, as is customary at military burials, Summer and Tim's mother were each given folded American flags. In addition, his mother received the Florida state flag that had hung at half mast over the Capitol in his honor.

Tim's stone under the persimmon tree reads that he died in pursuit of "Enduring Freedom." That's a fine inscription, but the end of a note Tim sent his family from Afghanistan rings truer: "The desert is vast. You can see a long way. I watched children beg for food, and I gave them all I had."

5

ST. MICHAEL'S CEMETERY, PENSACOLA

Pensacola has much in common with St. Augustine. Both have been capital cities, Pensacola of West Florida and St. Augustine of East Florida. Both have flown many flags—Spanish, British, Confederate, and American—to which Pensacola (which makes sense given its location) adds French. And each legitimately claims to be the "oldest European city in the U.S." Pensacola was founded in 1559, six years before St. Augustine, but St. Augustine has been continuously occupied longer because Pensacola's founders decamped whereas St. Augustine's stayed.

Pensacola's first European incarnation was as Bahia Santa Maria de Filipina, named by a conquistador with the romantic name of Tristán de Luna who, together with 1,400 settlers, claimed it for Spain. Unfortunately, soon after the party had settled in, a hurricane devastated more or less everything and two years later the survivors, beset by famine and Indian attacks, gave up and left. Though Pensacola was still officially Spanish after that, no Spaniards would return to it until Juan Jordan de Reina in 1686. It was he who was said to have named the settlement Pensacola (after the Panzacola, the local Indians).

In 1719, the French and Indians drove the Spanish off. This was the first of the eight times Pensacola would change hands. Three years later, the Spanish reoccupied what was left of the settlement (not much, since the retreating French had burned everything they could).

When the 1763 treaty ended and the French and Indian War gave Pensacola to the British, the city's 722 Spaniards and assorted Catholic Indians fled east to what was still Spanish territory. The British decided to settle in a new location, three miles from the entrance to the bay. This location—Pensacola's third, featuring a street plan set up parallel to the water— would be its last.

Pre-British Pensacola had been a rough-and-tumble place, with its citizens living in constant fear of privateers but by 1783, when the British, beset by the American Revolution, returned the city to Spain, it had made considerable progress toward civilization. In 1821, the Spanish turned Pensacola, together with the rest of their Florida holdings, over to the United States and, for the last time, withdrew.

Forty years later, when Florida seceded from the union, Pensacola's seventh flag, that of the Confederate States of America, was raised over the city. But it didn't fly for long since that same year Union forces took control of the area. They burned so much of the city that by May of 1862, they had frightened nearly all its 2,876 residents away. The Union would control Pensacola for the rest of the war, and nearby Fort Pickens, to which the Union Army had evacuated when Florida seceded, would make history by being the only never-captured Union fort in a seceding state. At the end of the war, Florida rejoined the Union and Pensacola changed hands for the eighth and final time.

Given Pensacola's long history, you won't be surprised to hear that St. Michael's, an eight-acre site in the middle of town, is (with Tolomato in St. Augustine) the oldest cemetery in Florida. Though it wasn't formally established until 1807 (by mandate of Don Juan Ventural Morales, the then territorial governor), British plans of the city prove that the area was a burial ground before that, at least as early as 1778. Pensacolans who died before the British era were buried in another cemetery but no one knows where that cemetery was, other than that it was near the water. Reports suggest it was abandoned because storms kept undoing its burials.

St. Michael's is smaller now than it was when it was founded. A map drawn by a land owner named Brosnahan in 1819 suggests that even by then the Catholic church (they owned the land) had diverted some of St. Michael's to other uses. Because there are no known maps drawn between 1840 and the 1870s, the exact evolution of the cemetery's boundaries after that isn't clear, but one thing is sure: that if a certain Union general had had his way, there wouldn't be anything left of it.

According to a journal written by a volunteer from Vermont during the occupation of Pensacola, a General Dow decided that grave markers might shelter the enemy or impede the progress of fires he intended to set. Consequently, he ordered his troops to knock them down. Some of his soldiers hung back, but others did what they were told and in the process a good deal of the eastern section of the cemetery was destroyed. After that incident, St. Michael's didn't change substantially and an 1884 map of Pensacola shows it in exactly the form it bears today.

Over the course of the twentieth century, Pensacolans forgot the history that lay in their midst, to the point where homeless people were sleeping in mausoleums and unchallenged vandals were prying stones loose to smash other stones. In those sad days only weeds and broken bottles graced the cemetery's walks. Finally, in 1999, an especially brutal series of vandalisms alerted the community to what it was losing. Today, St. Michael's is a jewel set between wide streets in the heart of town. And though the shadow of the civic center falls over it and a freeway rises nearby, inside its quiet confines time seems not to exist. And except for a few hurricane-damaged stones awaiting government reconstruction funding, its grounds bear no suggestion of their former condition.

The path that leads us through St. Michael's wrought-iron entrance gates is what's left of a colonial road that ran through the "new" 1887 section of the cemetery. Alcaniz Street, outside the gates, was also a road in colonial times, as was the road on the eastern side of the cemetery where the parking lot is now.

Some of the burials in this part of the cemetery are layered, new graves over other, older ones. In 2001, a work crew repairing some steps leading down to the Manning/McClelland crypt came across an obviously earlier corpse. Apparently, whoever had installed the crypt had simply ignored it. One of the crew, a young Creole man, reburied the body and painted a cross on the riser of the bottom step near where it lay.

Though St. Michael's lies in the heart of modern Pensacola, it would have been on the outskirts of the colonial town. If you look south toward the bay, you'll notice a slight rise in the ground. The large oaks that lie along it are all that's left of the hammock that sheltered the original cemetery. Well into the nineteenth century, if you'd walked a little ways beyond those oaks, you'd have come to a salt marsh. Marshes flanked the whole city on the bay side until late in the nineteenth century, when they were filled, not to build on but to accommodate garbage.

Except for the oaks, all the trees you see have been planted, among them a number of palms (they don't grow wild in this part of the state). Palms are highly symbolic to Christians: they represent not only Christ triumphant but also the victory of the spirit over flesh. Other trees here also have resonances. Cedars suggest healing, cleansing, and protection; flowering fruit trees, regeneration. For some Europeans, pears have particular significance, since in parts of that continent, a pear tree is traditionally planted to celebrate the birth of a child.

There are a number of clumps of bulbs in this part of the cemetery. Margo Stringfield of the University of West Florida has been studying the horticulture of St. Michael's as part of a larger investigation. She told me that most of the bulbs are lilies and that since planting lilies on graves went out of fashion after the 1880s, you won't find many on sites later than that. Stringfield's students are in the process of dividing the lily clumps, leaving only one bulb in the center. When the divisions are finished, the grave sites will have been returned to their original appearance. The project will then sell the extra bulbs to raise money for St. Michael's ongoing restoration.

There used to be a good deal of statuary here but vandals broke and stole so much of it that what you see today is only the few pieces that escaped: an urn, some small virgins, some lambs on children's graves. For some reason, two striking large sculptures seem to have been left alone. By coincidence, they're identical: a life-sized young woman leaning on a cross and looking sadly down at the earth

Some of the family plots here are enclosed by wrought-iron fences. But since wrought iron was expensive, many families resorted to substitutes. The Vidal enclosure is a good example: from a distance the surround looks like wrought iron but when you get closer you see it's actually wire. Among the graves in this plot is a small shell-encrusted mound, presumably a child's. Maybe the Vidals wanted to use stone but couldn't afford it so they did the next best thing.

Several of the mausoleums in St. Michael's reflect the Victorian fascination with Egypt. There's even one shaped like a sphinx. The most expensive though, built for the family of an Irish timber baron named Sullivan, is a classical affair. But the Sullivan mausoleum, lavish though it is, isn't the most expensive monument in St. Michael's. That cachet belongs to the memorial for John Hunt who died in 1851. It was made by a stone cutter in New Orleans and was said to have cost the family $4,300, a fortune in those days. Hunt's memorial consists of a rope-draped sailor's cross overseeing a marble scroll that proclaims Hunt to be "a Son of South Carolina." What made it so expensive was its use of both brownstone (the cross) and marble (the scroll). The brownstone, by the way, is the same brownstone that characterizes houses in New York City. Its color contrasts beautifully with the sugar-white marble scroll and the slightly darker marble base.

Though St. Michael's covers a relatively small area—only eight acres—it includes 2,750 visible graves. There are many more burials than that. Besides the ones that aren't apparent because an area was used twice, many markers have vanished for the usual reason (they were wood).

Pensacola, unlike Tallahassee, was never segregated by ethnicity so African American graves are mixed in with the rest. Ms. Stringfield pointed out one marker as typical. It was sweetly shaped, like a child's drawing of a house. She also mentioned other aspects indicative of African American burials: a shell at a grave's foot, for instance, or certain inscriptions, such as "Mother is gone but not forgotten." Possibly the most striking African American monument here is the large black marble slab dated 2003 that marks the final resting place of Wallace C. ("The Cat") and Miriam H. Mercer. On it is an inset of a piano (Miriam) and a saxophone (Wallace). What the stone doesn't say is that Wallace Mercer was Pensacola's first African American disk jockey.

Perhaps because of Pensacola's long history as a port, some of the memorials here reflect ethnicities not characteristic of cemeteries elsewhere in Florida. There are, for instance, a number of Bavarians, whose graves tend to feature a particular kind of ornate cross. An exception to that rule is the side-by-side metal memorials to a Captain Christian Pharo and a Gunner Anderson from a ship called *Gertrude*. Both men are identified as Bavarian, and both died in September 1867, whether from shipwreck or fever, the markers don't say.

One of the Italian families here is called Giardina. The family's Papa, a mid-nineteenth century immigrant from Sicily, parlayed hawking fruits and vegetables from a pushcart on the docks into a thriving vegetable wholesale business. For years following his death in 1905, rumors circulated that he'd been a member of the New Orleans mafia and that his death had been a hit. Actually, he died of a less romantic cause—typhoid in the middle of a yellow fever epidemic—but I can just hear the kids saying darn, we liked the other story. Tell them this one's a good story too, worthy of Horatio Alger. Then tell them who Horatio Alger was.

There had been many yellow fever epidemics before the one in which Papa died. Not far from the Giardinas, side-by-side box tombs contain seven members of one family, all of whom died of the fever between 1849 and 1853. One of the tombs contains three children, another two, a boy and girl who died within days of each other. Back then, it took a certain courage just to live here.

Speaking of courage, in the far southern corner of the cemetery, a quiet stone commemorates Delitey Kelly. When Delitey's father enlisted in the Civil War, ten-year-old Delitey and her mother went along as nurses. The little girl wasn't just a spectator. She ministered to fallen soldiers in the middle of battles, was captured and released, and was at Appomattox when the war ended. In 1931 she became the first woman in Florida to be granted a Civil War pension of her own. She was buried in an unmarked grave for almost fifty years until 1998, when her descendents placed a stone in St. Michael's in her honor.

No essay on this cemetery can fail to address the memory of the man who's been called both "king" and "father" of his city. His name was Don Francisco Moreno (d. 1883) and his Spanish inscription proves that someone in his family had a sense of humor. It translates as: "Here sleep two of his wives, some of his children and an unknown Yankee Captain that no one would claim."

Moreno's title as the father of his city comes close to being literal, since when he died in 1883 at the age of ninety-two, he left twenty-seven children, seventy-five grandchildren, and 127 great-grandchildren. His prowess was the result of several marriages. His first wife was Josefa Lopez, whom he married when he was twenty-one. When Josefa died six years later, he married her sister Margarita. Eleven years after Margarita died, he married for the final time. The lucky woman was Mentoria Gonzalez. She was sixteen when she accepted the Don's proposal.

That Moreno was called "king" had to do with the prominent role he played in his city's economic development. He was rumored to have been such an energetic Pensacola booster that before he formally opened the city's first bank, he kept a chest full of gold under his bed so he could immediately lend money to would-be investors. Besides his civic enthusiasm, there were two other reasons for the Don's success: the prestige and contacts he must have drawn from fifty-five years as Spain's official representative in the city, and the fact that for most of his life, he was business-oriented enough to swear allegiance to whoever was in charge at the time.

I say "for most of his life" because when Florida seceded from the Union, the Don, who owned several hundred slaves, took the Confederate side. He lost four sons in that war, two to battle and two to the northern cold. He also lost the 150 pigs the Yankees slaughtered to feed their troops. Still, through all the chaos, he managed to hold on to the bulk of his wealth, and he and his gold-headed cane were to be fixtures in the city for the rest of his life.

There's one other luminary here who can't be ignored—but I won't say much of him now since he has a whole story to himself. He was Manuel Gonzalez, who lived in Pensacola during the second Spanish period. His grave is in a fenced plot near the center of the cemetery. Four palms mark its corners and some of his descendents have placed a bench inside it. Many bricks around the cemetery are stamped with his insignia. Others bear the insignia of one of his sons-in-law, a man named Yniestra.

The Sierras, neighbors in death to Don Manuel, were a prominent nineteenth-century family. The senior Sierra, Eugenio, was a doctor who arrived in 1885 to work in the Spanish royal hospital. He died in 1849 at ninety-nine, having actively practiced medicine for his entire adult life. His daughter married another doctor and she and her husband lie here as well. Around the Sierras are several other family plots, all related to Sierra descendents. If you have time, untangling the generations could be as satisfying as getting what used to be a chaos of yarn wrapped neatly around your facing hands.

A few steps from the Sierras and their kin is a square of white glittery marble. The back explains that James Biddle, who died at twenty-one in 1828, had "at the age of fourteen left his father's house and the delights of home for the irksome and adventurous service of the navy, and sharing the ills of a sickly climate, he became the victim of disease." "This stone," the inscription continues, "is placed as a mark where rest his remains on a distant shore and is the last tribute of affection to a much loved brother."

There are some sights here at St. Michael's that I found especially touching. One of them is a stone near Biddle's that carries the words "Dear Mother," with the word "dear" almost shattered. The stone wasn't broken by vandals—a tree limb fell on it during a storm—but it struck me as poignant that the word "Mother" survived intact. There's also a worn cross for a child that has a dove flying diagonally across it and a gravestone embedded in the roots of a huge oak, as if the earth were trying to take back the person who lies under it. And, for the curious, there's an almost unreadable Spanish stone, clearly early, set in concrete behind the Sierra family plot. Those are a few of my favorite places here. When you visit, you'll find your own.

I've had to gloss over many details of burials at St. Michael's because so many of the details have been lost. But they may soon be known since the cemetery and its surrounding area have been the subjects of a GPS survey by Margo Stringfield and her research team. When it's finished, we'll know for certain what underlies what we can see. This level of historical understanding of a cemetery, Stringfield told me, is as far as she knows, unique in the United States and probably in the world.

Stringfield's is certainly important work. But to me what's unique about St. Michael's aren't the specifics of its history but the way its grounds radiate peace. You wouldn't think such stillness would be possible. Streets run on all its four sides. A civic center and an interstate dwarf it. And yet, if you listen, you'll hear the shush of the ocean in passing cars, and sense the way time seeps into the earth by the way your bones mirror those of the men, women, and children that lie under you, wherever you are when you read these words.

SPOTLIGHT: HOW A YOUNG MAN CAME TO THE NEW WORLD AND WHAT HE FOUND THERE

Don Manuel Gonzalez was born in 1767 in a Spanish port called San Vicente de la Barquera. Since his parents were well-regarded not just in the town but in the whole province young Manuel's prospects were of the finest, yet the older he grew, the more he yearned to escape. The source of his restlessness was almost surely his sea captain uncle, a frequent visitor who was never short of romance-laden stories of America. It's easy to imagine Manuel as a grey-eyed little boy, staring into the flickering light of a dying fire as his uncle describes the tangled forests of that new land and the strange customs of the savages that live there.

Years later, when Manuel was a prominent citizen of Pensacola, he would entertain his own children with tales of his adventures. One of their favorites was the one of how, as a rebellious young man, he had escaped Spain forever. Though most of Manuel's stories have been lost, we know how this particular one went because his last surviving child repeated it to a family historian named Leonora Gonzalez and she wrote it down.

It seems that by the time he reached his teens, Manuel had become so besotted with the idea of a life of adventure that he persuaded his uncle to take him away. Their plan was to go first to Madrid, then via the uncle's ship to Buenos Aires. Accordingly, one winter night near the time his ship was to sail, Manuel's uncle pulled up on the cobbles outside his brother's home. He was riding one horse and leading another, having taken the precaution of wrapping both horses' hooves to muffle any sound they might make. Manuel mounted the second horse and, without saying goodbye to his parents, he and his uncle rode off into the night.

Once the pair got into open country, they unwrapped the horses' hooves and galloped at a good pace along the frozen road, but somewhere on the journey—and exactly what happened we don't know because Manuel didn't say—the two quarreled and Manuel's uncle abandoned him in Madrid.

We don't know exactly when Manuel left that city, but we do know that by 1783, when Spain regained Florida (and a good deal of Louisiana) from the British, he was living in Cadiz. We know that because that was the year he volunteered for the army being raised to go to America. We also know what he looked like at seventeen because his enlistment papers described him as having grey eyes, chestnut hair, and a thin beard. They also specified that he had two moles near his mouth, and another on his cheek.

After what must have seemed a rough crossing to someone who'd never been to sea, Manuel landed with his regiment in Pensacola. Since he stood out among the new recruits, he was soon made an officer. Eight years later, he was named Indian Agent for Spanish West Florida.

"Indian Agent" was an office Spain had created early in its tenure in Florida as the result of a letter a Creek/Seminole leader named Alexander McGillivray had written the incoming governor. The letter was a veiled threat. It suggested that if Spain didn't make itself agreeable to the Indians by provisioning them and allowing them free trade, Americans fleeing the tax increases that were Congress's attempt to pay its war debts, probably would. And if they did, the letter implied, the balance of power in Spain's new territories could shift in unfortunate ways.

Manuel's job as Indian Agent meant spending months riding through the Louisiana interior on paths so narrow that the only way to accompany anyone was in single file, and so complicated that they were marked using not one system but several. In spite of the redundant marking systems, most outsiders got lost, but Manuel, who had a highly developed ability to focus, almost never did. And since he set out on his trips with only a coffee pot (which the family still has) and a sack of corn mixed with sugar, he must also have known where to find game, and which plants were edible and where they grew. Eventually, Manuel learned the local languages so well that he compiled a dictionary of their dialects, a dictionary that has, unfortunately, been lost.

For most of the thirty years Don Manuel (he was given the honorific later) spent as Indian Agent, relations between the Spaniards and the Indians were smooth. Almost every day according to a contemporary account, caravans of hundreds of Indian ponies carrying beef, poultry, venison, and honey for sale would arrive in the Pensacola area. The influence went both ways. Some Indian women learned to spin and weave, and many families abandoned the gathering life and began to till their lands.

Here's a quote from a contemporary review of Don Manuel's military career: "He is known for his fine practical sense, open-hearted generosity, and spotless integrity." The fact that he was cited for integrity probably meant that he hadn't acquired the habit of demanding the *mordidas* (bribes) expected back then by most people in his position. Despite this restraint, he became an extremely wealthy man. By the early nineteenth century, land grants from the Spanish crown had given him the lion's share of Pensacola and the area around it. In 1809, he donated land for a plaza the city fathers named after Ferdinand, the Spanish king Napoleon had deposed. They were patriotic in those days as evidenced by the fact that around that time, they also named many streets after battles in which Spain had triumphed.

In June of 1796, when Manuel was twenty-nine, he married Maria Louise Bonifay. Maria had grown up in a privileged family in Martinique. When she was fifteen, one of the family's slaves warned her mother Marianne that a revolt was imminent and that if she and her children didn't immediately go to the boat that was waiting to carry them to a ship anchored offshore, they'd be killed. Leaving her husband behind— she would never see him again—Marianne and the children boarded the ship and were carried safely to New Orleans. From there, the family made its way to Pensacola where Marianne petitioned for and was given land at the northeast corner of Alcaniz and Government Streets.

Manuel called on the Bonifays soon after they moved to town and soon after that, Maria accepted his proposal of marriage. After Marianne paid Manuel a dowry of seven hundred Mexican pesos and a teenaged Negro girl named Maria Francisca, the couple was united to the delight of all concerned. There's no indication that their union was ever anything but happy.

The newlyweds settled into Manuel's home, Gonzalia, also called Fifteen-Mile House because it was fifteen miles from the city proper. Seven years into their marriage, Spain sold Louisiana to Napoleon and moved its capital, which had been New Orleans, to Pensacola. The arriving governor wanted to make his mark on the town by redoing its entire layout, but when his plan was rejected in Madrid, he contented himself with renaming the existing streets in Spanish (since when the British laid out the town they had, naturally, used English names).

This same governor (who owned a sawmill) set off a real estate boom by granting lots to all comers, with the provision they be built on. In this way, Manuel acquired several new lots to join the four hundred arpents of land he'd been granted as a result of his service in the military and the 1600 arpents of Crown land he had been grazing his cattle on for free (with the rationale of keeping beef affordable).

In those days, Don Manuel and Maria employed a number of stockmen to help them manage their ten-thousand-head herd, stockmen paid mostly in kind—with every seventh calf. A couple of stockman stood out. The first was an older man named José who, always, no matter what the weather, arrived at the hacienda dry. His friends couldn't figure out how he did it, so they finally followed him. It turned out that there was a simple explanation. When he saw bad weather setting in, José would stash his clothes in his saddlebags and ride naked except for his hat and his spurs. Another stockman, Pablo, was never seen to spend anything he was paid. After he died, treasure hunters spent a good deal of fruitless time digging for his gold.

In the first years of their marriage—in fact all the way until 1813—the Gonzalezes enjoyed an idyllic life. They had children they adored. And they both loved to entertain, which they did lavishly. They even kept a stable of fine horses and a private racecourse so family and friends could try their luck.

But in 1813, things changed. For some time America had been asserting a claim to West Florida. Finally, in that year it looked as if President Madison would press his claim by taking military action against Mobile. Mobile being uncomfortably close to Pensacola and the Spanish treasury being depleted, the government called a meeting to warn its prominent citizens, Manuel among them, that an attack was imminent, and to ask for their financial help.

The Spanish had been right to worry. On the 15th of April that year, Mobile fell. But America wasn't the only source of trouble in the area. Around the same time, the British were inciting Indians in Alabama and Florida (using Tescumah, a fine orator) to fight the Americans. The result was Indians wandering the streets of Pensacola offering other Indians and Negroes five dollars for each American scalp.

Though Spain was theoretically neutral when it came to

Britain and America, the governor wanted to discourage the solicitations because he was afraid that all this talk of scalping was leading up to an Indian revolt against white men in general. In this, he was prescient; as it came out later, Tescumah had all along seen his alliance with the British as only the first step. In any case, since Don Manuel was famous for his skill with the Indians, the governor asked his advice. The Don, according to his son Celestino, said, "I should know what to do had I your power," to which the governor responded, "Act then as if you had!" which the Don did and, again according to Celestino who didn't explain the details, the solicitations soon trailed off.

But that didn't end the Indian problem. In August that year (1813), rumors of hostile Indians in the area drove some 553 mostly civilian men, women, and children to shelter in a stockade built by a half-Creek half-white man named Samuel Mims. At noon on August 30, the stockade came under attack and by dusk, nearly everyone inside was dead. The Indians then impaled their victims' scalps on sticks, rode into Pensacola, and presented them for payment.

Andrew Jackson was at home recuperating from a severe bullet wound at the time, but when he heard about the massacre, he got so angry that he put his arm in a sling and rejoined his regiment. After a day's ride he and his men caught up with a group of Indians and, according to Davy Crockett, "shot them like dogs." After several more defeats, the Indians' leader, a man named Weatherford, surrendered to General Jackson. Weatherford said that he himself was ready to die, but he begged Jackson not to kill the women and children who had been hiding, and starving, in the woods since their men had been killed. The general replied that he (Weatherford) had shown such bravery that if he would agree to live peacefully, he (Jackson) would spare even his life. The reformed Weatherford became a respected plantation owner. There's a monument to him north of Fort Mims, Alabama.

The next year, trouble would reach Pensacola from another quarter. While Jackson had been out fighting the Indians, the British had burned Washington. President Madison decided that the key to defeating them would be to attack their strongholds in the south. So in November 1814, he sent Jackson with a force of three thousand men to Pensacola to capture three nearby British-controlled forts—Barrancas, St. Rose, and St. Michael's.

When Jackson and his advance guard reached Gonzalia, which was, you remember, fifteen miles out of town, he found Manuel and his oldest son Celestino at home. Jackson indicated through his interpreter that he wanted Celestino to guide him to Barrancas. The Don said no. Though his life and property were in the general's power, he said, his honor was his own. And he, Don Manuel, would rather pierce his son's breast with a sword than see him a traitor. At which General Jackson is said to have withdrawn his demand, extended his hand to Don Manuel, and declared, "Sir, I honor a brave man." Thus began what would be a lasting friendship.

In 1816, Manuel petitioned for title to the 1,600 arpents of Crown land on which he'd been grazing his cattle, and also for permission to build a market. He was given title to only 800 arpents but his second request was granted and his new market became the center of civic life in the town, especially, according to one of Manuel's descendents, its coffee stand that sold a brew that suited the Spanish temperament: "black as night, strong as love, and hot as hell."

Two years later, Don Manuel again petitioned the Crown for title to the rest of his 1,600 arpents of land. This time, his petition was successful. But the date on which it was granted would cloud the Don's title because of a provision of the treaty by which Spain ceded Florida to the United States.

Most of the treaty impacted Don Manuel and his family positively. It extended freedom of religion and full American citizenship to all inhabitants of the former Spanish territories. It also validated all Spanish land grants made though January of 1818, provided the owners had developed their properties by then. The negative part for Don Manuel though was that it declared null and void any grants made after January 1818, which meant that, since he hadn't developed that land, he would have to fight for his last 800 arpents.

When it was clear the Americans would take over, though many friends of the Gonzalez family left Pensacola for Havana or Spain, Manuel and Maria decided to stay. For one thing, Manuel was deeply invested in the area and neither he nor his immediate family wanted to leave. For another, he was convinced he had a good argument for keeping those 800 arpents because his original petition had asked only for legal recognition of a concession already given him.

President Monroe wanted Manuel's old acquaintance Andrew Jackson to govern the new territory. But Jackson's wife Rachel was against it and Jackson himself wanted to stay in the army, so he wrote the president declining the offer and sent the letter to the post office. But after rereading the arguments the president's delegation had made in their original tender, Jackson decided to leave his decision to chance. If his letter declining the governorship hadn't left the post office, he said, he would go. Accordingly, a fast rider was dispatched to Nashville. When the rider brought the letter back, Jackson crumpled it in his hand and wrote another accepting the post, with the understanding (a concession to his wife) that he would leave it as soon as the government was organized.

In April, 1821, the first-couple-to-be arrived in New Orleans on a boat which also carried their freshly glassed, broad-lace-curtained, upholstered-in-Morocco carriage. Rachel Jackson relished New Orleans: "Great Babylon is come up before me," she wrote. And: "Oh the wickedness, the idolatry of this place! Unspeakable riches and splendor!" But she wasn't so keen on what she saw on the way to Pensacola, pronouncing the landscape sand, pines, yams, and very little else. The only positive statement she made had to do with the magnolias, on whose scent she remarked.

On June 17, 1821, the Jackson entourage arrived at Gonzalia where Jackson and his wife spent ten days (their troops camped at a distance). In July, when Jackson was setting up his government, he offered Don Manuel the position of justice of the peace. The appointment carried an unspecified salary and required its holder to swear allegiance to the United States. Manuel swore, and signed on the line.

Four months after his arrival, Jackson went home, never to return, leaving a subordinate named Walton to govern in his absence. In the spring of the following year, 1822, the U.S. Congress merged East and West Florida, named Pensacola as the temporary seat of government, and appointed W.P. Duval governor. Duval arrived in June and called the first session of the legislature.

While the legislators were making their way to Pensacola, a ship arrived from Havana with a cargo of fruit. The ship underwent the routine twenty-four-hour quarantine for ships arriving between June and October, but its captain didn't report one critical fact: that in the course of the passage two crew members had died of yellow fever. When the ship was cleared and the crew opened her hatches—the trip had been unusually long, some forty days—they found that most of their cargo was rotten. They sent the few fruits that looked sound to market. Eight days later, on July 25, 1822, yellow fever struck Pensacola so virulently that all public buildings were closed, troops were sent to camp in the woods, and many families left their homes and did the same. And in August, rather than risk the fever, the legislature moved its session to Gonzalia. Thus it was that most of the first laws passed for newly merged Florida were passed within the Gonzalez family walls.

Possibly in return for his services during this crisis, Governor Duval appointed Don Manuel quartermaster general. This was a highly powerful post since its role was to oversee supplying the military. By this time (August 1822) the Gonzalez operations included a thriving brick-making concern, evidence of which survives to this day in the form of Gonzalez-stamped bricks to be found in many older buildings and in the funerary architecture of St. Michael's.

The greatest excitement at Don Manuel's from that period until the end of his life, besides getting final title to all 1,600 arpents, was probably witnessing the marriages of his ten children. When he died in March of 1842 at age seventy-five, he was so beloved locally that the morning he was buried, stores and businesses closed their doors in his honor. His *Pensacola Gazette* obituary, a lovely specimen of Victoriana, radiated the esteem in which the town held this boy who had left home penniless in the middle of the night: "There never was a man in whom were more perfectly blended than in the deceased, the soft and tender virtues of the husband, the parent and the friend, with a high toned and lofty sense of honor and integrity." "Peace to his ashes," concludes the obituary. To which we can only say "Amen."

PART II

NORTH CENTRAL AND NORTHEAST FLORIDA

6

MICANOPY HISTORIC CEMETERY, MICANOPY

Micanopy, just south of Gainesville, is the oldest continuously settled inland town in Florida. Its earliest residents were Timucuans, followed in the mid-1700s by Seminoles, whose capital, Cuscowilla, was centered near the intersection of present-day Cholokka Boulevard and Ocala Street. In 1821, the year Florida became an American territory, Edward Wanton built a trading post here. The post attracted more settlers to the area and soon, like mushrooms after rain, shops and small businesses sprang up to serve them.

In 1835, the Seminoles went to war against whites over the Indian Removal Act. To protect the population, the federal government built first Fort Defiance then, when it burned down, Fort Micanopy. Both forts are gone now and no one knows where they were. They must have served their purpose though, since the only local casualty of the Seminole Wars was an army wife named Mrs. Montgomery (no relation to the Lucius you'll be hearing about) who was killed in an ambush while being convoyed from Fort Micanopy to Fort Wacahoota.

Micanopy takes its name from Chief Micanopy (d. 1847), one of the few Seminoles who stayed in the area after the wars. The town was originally called "Wanton" after its founder, but—perhaps because "wanton" had the disadvantage of being synonymous with "slut"—after a period in which both names were used, "Micanopy" prevailed.

Micanopy prospered between the turn of the twentieth century and World War II, but so few people returned from that war that it went into decline. Finally, in the 1960s, the town got a new lease on life when hippies, artists, and craftsmen from Gainesville moved there, attracted by its small town charm. And almost half a century later, Micanopy is still charming and still a small town. Its population hovers around seven hundred, roughly the same as it was a hundred years ago.

Micanopy's appeal has something to do, I think, with its lack of pretension. It boasts only one grand residence—the Herlong Mansion, now a bed and breakfast—and one commercial street, tree-lined Cholokka Boulevard. And its "commerce" consists not of malls but of dusty antique shops full of interesting oddities, an antiquarian bookstore, and two or three little restaurants patronized as much by locals as tourists. Among the locals, I know an antique store proprietor who absolutely never misses the sandwich-shop-cum-ice-cream-parlor's Thursday special: chicken and dumplings.

Besides the Micanopy Historic Cemetery, two other interesting burial grounds grace the area: Haynes Memorial Historic Cemetery, home mostly to African Americans, and Oak Ridge in nearby Rochelle. Oak Ridge was officially opened in 1865 on land donated by Madison Starke Perry, the then governor of Florida. Perry—perhaps the only politician on record who can claim a city for each of his names—is buried there, as are a number of Confederate soldiers.

The Micanopy Historic Cemetery is on Smith Street, a longish walk or a short drive from Cholokka Boulevard. You'll know you're in the right place when you see the brick arch proclaiming 1826, the year the cemetery was founded. The Micanopy Cemetery Association, a nondenominational citizen's group, has run it since 1905.

The association's records can be found in the archives of the Micanopy Historical Society, and they make fascinating reading. They include, for instance, a 1906 sexton's contract in which one F.R. Sadler agrees for the sum of 108 dollars per year to rid the cemetery of debris during the first week of each month unless prevented by bad weather (in which case as soon thereafter as feasible); to use surplus earth from new graves to fill any plots which have subsided; to keep the stones in plumb (and if he can't do it alone, to hire an assistant); and to refrain from throwing leaves or trash over the wall. Instead, he is to burn them in an inconspicuous area and remove the evidence afterwards "for it is unsightly." In return for the satisfactory completion of the above (and other) tasks, the Association contractually agrees to send grave-digging jobs Mr. Sadler's way.

According to the Cemetery Association's bylaws, the grave sites here belong to their inhabitants, so when you're buried in Micanopy, you become king or queen of your own little country. Some people say you won't be accepted by the community unless you've declared your commitment to such permanent citizenship. Diana Cohen, who curates the Historical Society's archives and has lived here almost thirty years, told me that the locals shunned her until she bought a cemetery plot. After that, she said, they considered her one of them, and she and a friend of hers often talk about how when they're dead, they'll lie side by side and gossip about the rest of that ex-recalcitrant lot. Ms. Cohen also commented that in the North, where she grew up, what people care about is who they'll be buried near, whereas here in the South, what seems to matter isn't your neighbors but that your individual soul has a resting place—in Ms. Cohen's case the cemetery we're about to visit.

Shady paths featuring live oaks festooned with pale green moss invite you into the grounds. Some of the oaks are so large that if two large men were to stand on opposite sides of the trunks and reach around, their fingers wouldn't meet. Not only that, but if you're lucky enough to come in spring—early to mid-March in this part of Florida—explosions of pink and white azaleas will leave you in no doubt as to where the state got its name.

You may notice (if you don't, your feet will) that for a small town cemetery, this one covers a lot of ground, so much ground that even after all these years, it's not full. But unless you live here, don't bother asking. When too many tourists did, the town decided, in the interest of historic preservation, to limit new burials to people who died with Micanopy zip codes.

Whether we can be buried in a cemetery or not, though,

I think most of us who visit want to leave feeling less the stranger than we did when we came. That's where inscriptions come in. Sometimes all a stone tells us is a name and two dates. But sometimes—and this is the fun of wandering—we come away with a real sense of who this person was. Also, the sum total of a cemetery's inscriptions can be revealing. We can go home knowing which extra-local events mattered here (which wars, for instance), and also, by reading the causes of death, what the area's health hazards may have been.

In most of premodern Florida, standing water triggered outbreaks of malaria, cholera, and yellow fever almost every spring. But here in Micanopy, in spite of the fact that a few gravestones mention "bilious fever," water seems to have drowned more people than killed them by disease.

Micanopy's most infamous drowning happened in 1871 when an excursion ship called *The Flying Cloud* capsized on Orange Lake. According to eyewitnesses, a man named Frank McIlvane caused the accident by dipping the sails in the water "to scare the girls." The first two times he did it the ship righted itself, but the third time it capsized. Two of the seven victims of that incident (some say three) are buried here. You'll come across a number of other inscriptions that mention drowning as well. I feel especially sorry for the several mothers who lost children this way, starting with Mrs. Emerson, whose ten-year-old son Roy drowned in Levy Lake. Her particular ordeal came to life for me when I heard that Emersons are still living in the area, and still on Emerson property.

Here, as in most cemeteries, you'll find war dead. Some Civil War graves are marked with two stones because the memorials the Confederacy had promised its fallen tended to arrive so belatedly that by the time they did many soldiers' families had erected their own. Most families abandoned the extra memorials—several are lying against a tree outside the Micanopy Museum—but a few took them to the cemetery. Just a couple of years ago, a hundred and fifty years after the fact, the Powell family rescued its ancestor's stone from the museum and installed it beside the original.

The most prominent citizen whose memorial mentions World War I is Leon Thrasher. A small man whose nickname was "Skeet" (as in mosquito), Thrasher was famous for developing a state-wide system of paved roads to replace the almost entirely unpaved ones of the time. A single World War II casualty, Joe Chamberlin, lies here, as well as a few men and women who died in other wars.

Because Micanopy was never a wealthy town, its cemetery doesn't have a lot of statuary. The largest is the angel that watches over Annie Barr. But that doesn't mean there's not plenty to stimulate the imagination. Take the side-by-side graves of John Ley and his wife, both of whom died around the turn of the twentieth century. John Ley was a Methodist minister whose stone describes line after line of his good works finally concluding, "Servant of God, Well Done." His wife Martha's inscription, by contrast, consists of one sentence: "She hath done the best she could." Since Martha outlived her husband by seven years, the inscription can't be his verdict on her life. So whose was it? And "The best she could" seems unfairly judgmental, considering the fact that she lost three children, one at under a year, one at a year, and a third at three. Couldn't the writer have praised her courage instead? Then there's the case of Dancy Hall who died in 1851, leaving "a husband and eight children." One wonders what happened to the children when, a year later, her husband died too.

One don't-miss grave belongs to little Susie King, who died in 1897 when she was twelve. It's not the grave that makes Susie unforgettable. It's the diorama—when I last visited it consisted of plastic figures—that introduces it. There's a story behind the display. The empty glass case by Susie's grave once contained a stone lamb. After it was stolen, Micanopy's school children took Susie on and it's they who arrange and tend the scene you see. Beside Susie is a faint brick outline. That's where her sister's baby, who died at birth, is buried. That the baby has no stone suggests the family may have been poor (for most of Micanopy's history, anyone here who died destitute could be buried without charge).

The town's oldest grave belongs to a James Martin, who left this life in 1826, only five years after Edward Wanton founded his trading post. His wife Minnie who died six years later is also buried here. Unfortunately, no one alive knows anything about them beyond what's on their stones. It's enough to make you want to leave some notes behind so that hundreds of years from now, you won't be that unknown name.

Luckily, Micanopy's been small enough for long enough that most of its deceased occupants *are* known. One of the cemetery's larger family plots belongs to the Thrashers. A twinkly long-time resident, John Thrasher III, says there have been Thrashers in Micanopy since 1876, when his grandfather, who was twelve or so, moved here with his family. After clerking for ten years in Benjamin's Mercantile Store, the boy—now a young man—founded his own operation. When he retired in 1931 to deal in cattle, mules, and land, he passed the store on to his son, Thrasher's father. Thrashers ran the store for the next forty-two years until Thrasher sold it and the fenced area around it (where his grandfather had traded livestock) to the town of Micanopy for a museum. The new small building on the far side of the store's yard, by the way, is home to the Historical Society Archives.

The wildest character in the Thrasher family, according to John, was his Aunt Rubie, who died in 1960. Before John's school teacher mother married Rubie's brother, she and Rubie had been close friends. But then, in 1914, the young couple came back from their honeymoon to live with the young man's parents and Rubie, who was still single. On the couple's first day home, Rubie set the breakfast table a place short, and when her new sister-in-law came downstairs, she told her there was nowhere for her to sit because she, not being a member of the family, didn't belong there. And that was just the beginning. Life with Aunt Rubie turned out to be so difficult that the newlyweds lasted a year then left the family home to board with the Montgomerys.

The following year, 1916, Rubie married and moved to Georgia. Two years later, her husband died of gas inhalation (some family members suspected suicide) while Rubie was visiting her parents in Micanopy. Rubie lived at home after that, first with her parents then after 1939 when they died, alone. She hardly ever went out except in winter when she'd cross the street to the store to warm herself at the kerosene stove.

During this time, she was hospitalized several times for mental breakdowns and taken to the Mayo Clinic, which didn't seem to know what to do with her.

Possibly because Rubie often forgot to eat, she used to faint on the street. When this happened, whoever found her would deliver her to Thrasher's mother, who'd care for Rubie until she could find someone else. At one point, a Micanopy family complained publicly that the Thrashers were abusing Rubie, to which the Thrashers said, "*Fine, you take her.*" When the family did, according to John Thrasher, Aunt Rubie proceeded to make their life a living hell. She'd sit there like a princess and expect to be served and picked up after and, he said, to add insult to injury she'd complain loudly when things weren't to her liking.

One day I was telling a friend about the Thrashers' troubles with Rubie and she said, of course, every family has a crazy aunt. And that's, I think, one of the most rewarding things about going to cemeteries; that the more we visit, the bigger and more entertaining our family gets, as over and over again we find not strangers but ourselves.

SPOTLIGHT: THAT MICANOPY AFFAIR

One of the more notorious occupants of the Micanopy Historical Cemetery is Dr. Lucius (H.L.) Montgomery (d. 1924), who for many years practiced medicine in partnership with his father. The senior Montgomery (also named Lucius) had trained as a surgeon on a battleship during the Civil War and was, unlike his son, eminently respectable. We know he had moved to Micanopy by 1854 because that was the year he became a founding member of the local Presbyterian church. He died in 1914 and is buried by his wives—Madora, who was only eighteen in 1870 when she drowned in Orange Lake, and Lou who in 1876 gave birth to Lucius. The family home stood in an orange grove behind the ornamental brick wall you can still see on Smith Street.

The younger Lucius's childhood passed by unrecorded but not so his adulthood. His philandering got him into some public, and highly entertaining, trouble and his drinking landed him in jail on at least three occasions. I'd assume that since no one ever said the doctor was crazy, whiskey had to have been a factor in his putative stark-naked ride down Cholokka Boulevard one afternoon.

In spite of the preceding, of which we'll hear more in a minute, Doctor Montgomery was reputed to have been a talented doctor. He was also a talented, some would say, huckster. As a sideline to his medical practice, he sold a patent medicine of his own invention that he called "Tropical Imperial Tablets." His ads pitched Tropical Imperial to women "in all states of bad health, especially with pains in the back and ovaries," asserting that after inserting these tablets, "weak and delicate ladies will be surprised at the tonic effect received." Although Doctor Montgomery's tablets may have in fact been helpful for fevers and so on, his customers understood that their true purpose was contraception, something that would, given the religious environment of the time, have been impossible to advertise openly.

The ads for Tropical Imperial claimed that its potency was guaranteed by the government "under the Food and Drug Act of 1906." To this institutional warranty Doctor Montgomery appended one of his own: that if any pills arrived crushed or broken, the customer should save the powder and pieces until they filled "three or four boxes" then ship them back. He would then, gratis, remake them into tablets and return the result.

The formula for Tropical Imperial is in the Micanopy Historical Society archives. It involves quinine, bismuth, gum Arabic, sugar, starch, and last but not least, Listerine. The trade it represented must not have been *too* profitable since after the doctor died, his widow, Geneva, tried to sell the formula to a family friend who said he wasn't interested. Neither, it turns out, was anyone else.

Besides being an inventor, the doctor had a musical side, manifested especially when he was in jail and had plenty of time. His musicality—though for all we know it may have been broader—consisted of ditties he wrote for the burlesque.

One of these songs suggested an encore involving a Maltese cat and some double-entendres regarding feline care.

With this background, we arrive at the doctor's first and only public airing as a reprobate: the 1889 Presbyterian church trial, dubbed "That Micanopy Affair" by the Gainesville newspaper which must have sold briskly since almost every issue contained charges and countercharges launched by the parties involved.

The Micanopy Affair began when Presbyterians felt forced "in order to maintain the honor of Christ's Church," to prosecute Dr. Montgomery for adultery because potential congregants were refusing to join the congregation because of rumors concerning his escapades and some elders were threatening to leave it for the same reason. Their immediate case, the "affair" in question, involved a comely orphan clerking at the store.

One afternoon, after the hearings had begun, the doctor, who had been ranting for some time against what he described as unjustified attacks on the young woman's honor, threatened Reverend Shearer on the street with a whip. Shearer reported the incident to the sheriff, who sent assault charges to a grand jury. The jury validated the charges but the sheriff—who had in the meantime changed his mind—overruled its verdict, so the Presbyterian conclave added "speaking abusively to a clergyman in pursuit of his official duties" to its original charge of adultery.

A spate of letters to the paper followed the incident on the street. The doctor, railing against the assault on the young lady's name (though not denying the adultery itself), claimed he had given Shearer "a good cowhiding." Besides that, he said, the church should vacate the verbal abuse charge because he, the doctor, had examined the session books and not found any duty assigned to Shearer which he, Shearer, might have been pursuing at the time the doctor abused him. The doctor also opined that Shearer was an agent of Satan and had been "evolving downward instead of up." In response, the reverend wrote an article that began by outlining the doctor's infamies and went on to assert that he had in fact been acting in the line of his duty and that furthermore, "the cowhide never struck me at all else he (Dr. Montgomery) might not have come out as well as he did."

Before it was over, the Micanopy Affair would produce a good deal more of this kind of thing. A young man who worked for the doctor, one "little" Mac Curry was rumored to have been the one to ice the case against his former employer (he was fired when it broke). This rumor was supported by an article published under Curry's nickname ("Bootlick") in the Gainesville paper, in which he said that he knew the doctor and the young lady had been in his bed on several occasions because, having "pinned the covers different ways," he had returned to find them disturbed. That "Bootlick" had been involved in making the case against the doctor was confirmed by a letter from a church member who said he had heard him ("Bootlick") testify to the conclave that he had come into his room one day to find the young lady in question reclining on his bed and the doctor sitting on it beside her.

Set against this was a second article, also supposedly authored by "Bootlick," denying authorship of the first, and ending with the statement that while "'Bootlick' doesn't fear the allegations against him are intended to cause him PERMANENT damage . . ." the writer of the Gainesville piece "shows so much 'Bile' that, being something of a physician himself, 'Bootlick' recommends one dozen Smith Bile Beans, taken before going to bed, and one ounce of Quinine taken in broken doses afterwards as a Tonic only." Accompanying this second article was a letter signed by several church members, reporting that when they went to see "Bootlick," he denied everything.

Besides the controversy surrounding "Bootlick," there was another, even stranger one swirling around one J.M. Quarterman, who was said to have authored an unsigned article in a new Micanopy paper called *Lake View*, that recapped the case against the doctor and reported under the headline "An Elder Suicides" that Doctor Montgomery, having grown despondent over the above-outlined facts, was now no more. This article was followed by a flurry of testimonials from citizens denying both the facts of the case and the fact that the doctor was dead, as well as a note from the decedent himself saying that when his wife received condolences, and apparently she had received several, "it has been my good fortune to be able to reply to them." What ensued next was that in this same paper, Quarterman denied authorship of the suicide article and said he suspected one of his friends had started this rumor against him, expressing his disappointment in people he'd previously thought "as fair minded as the ordinary mortal one meets in a day's ride."

There was also the question of the doctor's wife. According to the doctor and to a letter in the paper supposedly written by Mrs. Montgomery (some people thought the doctor had written it himself), the Rev. Shearer had improperly upset her by calling on her to discuss the alleged adultery before he had even talked to her husband. In answer, Shearer, while admitting he had called on Mrs. Montgomery, claimed that he had done so only after the doctor had told him he had discussed everything with his wife. He added that he would surely have seen the doctor first, if the doctor hadn't been avoiding him.

From the above, you can imagine the stir the scandal as played out on the streets and in the papers, must have caused at the time. And if that hadn't been enough, there was a persistent rumor going around that it was the doctor who persuaded the young lady in the case not to testify. In any case, she didn't—not being a church member she didn't have to—which resulted in the church assessing a rather light penalty in the end.

"That Micanopy Affair" wasn't the last time the doctor would land in the papers. In June 1912, two articles about him appeared within a week of each other in the *Ocala Star Banner*. They were headlined, respectively, "Micanopy Man Causes Excitement in the Metropolis" and "Micanopy Man Runs Amok."

The first of these incidents was probably the more spectacular. Apparently, the doctor had become increasingly disorderly while visiting a young lady and her mother in Ocala, and when the women threatened to call the police, he pulled a gun on them and proceeded to slash the telephone wires. The daughter ran off and returned with a policeman who lived a few blocks away. But when the policeman reached into the doctor's back pocket for the gun, he came up with a bottle of whiskey instead, which gave Montgomery time to draw his weapon and threaten the policeman with it. The newspaper reported that at this point "the officer's life was . . . in peril and that it was an encounter whereby the agility of each of the men was pitted against the other." Luckily for him, the policeman turned out to be the more agile and the doctor was arrested. When his friends bailed him out, the doctor wanted to demand his gun back but his friends talked him into giving it up.

The second incident was even more action-packed than the first, which explains the use of the word "amok" in the headline. "After exceeding the speed limit and damaging his auto" said the *Star Banner*, "the doctor . . . went to Carmichael's downtown saloon and raised a rough house. When the Marshall went to arrest him, he drew his gun and caused the officer quite a tussle. After the Marshall booked him into the city jail he was given the freedom of the corridor but hardly had the key been turned on him when he began an attack on two or three negro prisoners. The Marshall tried to put him in a cell but was met with another assault. He called backup who tried to reason with the doctor but was also attacked. Being used to this sort of business, the officer hustled him (the doctor) into a cell where he will probably remain until morning." It's clear that the doctor hadn't learned much of a lesson from the first incident since a week later he had already rearmed himself.

The two fracases I've just described weren't the only times the doctor had been arrested. In the Micanopy Archives there's a 1916 letter to a friend in which the doctor asks that his shaving implements be brought down to the jail. It mentions his familiarity with the dinners there and also reveals his sense of humor: "The hone (blade-sharpener) is wrapped up in brown paper in the bottom drawer of bureau in the bed room," the doctor says, and follows that instruction up with: "Don't bother that long-barreled 22 pistol in there, damn you!!!" I might also cite the words of the doctor's newest burlesque song written out in the letter, but you'll have to take my word for the humor of those, because they aren't immediately printable.

To give Dr. Montgomery his due, it's only fair to report that he was popular enough with the locals that some of them defended him in writing during the Micanopy Affair (though no one spoke up in the later incidents). But it's not the doctor's virtues that have kept him newsworthy. It's his faults. My grandmother used to say that a lady should be in the paper only three times in her life: when she's born, when she marries, and when she dies. In this respect, as in so many others, the doctor was no lady.

7

THE HUGUENOT CEMETERY, ST. AUGUSTINE

In Miss Adams's fifth grade class in Mill Valley, California, I learned that St. Augustine is America's oldest city. Fair enough for fifth grade, but the truth is more complicated. St. Augustine is oldest only if you add "continuously settled" and if you're counting only Europeans. The first of those to settle the area—excluding the French, who had a fort nearby—were the six hundred colonists who arrived with Pedro Menéndez de Avilés in September of 1565. Menéndez named his city-to-be for St. Augustine because it was on Augustine's feast day that the expedition sighted land.

Within weeks of their arrival, Menéndez and his men, out of concern for the safety of Spanish treasure ships bound for Europe, attacked Fort Caroline, killing most of its inhabitants. They were also responsible for the deaths of over three hundred Huguenot would-be settlers who had had the bad luck to run aground in Matanzas Inlet (named for that incident). Since the Huguenots, whose group had included women and children, hadn't been soldiers, Menéndez couldn't claim that slaughtering them had been militarily necessary so he used religion (he was a devout Catholic) to justify what he'd done, explaining that it wasn't Frenchmen he'd killed but heretics.

And in fact, Menéndez was as interested in religious as he was in political domination. Soon after his arrival, Jesuits under his protection set about converting the population and soon after that, Catholicism was proclaimed the state religion of Spain's new possession.

In spite of the expulsion of the French and the efforts of the Jesuits, life in early St. Augustine was difficult. Indians were a constant threat, and so were English pirates, who burned the city several times in its first century.

In 1672, the Spanish began to build the Castillo de San Marcos as a hedge against possible hostile incursions by the British, who by that time were an established presence in the Carolinas and Georgia. It turned out to be a good move because in 1693, with the Castillo nearly complete, the British attacked the city from the sea. When the first attack failed, they tried again, but the second attack got no farther than the first. Some say what thwarted them was the fact that the Spanish had built their fort using a conglomerate called coquina. Coquina isn't hard like stone. Instead, it's so soft that British cannonballs, rather than reaching the inside of the Castillo where they could have done some damage, lodged harmlessly in the walls.

In 1763, the Treaty of Paris that ended the French and Indian Wars gave the British by diplomacy what they hadn't been able to win militarily. But twenty years later, after the British defeat in the Revolutionary War, the second Treaty of Paris returned Florida to Spain. The character of St. Augustine had changed since the first Spanish period. The aristocratic Spaniards that once dominated it had been largely superseded by lower-class Minorcans, former indentured servants who had moved north to St. Augustine from a failed British development in New Smyrna.

In 1819, Spain signed the Adams-Onis treaty, ceding Florida to America. In 1821 when the handover actually took place, large numbers of politicians, bureaucrats, landed gentry, settlers, failed plantation owners, land speculators, and tradesmen moved to the new territory, and especially to St. Augustine.

That same year, the city suffered its most serious yellow fever epidemic to date. The epidemic's timing was no coincidence since the newcomers had no immunity to the disease, unlike the natives, most of whom had contracted mild cases of it in childhood. The first recorded person to die in the outbreak was a recently appointed judge named Thomas Fitch.

His demise was quickly followed by many others. In the middle of the epidemic, one soldier wrote of "thirteen or fourteen [deaths] a day," and estimated that by the time of his letter, 132 civilians and forty soldiers had died. A newly arrived priest conducted ninety-five funerals in his first two months. Eventually, the pace of death accelerated so quickly that the bell the church traditionally rung when someone died was silenced out of respect for the ill and failing.

It was characteristic of that particular epidemic that young men in their prime were as likely to catch the fever as anyone else. William Worthington wrote of one such, his friend Jean Penier, who died leaving a wife and children: "He was at my house Tuesday night, gay . . . and delightful. Alas on Thursday night, he breathed his last." By the end of 1821, the city fathers had had to establish what is now called the Huguenot Cemetery because Tolomato, St. Augustine's only official burial ground at the time, was refusing to accept victims of the epidemic who weren't Catholics.

Paradoxically, within a few years of the end of the epidemic, St. Augustine became a tourist destination for droves of invalids suffering from respiratory diseases. One explanation for the city's popularity as a spa may have been that until the mid-1800s, it was the warmest place in the continental United States that offered lodging (only boarding houses at first, but by the 1840s, hotels like The Planter and Florida House, both of which later burned down). Though those first visitors may have come for the air and sea breezes, we can assume they found other pleasures when they arrived, like the sweep of bay out from the fort, like its water sometimes calm, sometimes glittering with sun, wind, or stars.

Pleasures aside, whether visiting St. Augustine would actually help you get well depended on the nature of your disease. Sufferers arriving with bronchitis tended to recover and go home, but those unfortunates hoping to conquer tuberculosis—the nineteenth century's prototypic wasting ailment— tended to die. The Huguenot Cemetery is home to many such accidental citizens, called "strangers" even in their newspaper obituaries.

In 1845, Florida became a state. When the Civil War broke out, though Florida aligned itself with the Confederacy, St. Augustine was captured by the Union early on and remained under Union control until the war was over.

In the late 1870s, when Henry Flagler visited the city, he was so repelled by the hacking coughs of its tubercular visitors he couldn't leave fast enough. But after a second, honeymooning, visit in the 1880s, he decided to turn St. Augustine into a refuge for the rich—in his words "the Newport of the South." On the theory of "build it and the wealthy will come," he constructed two ornate hotels and bought a third. And when, in the late 1880s, his railroad finally linked St. Augustine to the northeast, the rich did come. Around the turn of the twentieth century, they deserted it in favor of south Florida, but by that time the city was so well established as a tourist destination that all that really changed was the composition of its visitors—middle rather than upper class.

Reflecting the fact that in the Victorian era, burial grounds had became tourist attractions, the first guidebook to Florida, written in the 1840s, specifically mentions both Tolomato and the Huguenot Cemetery.

The latter, the subject of this essay, occupies a shady fenced-in area directly across the street from the Castillo de San Marcos. As you've just read, it was established during the 1821 yellow fever epidemic to accommodate non-Catholics needing burial. At the time of its founding, a certain I.G. Happholdt, who departed this life in August 1821, a month before Judge Fitch, was already buried there. Whether Mr. Happholdt had company no one at the time knew and, in spite of efforts expended since, no one knows now.

Four years after the cemetery was consecrated, a landowner named Lorenzo Capella produced a Spanish deed as proof that the property it stood on was rightfully his, and demanded burials stop immediately. But the controversy didn't last long because soon after he raised the issue, Capella sold his land to a Reverend Alexander, a parson of no fixed denomination, who reopened the cemetery. Unfortunately, Alexander proved to be a poor supervisor, and he allowed the cemetery to fall into disarray. In the fall of 1827, for example, when the fence surrounding it blew down, he did nothing to prevent its remains being cannibalized for firewood. Things were so bad that the Huguenot's sad state was commented on by no less a personage than Ralph Waldo Emerson, who had come to St. Augustine to recuperate from bronchitis.

In 1830, the Reverend Alexander deeded the land on which the cemetery stood jointly to the Episcopal and Presbyterian churches. At the end of a series of events involving both churches and the city, the Presbyterians assumed the trusteeship of the property and in 1860 established a board to maintain it jointly with the Episcopal church.

In 1884, in response to pressure brought to bear by a luxury hotel—the San Marco, that had recently been built nearby and did not want an active cemetery as a neighbor—the city shut down both the Huguenot Cemetery and Tolomato.

After its closure, the Huguenot Cemetery entered a long period of decline. It's now being restored under the sponsorship of the Friends of the Huguenot Cemetery, an umbrella organization backed by the Presbyterian church. Though it's physically open only on Saturdays from eleven to three when docents give tours, the grounds are available 24-7 to anyone who cares to look through the fence. And it takes only a few contemplative moments to conjure the winding walkways and the vanished trees that once stood here, their branches bent to shelter mourners from the sun.

"Huguenot" wasn't the cemetery's original name. It was established generically as "The Public Burying Ground." Later, that name morphed to "The Old Protestant Graveyard." Finally, in the middle of the nineteenth century, someone, perhaps an enterprising tour guide, came up with its present name. Whatever its origin, "Huguenot" was never an accurate descriptor since it is inhabited by only one person identified as Huguenot. Perhaps "Huguenot" was meant to be a generic for "Protestant," though that's not accurate either since at least one Catholic is buried here—Manuel Crespo, whom Tolomato had refused because he was a Mason.

If you stand across from the Castillo and face into the cemetery, you can get a sense of the wide variety of its markers.

There are marble, granite, and sandstone. There are even a few memorials made of coquina, the same shelly material that was so successful in repelling the British. The reason for the hodgepodge is that since there was no supplier of gravestones in St. Augustine in the nineteenth century, people had two choices: improvise or order from out of town. "Out of town" tended to mean Charleston, partly because many of the dead came from there and partly because in those days Charleston was famous for its architectural stonework. Certain masons like T. Steel, J. Walker, and J. White used to sign their work the way an artist signs a painting, thereby memorializing themselves as well as the persons their carvings commemorated.

The styles of the memorials in the Huguenot Cemetery parallel the evolution of nineteenth-century funereal fashion. In the 1830s, Egyptian obelisks and slender monuments inspired by Greek revival architecture were popular. By the 1850s, memorials had thickened and tended to carry resume-like inscriptions, to wit: "He graduated Yale College" or "He graduated from the College of Charleston, South Carolina, and was awarded first honors by the medical faculty of that city." Later in the century (remember that the cemetery closed in 1884), sentimental motifs like urns, weeping willows, and clasped hands began to appear. In general, the later the burial, the more ornate the memorial.

In addition to its stone markers, the Huguenot Cemetery contains a few box tombs, all of which are empty. And for a very practical reason—box tombs required extensive work and corpses don't keep, so by the time the tombs arrived their intended bodies had had to have been buried. To give you an idea of how long such delays could get, in the case of one box tomb, fourteen years passed between order and delivery.

Although cemetery rules prohibited families staking out plots, they used to do it anyway, most commonly with wrought-iron fences and gates or coquina strips at ground level. At one time there were also many plots designated by wooden fences or planks laid into the ground but, being perishable, those are long gone.

Many more people were buried here than is apparent today.

Some now-unmarked graves once had stone markers that were broken or stolen, but many more had wooden crosses put up by families who couldn't afford anything else. In addition to the graves whose markers have vanished, there are an unknown number of indigent graves that were never marked at all. We do know, though, that one of those belonged to an individual from "Hindestan."

Among the indigent graves are three people who were on their way to the city during the Seminole Wars when a band of Indians led by Chief Coacoochee waylaid their wagons. One of the three was a musician on his way to join a theatrical troupe. When he didn't appear, the troupe performed without him—and without the costumes he'd been carrying. Some accounts report that Indians were later seen wearing them. In any case, records show that those three burials cost the citizens of St. Augustine $45.50: $24 for coffins, $12 for grave digging, and $9.50 to pay mourners (since the dead had no friends in the city). The cemetery also used to house several marked graves of soldiers killed in those wars but years ago, both bodies and markers were moved to a military cemetery across town.

There's always social information to be gleaned from the inscriptions on graves. In this case, even the most casual reading will tell you that many people buried here were successful professionals—judges and politicians, for example. Some of the earliest of those may not count to St. Augustine's credit since they died within a year of their arrival, but others were prominent officials who spent much of their lives here. Among the latter is Joseph Lee Smith who succeeded to Thomas Fitch's judgeship and fathered Edmund Kirby Smith, a famous Confederate general.

There's another, unrelated, Smith here who should be much better known than he is. His name was Buckingham Smith and he lies somewhere near his wife's slender, graceful obelisk (his grave isn't specifically marked). If Smith wasn't *the* father of Florida history he was certainly among its fathers. He was the first person to translate the Spanish documents that would make Florida's past come alive for later generations. He was also the first to understand how important those documents, which at the time existed only in Spain, would be. Smith had learned Spanish growing up in Mexico. When he moved to St. Augustine, he developed such a passion for Florida's colonial history that he obtained diplomatic appointments to Spain and Mexico so he could do research in their archives. Over the course of his lifetime, Smith would translate many important documents, the most famous of which is probably De Soto's account of his expedition to the New World.

While the other Smith family in this cemetery—who were originally Connecticut Yankees—spawned a Confederate general, Buckingham Smith took the Union side when the Civil War broke out, and worked tirelessly for that cause. In his will—perhaps partly because he and his wife had had no children—he left his estate to benefit the black community of St. Augustine, thus establishing the oldest continuous social welfare organization in the nation's oldest city: the Buckingham Smith Benevolent Fund, in aid of indigent, elderly blacks.

I'll leave you with one of the many ghost stories whispered in St. Augustine's streets after dusk falls. In 1882, one of the city's post-Civil War arrivals, a judge named John Stickney, embarked on a trip to Washington despite having fallen ill with dengue fever. He died within a week of reaching his destination. When he was sent home, a delegation from the Duval County Bar met his remains at the Jacksonville train and conveyed them to St. Augustine for burial. Twenty years later, his children decided they wanted to move his body to Washington, so they hired a gravedigger to unearth it. The action at Stickney's grave attracted a sizeable group of men who were by all reports in various stages of inebriation. Not especially intelligently, as the gravedigger opened the casket he handed Stickney's bones up to the drunks. Only when he was reassembling the corpse for transportation did he realize that several gold teeth had disappeared. It wasn't long after that incident that Stickney was first seen, pacing transparently around the area in search of his missing teeth. And if you walk the streets with lanterns some dark night, you may spot him too, especially if you happen to be a tourist guide.

Some years ago Frances Kirby Smith's granddaughter, who was visiting from Sewanee, Tennessee, decided to pay her respects to her grandparents. But when she got to the cemetery, she was shocked to see that though her grandfather, Joseph Lee Smith, was suitably commemorated on an obelisk her grandmother's name was nowhere to be found. To remedy the situation, she hired a stonecutter to add Frances's name to her husband's memorial. What the granddaughter didn't know was that the reason Frances wasn't mentioned on the obelisk was that she wasn't there. Unusually for her time, she was never buried by her husband; instead, she lies in an unmarked grave in Palatka next to her sister Helen. Still, no matter where she physically is, Frances deserves to be remembered. This is her story.

Frances Kirby was born in Connecticut in 1785. In 1803, she became engaged to Joseph Lee Smith who was considered quite a catch. (His son Edmund, who took after him, was said to have been the handsomest man in the Confederate army.) But looks weren't Joseph's only asset. He was also intelligent, so much so that when he became a judge, not one of the 1,000-plus cases he heard was ever reversed. That Joseph was equally articulate in private life is obvious from the many letters he left behind, beginning with the one he wrote Frances's father, asking for her hand.

In 1804 when the couple married, Frances was a girl of nineteen whose high-strung nature, her father said, was "tempered with much warmth." This warmth would serve her well when at the age of seventy-seven she used it to get intelligence for the Confederacy from the Union soldiers she regularly entertained in her St. Augustine home. But let's turn the hands of the clock back.

In the first fourteen years of her marriage, Frances had three children, all born in Connecticut: Ephraim and Frances, born in 1806 and 1812 respectively, and Josephine, born in 1818. Six years after that, her fourth and last child, Edmund, would be born in St. Augustine, where her husband had moved to become a judge. Edmund would grow up to be a general, fighting in the Civil War on the Confederate side. It's Edmund, not his father, after whom so many schools and roads in Florida are named.

Frances and Joseph ended up in St. Augustine as a direct result of the 1821 yellow fever epidemic that swept that city. When President Monroe was filling positions in the newly acquired Florida territory, Joseph wasn't on his list but when the president's first choice for the federal judgeship for the Eastern District of Florida died of the fever before he could assume his duties, Monroe appointed Joseph to replace him.

Joseph decided to establish himself in his new environment before he brought his family from Connecticut, so when he stepped ashore in St. Augustine for the first time he stepped alone. He found the city still in the grip of the epidemic that had killed his predecessor and before it played out would sicken twelve hundred of its seventeen hundred or so citizens. Soon after Joseph's arrival, he himself fell so ill that he was given up for dead. He was lucky enough to recover but because yellow fever, like malaria, has a way of coming back he would suffer from it at intervals for the rest of his life.

Sickness aside, Joseph's initial impressions of St. Augustine and its citizens were less than favorable. He found the population—mostly Minorcans and opportunists from the North—a coarse lot and its love of pageantry in execrable taste. After Mardi Gras, he wrote Frances that he had experienced "a succession of masquerading shows of the most grotesque and ludicrous character." I think it's safe to assume that Joseph wasn't alone in this view and that, until they adjusted, most people of his intellectual ilk felt deeply relieved when Lent began.

Two years later, in the fall of 1823, Joseph brought his wife and children to their new home, a Presbyterian parsonage on the site (and in the style) of what is now the Columbia Restaurant on St. George Street. Though they would later rent the Segui house on Aviles Street, it was the parsonage that in 1824 welcomed the family's last child, Edmund (they called him "Ted") into the world.

Over the course of the next several years, Frances spent a good deal of time up north. Homesickness doesn't seem a plausible explanation for all this traveling since Frances's letters make it clear that she liked the South. In one of them, for instance, she contrasted (her words) the "courteous and refined" St. Augustinian way of life with the brutish habits of the northern hoi polloi. And her preference only strengthened with time. When the Civil War broke out, she was so fiercely loyal to the Confederacy that she became a spy.

So if Frances wasn't going north because she preferred the life there, why did she go? The answer is probably that, as her letters also reveal, she and Joseph didn't get along. Their differences must have been chronic too, because when Joseph died of apoplexy in 1846, it came out that he had willed the family home not to Frances, which would have been usual, but to her children. And when Frances herself died, she was buried not by her husband, which again would have been the custom, but beside her sister Helen in Palatka, a considerable ride away.

Joseph seems to have been something of a philanderer. There were persistent rumors that he had fathered, by one of the family slaves, a son named Aleck Darnes. The boy grew up to become the first black physician in Jacksonville and an early friend of James Weldon Johnson. And the rumors were probably well-founded since, judging from their photographs, Aleck and Joseph looked a good deal alike. And even if Aleck had been the only time Joseph strayed, it might still have angered Frances to the point where she avoided him as much as she could. Religion may have entered into it, too. We know from her letters that Frances took her faith seriously. She wrote Edmund once that the book he'd mentioned reading had questionable values and she would try to find him something more suitable. She also often closed her missives like this: "May He who keeps our destinies in his keeping, hold you in the hollow of his hand."

Soon after Joseph died, Frances wanted to sell several of the family's slaves, including Aleck. The older children were amenable to the proposal, but Edmund opposed it because, he argued, the slaves were part of the family. In the end, he prevailed, and Aleck and the others stayed.

In 1860, Lincoln was elected president. Later that year, South Carolina seceded. "The secession ball is rolling!" Frances exulted, and immediately donated fifty cents toward a flagpole destined for a Confederate flag to be erected in the plaza. While the pole was being readied, a group of women busied themselves sewing the flag and when it was finished, ceremoniously hoisted it. Frances must have felt something swell inside her as she saw it lifted wide by the winds coming off the harbor. "I never expected to live to see a Revolution," she wrote, but "our cause is a just one."

Events moved quickly. Within a month of the flag raising, the Confederacy commandeered civilian steamers on the St. Johns to transport weapons from Jacksonville. Soon, Southern officers all over the United States were resigning their commissions and coming home. Around this time, Frances forwarded some of Edmund's letters to Jefferson Davis as proof of her son's loyalty. Davis must have believed the sentiments in the letters because when Edmund reported for duty, Davis gave him a command.

Not all St. Augustinians sympathized with the Confederacy. Many, like the Burts, the Pecks, the Andersons, Miss Sarah Mather, and Edmund Jackson Davis, who became a Union general, were firmly on the other side. And so many local blacks fought for the Union cause that after the war, St. Augustine had two chapters of the Grand Army of the Republic (the organization of Union veterans), one black and one white.

Those who did support the Confederacy were passionate. Some local women even dressed in men's clothing and joined the army. Frances, being in her mid-seventies, was too old to follow them, so she busied herself by doing what she could for the war effort, which consisted at first of arranging the transportation of mail to local Confederate troops fighting elsewhere.

On March 10, 1862, the Union steamer *Wabash* landed at Fort Marion (as the Americans had renamed the Castillo de San Marcos after the Spanish left). The mayor (whom Frances sardonically called "Old Bravo")—together with the council, which was, according to her, "much like him, all low ignorant

Minorcans"—immediately surrendered by raising a white flag over the fort, then added insult to injury by helping the invading army occupy it. Frances never did get over her contempt at the alacrity with which the mayor and his cronies had given in. She liked to say that they had raised the white flag "as soon as two rowboats had rounded the point."

Most of Frances's female contemporaries shunned the craven administration too. When "Old Bravo" invited a certain H. Juster to attend the raising of the new flag, she refused, saying "I would see them all in a bad place first," a sentiment Frances certainly shared. In fact the minute it was clear that the Yankees were going to take the town, some women, Anna Dummett and Sally Hardee among them, rushed into the plaza and chopped down the flagpole. The federals might fly the stars and stripes over the fort but they were never going to be flown over the plaza.

At first everything went as well as could be hoped, considering the city was under occupation. The new administration promised the locals "the quiet possession of our property and every thing to go on in the good old way, ample supply of provisions at cheap rates &c &c."

But then the Yankees proclaimed martial law and everything changed. St. Augustinians had to take a loyalty oath before they could buy food or move around the city. Armed men patrolled the narrow streets at all times—Frances could see them out her window. Sentinels stood watch at every corner. No one was allowed out at night without a pass. Nor was anyone allowed to leave town without permission. This last rule was enforced by lines of soldiers, posted within earshot of each other at every possible entrance and exit point to the city.

Eventually, the administration began seizing any property that looked untenanted. This kept Frances, who feared losing her home, a virtual prisoner for weeks on end. Most of this time, she was living by herself since one effect of the Yankees' arrival, according to contemporary reports, had been that many servants—the number included Frances's—no longer felt responsible so were running free in the streets.

"We are under the hands of an oppressor," Frances wrote,

"the avowed aim of whom is to subjugate us, to exterminate us, to starve us even, into submission." She took comfort only in the fact that, at least according to her, the occupiers' only known converts were unionists and tradesmen who had never stopped thinking of themselves as Northerners. Frances waxed especially vitriolic about the latter who, she thought, having become strong by exploiting the population, were now opportunistically turning against it.

Though Frances said what she thought in her letters, she acted in an accommodating and realistic way in public. She took the Union's loyalty oath. She even entertained its soldiers in her home, a situation not as unnatural as it sounds if you remember that two of her sons and a son-in-law were career army officers so she might have known some of her guests socially from before the war. What the Union officers being served dinner didn't know, however, was that this apparently harmless old lady was passing on to Confederate agents every single piece of military information she could overhear.

The relative ease of the occupation's early days didn't last, and life became progressively more difficult, particularly when it came to food. Some former slave owners (whose slaves had decamped after they were told by the occupiers they were free) applied for Union assistance. In some cases, the former owners weren't so much in need as simply throwing up their hands because they were unwilling to do the work their former property had done. Others, though, were asking for help because they were genuinely short of resources.

At one point Frances had nothing to eat but some stolen white beans and the little milk her starving cow could provide. But "strange things happen, sitting sorrowfully," she wrote about the day two soldiers came to the house, inquiring for "an old widow lady, a Mrs. Smith." Upon learning that Frances was Mrs. Smith, they proceeded to sell her sugar, bacon, flour, and brine, all at a good price. She never found out how that came to pass, and it never happened again.

As the occupation continued, some Confederate supporters in the population began quietly to rebel. Many people stopped attending church, for instance, because of pro-Union remarks made from the pulpit. Frances herself stomped out one Sunday and never went back because prayers were being offered for "Old Abe."

In May 1862, fourteen months after the invasion, some soldiers playing ball in the plaza stopped for a minute to hack at the stump of the flagpole that threatened to trip them. You'll remember that the stump was what remained after Sally, Anna, and others had cut the flagpole down to stop the Union flag from being raised. What happened next was that two or three young Minorcan girls rushed up, gathered the chopped-off splinters to their breasts, kissed them, and carried them away. It was said that something similar had happened on another occasion with some ashes left over after the Yankees had tried to burn the stump. About that time as well children began to be seen around town, playing with replicas of Confederate flags. In response to these behaviors, the Yankee commandant, a Colonel Bell, posted a notice in several locations around town. The notice was not gentle: "Certain disgusting exhibitions of Treason having been made by some women of the City, it is ordered that any persons showing any evidence of Treason by word or act, will be arrested at once, and placed in Confinement as Traitors, by orders from Headquarters. Rebel flags having been waved by children before houses in the City, it is ordered that upon another occurrence of the kind, the house will be immediately seized, and all the inmates placed in confinement."

And the Yankees meant what they said. One by one, rebellious women were ushered out of town. On April 2, 1863, Frances wrote, "This is a dark dark day. At 4 o'clock this afternoon, my sister Helen, Mrs. Putnam, left her home, expelled from it by order because her husband . . . is called a secessionist." The charge was false, according to Frances, who confided to her journal that "he has not born arms against the Union."

"I," Frances wrote in the same journal entry, "am permitted to remain on account of age, seventy-seven years' infirmity, and poor health." But Frances's reprieve didn't last. Two months later, soldiers arrived and she too was escorted out of town. She managed through Edmund to contact General

Beauregard, who sent a carriage. She spent the rest of the war in exile in central Florida. When it ended, she returned to St. Augustine and lived out her life as an unreconstructed Confederate patriot. The merits of Frances's cause aside, how can you not admire her courage? And when you stand at her obelisk, it doesn't matter whether she is lying under it because it's not her physical presence that matters. It's the part she played among women who emotionally and morally prevailed over their occupiers because however pressured they might have been by deprivation and insult, they did not yield.

8

EVERGREEN CEMETERY, JACKSONVILLE

Evergreen (established 1880) has a breadth of story its cousin across town, Old City Cemetery (established 1820), can't match. To some extent, that's a function of Evergreen's size. At 169 acres (not counting three adjoining Jewish cemeteries whose burials it manages) and 70,000-plus burials Evergreen is one of the largest burial grounds in the Southeast. Another plus is its affiliated organization, the Pilot Club, whose frequent tours bring Jacksonville's past to life—from the city's founding in the 1820s to its experiences during the Civil War; from the 1888 yellow fever epidemic to the Great Fire of 1901 that devastated most of downtown.

Evergreen also has the distinction of being the only cemetery in Florida to have appeared in Ripley's Believe It or Not. It was featured twice, first because it had the longest (at the time) continuous brick wall in the world and second for a heart-shaped tombstone on which a bereaved husband swore "I'll never marry again," then within six months of the funeral proceeded to do exactly that.

Evergreen's also unusual because it has an arboretum—and a unique arboretum at that: thirty-five acres of the offspring of historic trees. The area is curated by Jeff Meyer, an internationally known arborist who happens to live in Jacksonville. Meyer uses documents, journals, diaries, and photographs to identify still-standing trees that witnessed what happened in places like Monticello or Gettysburg or Andersonville. Then he collects seeds from those original trees and propagates them here in Evergreen. So far, the arboretum has 125 descendents of historic trees, and there are plans for many more. All you have to do is think, "the Thomas Jefferson Poplar," "the Patrick Henry Osage Orange" and without taking a step out of Jacksonville, you're traveling.

Evergreen's layout has evolved organically. Its original acreage was in the southeast corner but over the years it absorbed the adjoining Catholic, Greek Orthodox, and African American cemeteries. Though some of the absorptions were rectangular, others were oval, circular, or kidney-shaped, which naturally constrained the direction of the burials that filled them. The result of such nonstandard shapes is that unlike most historic Florida cemeteries whose graves face east, Evergreen's may face in any direction.

Though Evergreen's atmosphere is consistently park-like—its roads wend their way through grassy groves of live oaks, magnolias, cedars, and camphor trees—the materials and shapes of its memorials are anything but consistent. As far as I'm concerned, this lack of consistency is one of the place's greatest charms since it's so extreme that almost any kind of memorial you can dream up can be found somewhere in the grounds. And unlike many other historic burial grounds, Evergreen has few apparently empty stretches because most of its original memorials were stone and so have survived.

Evergreen offers a couple of unusual types of set-aside areas. The first is three sections—the largest about six hundred graves—which accommodate only babies Happily, these areas aren't filling up as fast as they used to. According to Evergreen's current director, Robert Mueller, in 1973 when he came onboard they were burying a baby a week, but now they bury only about ten a year.

The second unusual set-aside consists of rows of identical standing stones flanked by many more rows of identically formatted flush-to-the-ground plaques. These remember people who died in the Florida Christian Home. This was Jacksonville's first nursing facility. Though now it operates conventionally with payment by the month, it originally required patients to sign their assets over when they moved in, in return for being cared for in life and buried when they died.

If you're a Civil War buff, you might look for a marker dedicated to the crew of the *Hunley*, a Confederate submarine that went down in Charleston harbor shortly after it had itself sunk a federal blockade ship. You might also want to visit Frank Ironmonger, whose memorial is inscribed "The Youngest Soldier," because Frank had gone off to fight the Yankees when he was ten. The marker doesn't specify what Frank did in the war but if they weren't simply accompanying their brothers or fathers, young boys tended to be used as drummers or messengers. In any case, young Frank survived his experience and "died as he had lived: a gentleman."

Although Evergreen doesn't have a generic Confederate memorial, it does have one dedicated to the Union: a gorgeous white bronze soldier, looking wistfully north. There are also some Union soldiers' graves but it's not clear exactly who the soldiers were. They may have been part of the force that occupied Jacksonville during the war. They may have been killed in the Battle of Olustee/Battle of Ocean Pond. Alternatively, they may have survived the war and died later.

Among the other military dead are fifty or so American servicemen who died in Cuba during the Spanish-American War, the "splendid little war" as Teddy Roosevelt called it, fought between April and August of 1898.

Besides the servicemen's, the Spanish-American War was responsible for two spectacular local deaths. In June 1898, two months into the fighting, the federals decided to mine the St. Johns River. A Lt. Hart of the U.S. Engineering Corps was in charge of the operation. His second in command, John O'Rourke, was assisted by Edward Houston and a youngster named Hogart. The project's "office" was a shed on the St. Johns Bluff. One afternoon, Hart was dictating a letter while across the room Houston was holding a plug for O'Rourke so the latter could test it by running current through it. Hogart was outside, tying his shoes.

Then disaster struck. The current O'Rourke sent was so strong it exploded the dynamite in the shed. O'Rourke died instantly on the spot. Houston's body, though, was propelled through the roof. Rescuers later picked up the larger pieces of him and laid them on a canvas. Hart was injured by flying shrapnel but he survived. The boy, Hogart, escaped entirely thanks to his recalcitrant shoelaces.

The Civil War was the first time in history that saw soldiers sent home for burial. In all earlier wars, the fallen had been buried on the battlefield or if retreat was hasty, left behind to be scavenged upon by vultures or dogs. But during the Civil War, thanks to the telegraph, families could be notified of a loved one's death, and thanks to the railroad, his remains could reach their destination before they rotted. At the start of the war, with both those innovations in place, casualties were routinely shipped home, south or north, as the case might have been.

But heavy fighting soon disrupted the process—communication lines were cut and rail service was irregular—so again many of the dead were laid to rest within shouting distance of where they'd fallen. Still, if undertakers had known during the war what became clear afterwards, they might have been able to save at least some of the dead from permanent exile. They did know that packing a body in charcoal (a separate charge on the family's bill) would preserve it even after a relatively long journey. But they didn't find out until 1868 how long this preservation could last.

Here, courtesy of the curator of the historical burial grounds in Lynchburg, Virginia, is what happened. A family whose son had been killed in 1861 asked an undertaker to hold his body until they could pick it up. In response, he did the usual: packed the young man's remains in charcoal. Seven years later, the undertaker realized he had never heard from the soldier's family and decided to bury the body himself. When he unpacked it to put it in a coffin, he found to his surprise that it had been perfectly preserved.

Now you've heard about some of the set-aside areas at Evergreen, I'll leave you free to discover the rest. But I do want to tell you about a few must-visit individuals and graves. The first of the individuals is Isaiah Hart, who's credited with having founded Jacksonville. Hart was a career robber of slaves and cattle who fled Georgia just ahead of the law. He arrived in Florida soon after the Americans assumed control and pitched a tent by the St. Johns River in an area called "Cow Ford."

Eventually, he sent for his family in Georgia and in 1822, he and some other settlers had the area surveyed and laid out in streets. They then named their new town after Andrew Jackson, Florida's territorial governor. Somewhere along the line, Isaiah converted to Christianity and repented of his former life. By the time he died, he was a prominent and respected member of the community. In 1861 when he died, his family laid him to rest downtown in a free-standing brick mausoleum topped with a stone spire. But no one took care of the place and finally Florida's rampant weeds overgrew it to the point where it all but disappeared.

It's a steamy July night in 1896 and you're the newspaper reporter who has finally located Isaiah's mausoleum in a particularly dank part of downtown. Pistol at the ready, you lift your lantern and step over the iron-bound door someone has torn off its hinges, and suddenly there it is: a grinning skull, tumbled from a broken wooden coffin. The corpse's bones are still draped in the remains of its burial suit and on its feet are black shoes, nearly rotted away. Around the walls are seven other coffins, apparently untouched. What a story! And it's all true. The reporter's gestures to drama—the night visit, the lantern, the gun—paid off in spades when he stepped across that threshold.

After the scoop about the Hart tomb appeared in the paper, so many people vandalized it—someone even stole the bones from the tipped coffin—that a Hart descendent had the entry bricked up. There things rested until, five years later, the mausoleum was destroyed in the Great Fire. What was left of it—Isaiah and his relatives' now-cremated remains, the original spire, and the engraved stone that had stood over the entryway—was moved to Evergreen. And when Isaiah was moved, his son Ossian (who governed Florida for less than a year before he died) was relocated from the Old City Cemetery to lie beside his father.

Evergreen is home to three passengers from the *Titanic*. Two of the three, individuals of Palestinian origin, survived the sinking and lived here until they died of other causes but the third, the Reverend R.J. Bateman, went down with the ship. Since in those days an unaccompanied lady was looked on askance, the reverend had gone to England to escort his brother's wife home. When the *Titanic* began to sink, he put his charge into a life boat and turned back. He was conducting a service on the tilting deck when the great ship juddered and toppled a stack that struck him on its way down. His death was witnessed by his sister-in-law from her boat, swaying on the swells. In the movie *Titanic*, the man depicted handing a scarf to a woman as she sits in a lifeboat is the Reverend Bateman. The woman is his sister-in-law. That scarf still exists. We know because more than eighty years after the disaster, some members of the family, in Jacksonville for a family reunion, brought it with them.

There are quite a few prominent people in Evergreen. You can visit the graves of a Pulitzer-winning poet (George Hill Dillon), a prominent student of Frank Lloyd Wright (Henry John Klutho), a highly successful Confederate general sometimes called "the Confederate swamp fox" (J.J. Dickison), several Episcopal bishops, five Florida governors, three U.S. senators, and a C.S.A. senator. Besides those worthies, Evergreen is home to many distinguished judges and business leaders from industries like mining, timber, coffee, and dairy farming. If Ripley's Believe it or Not were still in operation, Evergreen might have another claim to fame since it's possibly the only cemetery in the world where coffee and cream lie within yards of each other.

Among the dignitaries buried at Evergreen, I find Napoleon Bonaparte Broward among the most appealing. Posthumously modest, his stone carries only his name and dates (1857–1910) and refrains from mentioning the fact that he governed Florida.

Bringing up the rear (as it were) of our list of famous individuals is someone less dignified: Cora Crane, the notorious Madam who claimed to have been the common-law wife of Stephen Crane (whose famous story "The Open Boat" was set off the coast of Daytona Beach).

There are some unusual sights here. Take what looks like the melted bronze torso of a large animal. The torso started life as an elk—it's in the middle of an area where members of the fraternal order of Elks are buried—but vandals broke off its extremities so often that the cemetery management finally gave up and buried them nearby. The torso is all that's left.

There's also perhaps the only tombstone anywhere whose inscription directs its reader to "See Reverse Side." The stone belongs to Lawrence Towers Anderson also known as, it says, L.T. Carroll. The back of the stone explains that though Lawrence was raised by the Carroll family he was born an Anderson. At the bottom it adds the helpful information that "all of the above are residents of Wakulla County." The story behind this oddity is that when Lawrence died, his adoptive family buried him in an unmarked grave. This fact started a fight between the Carrolls and his birth parents the Andersons, the upshot of which was that the Carrolls agreed that the Andersons could erect this marker.

In the late Victorian era porcelain pictures set on flexible steel, called Delouches, were common in cemeteries. Unfortunately, like the elk, the Delouches in Evergreen were vandalized so often that the management banned them, which makes emotional as well as practical sense since looking at stones with desecrated Delouches feels like looking at someone whose eyes have been put out.

Three abandoned receiving vaults parallel Evergreen Avenue on the cemetery's east side. The story behind them goes back a hundred years. In the late nineteenth and early twentieth centuries, Jacksonville was a magnet for snowbirds because it was the only Florida port where large steamships could dock. In its touristic heyday, the city boasted four or five hotels with hundreds of rooms apiece, filled to capacity each winter by northerners escaping the cold. And, as would be statistically natural, every winter some of those people died. That the decedents couldn't be buried at home until after the spring thaw presented Evergreen with a business opportunity. To accommodate the corpses while they waited, the management built two receiving vaults, each containing twelve crypts each of which rented for $10 a month. Demand for the first twenty-four crypts proved so brisk that Evergreen soon added thirty-two more. As it happened, the expansion proved to have been a bad decision because as soon as Henry Flagler's railroad offered a way farther south, people took it. Now, the majority of winter deaths happened out of reach of Evergreen.

One of Evergreen's more successful ventures lies across the west side of the grounds: a lovely mausoleum containing three thousand single crypts and a few private "rooms" incorporating several crypts. At least four of the crypts are occupied by funeral home directors. One of them, a Mr. Kraus who owned a chain of such institutions, was so claustrophobic that he purchased a room with four crypts and ordered the bottom to be knocked out of each of the two upper "berths" so he and his wife could have breathing room above them.

The maps you'll find in a bin outside the office locate most of the places I mentioned as well as a few I didn't, so be sure to pick one up as you come in. I'm hoping that along with this essay, they'll convince those of you who enjoy variety in your cemeteries that Evergreen is the place for you. The very beautiful place for you.

SPOTLIGHT: SON OF EVERGREEN

Want to know what it's like to grow up surrounded by the dead? Not across the street from a cemetery, with a road between you and the graves, but right in the middle of one? Ask Bill Jennewine, whose family moved from Richmond, Virginia to a house in Evergreen in 1950, when Bill was five, and stayed there until the 1980s when his father retired as general manager.

The Jennewine family didn't have a history of involvement in the cemetery business. That they ended up where they did was a function of the economic atmosphere of the late 1940s. Back then, if you hadn't served in "The War"—which Bill's dad hadn't—you were going to have a hard time finding work. So when the senior Jennewine was offered the job of assistant general manager at Evergreen, he accepted it in spite of its several downsides: cemetery management wasn't the job of his dreams, the family would have to move, and the pay wasn't good.

The Jennewines, father, mother, and three small children—Jane, eight, Bill, five, and Betsy, two and a half—arrived in

Jacksonville in June, 1950. There was no air conditioning back then and Jacksonville in June was much more intense than Richmond had been in June, so the first thing the family noticed was the heat. On the other hand, the 1915 house they were given as part of Bill's dad's salary had been built for the climate, with wide porches and opening windows so living in it even at the height of summer was doable. Besides, since everyone was in the same boat in those days, being hot just felt normal and by the end of summer, the family had settled in. In the fall, Jane and Bill started elementary school and Betsy followed soon afterwards.

As little kids, Bill and Jane and Betsy didn't think there was anything odd about where they lived. What the cemetery was to them was an extra-large yard awash with flowers, trees, and creatures. Bill particularly remembers a couple of families of grey foxes who'd dug dens under large flat tombstones. The pups would come out to play on the grass but every time the children tried to sneak up on them, they'd scatter. One Sunday, Bill's dad caught a pup that was a little slower than the rest. He petted the pup's head while it blinked sleepily at him. Then he told the kids, "Look what happens now," and just barely lifted his hand. Zoom! The pup was gone, back to its mother in the trees. Unfortunately for the foxes, soon after that incident Bill's father decided they had to go. They were damaging the grounds and besides, he was afraid they'd become rabid.

Besides foxes, the cemetery was home to possums, raccoons, and rampant populations of grey squirrels. Bill remembers several baby albino squirrels but no albino adults because albino babies didn't survive, being too easy for hawks and owls to see. The cemetery had a few exotic visitors too, like the bobcat that wandered off the railroad track onto the grounds.

The saddest creatures on the place, according to Bill, were the non-wildlife. People seemed to think that a cemetery was the ideal place to abandon animals, so dogs and cats—especially puppies and kittens—often showed up there. Many were sick but even the healthy ones were moved off or destroyed out of concern for the family's own pets.

Bill and Jane's schoolmates never teased them about where they lived. On the contrary, most of them relished coming over to play, at least during the day. At night they were a lot less comfortable. In fact, as Bill got older, he'd take his high school pals, most of whom were Boy Scouts or played sports, on night walks just to see, as Bill put it, "the tough guys wither." Bill himself was iron-nerved where ghosts were concerned. When he was managing his high school football team, he regularly got home after dark. The bus would drop him off at the entrance and he'd walk the grave-lined mile to his house on paths lit only by the moon. Owls would sob all around him and the wind would blow the Spanish moss in eerie patterns. But, disappointingly for those of us who love spooky stories, Bill swears nothing worth telling happened on those nights.

Though there may not have been any ghosts, once the cemetery was invaded by scores of people looking for them. It happened when a local radio station hoping to raise its ratings reported strange sightings on the railroad track that runs through the grounds. At the time of the radio cam-paign, cemetery workers happened to be burning debris along the banks of a drainage ditch by lighting piles of moss and branches and leaving them to burn themselves out. The pro-cess took days and resulted in smoke rising from apparently undisturbed ground. Bill thinks it was probably the smoke that attracted the crowds. In any case, once they material-ized it was only a matter of time before some seeker after the occult fell through. The lady seeker who had burned her legs and lower body tried to sue the cemetery. Though her suit was thrown out, the incident got the cemetery board of trustees nervous enough to pressure the city to get the radio people to come up with another gimmick.

In the years he lived at Evergreen, Bill did hear one story which suggested a true ghost. It concerned a tombstone in one of the older sections that had an alligator carved on it. Since this was before Gator football, an alligator carved into a stone was unusual enough that it got Bill wondering why it was there. When he asked the old timers who'd been around when it was installed, they told him that the man who was buried in that grave had worked with alligators and supposedly had had some he raised. When he first died, they said, they'd had to be careful around his grave because a large alligator would be lying on top of it, for all the world as though it knew where its master was buried.

The one day that none of the Jennewine kids' friends would go near the cemetery was Halloween. Since no one came trick-or-treating there either, Bill and his sisters worked up their own fun down at the abandoned vaults that stood by the railroad siding.

The vaults were close enough to the cemetery fence to be visible to passing cars, so Bill and Jane used to hang a sheer curtain across their fronts and settle down to wait. At the first sign of headlights, they'd swing their flashlights around behind the curtains and make woo-wooing sounds as they whooshed them into the air. What happened next, Bill said, would be one of two things. Either the driver would squeal the tires as he stepped on the gas to get out of there, or he'd slam on the brakes to get a better look. The kids never got caught though, because no one was ever brave enough to get out of the car.

As you've probably gathered by now, Bill likes a joke. When he was in high school, a not-quite-facetious feud in his family gave him the perfect opening. Several of his father's family had served in the Union but his mother's ancestors had fought for the other side. This made for running discussions in the family as to the relative merits of Yanks and Rebels. So one day, just for the heck of it, Bill climbed the statue of the north-facing Union soldier and put a Confederate flag in its rifle barrel. That escapade had Bill's father looking for "the young punks" for quite a while.

On weekends and summers during high school and college, Bill worked in the cemetery grounds. One day he was mowing parallel swathes up and down an area of flat stones when he noticed something out of the corner of his eye. He thought, "that's a birthday cake," then shook the idea off, and went on mowing. The third time he passed the spot, curiosity overcame him and he got off his tractor to have a look. It really was a cake. Something had eaten the icing but you could still make out the letters. They said "Happy 6th Birthday" and a child's name. When Bill lifted the cake and looked at the marker underneath, he saw that the child in question had been less than a year old when she died.

Several times during high school, Bill would be mowing along when one or more of his wheels would sink into a grave. That was because at that time the cemetery was still allowing wooden caskets and, as we all know, wood rots. When Bill got stuck like that, he'd make a note of the place and the next day workers would fill in the grave to prevent further collapse. Not nice to have visitors sinking up to their armpits.

In the 1970s the board of trustees banned not just wood coffins but all copings (the borders used to mark family plots). Banning the copings was Bill's father's idea. He convinced the board that they could save on maintenance if they didn't allow new ones and if families would agree to allow the cemetery to remove the ones that were already there. Over the years, most families did agree, and Bill's dad used the extracted copings to build a fireplace in the shed where the workers took their breaks and ate lunch. The fireplace wasn't for show. The workers used it to warm their food, to warm themselves on winter mornings, and to dry off on rainy days.

One day Bill was digging a grave in a just-opened area near the back of the cemetery when his shovel hit a bone. When he found a skull, he stopped and called his dad. What Bill had unearthed turned out to be a yellow fever victim. Unmarked graves were so unusual for Evergreen that Bill hadn't known there were any. After that first discovery, Bill and the men he was working with came across many sets of remains, often mingled with such items as eating utensils and plates, cups, and glasses. The people in that part of the cemetery had died before anyone knew what caused the fever so survivors buried everything the victim had touched along with her corpse.

Bill tells a story that offers us a window into race relations in the first half of the twentieth century. The late 1940s and early 1950s—the Jennewines arrived in 1950—were the heyday of the Ku Klux Klan in Jacksonville. When Bill was young, Klansmen dressed in civilian clothes would show up for certain funerals. Then, before the service began, they'd duck behind bushes and change into their robes. When they reappeared, the cemetery workers—in those days, all of them were black—would hide. Only after the workers were sure the Klansman had left not just the grave site but the cemetery, would they come back to fill in the hole.

The Klan's overt activities in the area diminished throughout the 1950s. By the early '60s, Evergreen's ground crew was integrated via a couple of older white full-timers and six white part-timers, Bill and five other high school students.

When Bill was on duty wasn't the only time he saw odd sights. One day on his way home from school he came across some groundsmen beginning to close a grave. He slowed down out of respect for the dead, and as the casket was being lowered, he saw a man with an 8mm camera following it down into the vault. Bill's take on the situation is that the cinematographer was verifying that Uncle John was really in the ground and not coming up again.

Another time, Bill was hanging around on the porch one hot afternoon when he heard what was either a scream or a laugh coming from the Jewish section. One of the men Bill worked with had a similar laugh and Bill was afraid the man didn't know there was a funeral so he left the house and headed toward the shed to warn him to keep it down. On the way, Bill ran into his father, who told him not to bother. The screams (not laughs) Bill had heard, his father explained, came from the daughter of the man who died. She'd been wailing frenziedly as she tried (she was prevented) to jump onto her father's casket as it was being lowered into the grave. An act of remorse perhaps, said Bill's dad, since according to the funeral director, the daughter had told her father to "go to hell" just days before.

Bill lived in the house on the cemetery grounds all through college and every summer until he graduated, he would go home to work there. These days, he's migrated to central Florida, but he says that neither he nor his sisters would trade their childhoods for anything. How many children, after all, were lucky enough to have so much land to roam at will? And when Bill dreams of the place now, the dreams are almost always about the good times. In the end, he's a '50s kind of guy, with that sort of happiness. And he doesn't mind at all, in fact he's proud of it, that at his high school reunions, he's known— a la Tarzan of the Apes—as Billy of the Cemetery.

A child flying to Heaven (Tallahassee). Courtesy of mybluenothing (Casey Haseldon).

Family plot enclosure: detail (Tallahassee). Courtesy of mybluenothing (Casey Haseldon).

A Woodman of the World grave marker (Mount Horeb). Courtesy
of June Spear.

The Mount Horeb Primitive Baptist Church (Mount Horeb). Courtesy of June Spear.

Alvan Chapman in his study (Apalachicola). Courtesy of Apalachicola Municipal Library; Beverly Mount-Douds.

Panda in bamboo grove (Glendale). Courtesy of John Wilkerson.

Miss Nessie, the Shining One (Glendale). Courtesy of John Wilkerson.

Everyone (Apalachicola). Courtesy of Susan Cerulean.

The Magic of Place (Apalachicola). Courtesy of David Moynahan.

A baby fallen asleep (Pensacola). Courtesy of mybluenothing (Casey Haseldon)

An angel now (Pensacola). Courtesy of mybluenothing (Casey Haseldon).

Lester (Micanopy). Courtesy of Jamie Sanford.

A soldier (Micanopy). Photo by author.

Outsiders (St. Augustine). Courtesy of Jaeme Haviland.

Fare thee well (St. Augustine). Courtesy of Harold Fethe.

A great Confederate general (Jacksonville). Courtesy of metrojacksonville .com.

Above: Home from the sea (Jacksonville). Courtesy of metrojacksonville.com.

Left: Dr. Fager's winning stride, 1968 (Ocala). Courtesy of Bob Coglianese (NYRA).

The Great Wallenda (Bradenton). Courtesy of Authentic Wallenda Archives.

Tommy Hanneford, Hanneford Circus (Bradenton). Courtesy of Pat Padua.

Peace (Sanford). Courtesy of Christine Kinlaw Best.

Loved (Bradenton). Courtesy of Pat Padua.

The United States of America,

TO ALL TO WHOM THESE PRESENTS SHALL COME, GREETING:

Homestead Certificate No 3183
Application 1680

Whereas there has been deposited in the GENERAL LAND OFFICE of the United States a CERTIFICATE of the Register of the Land Office at Gainesville Florida, whereby it appears that, pursuant to the Act of Congress approved 20th May, 1862, "To secure Homesteads to actual settlers on the public domain," and the acts supplemental thereto, the claim of Sofia Charlotte Sjoeborg has been established and duly consummated in conformity to law for the south-east quarter of the north-east quarter the north half of the south-east quarter and the south-west quarter of the south-east quarter of section twenty in township twenty-one south of range twenty-nine east of Tallahassee Meridian in Florida, containing one hundred and sixty acres and six hundredths of an acre

according to the Official Plat of the Survey of the said Land returned to the GENERAL LAND OFFICE by the SURVEYOR GENERAL.

Now know ye, That there is therefore granted by the UNITED STATES unto the said Sofia Charlotte Sjoeborg the tract of Land above described: TO HAVE AND TO HOLD the said tract of Land, with the appurtenances thereof, unto the said Sofia Charlotte Sjoeborg and to her heirs and assigns forever.

In testimony whereof I, Chester A. Arthur President of the United States of America, have caused these letters to be made Patent, and the Seal of the General Land Office to be hereunto affixed.

Given under my hand, at the City of Washington, the thirteenth day of August, in the year of Our Lord one thousand eight hundred and eighty-three, and of the Independence of the United States the one hundred and eighth

By the President: Chester A. Arthur

By Wm H. Crook Sec'y.

S. W. Clark, Recorder of the General Land Office.

Sofia Sjoborg's homestead deed (Sanford). Courtesy of U.S. Bureau of Land Management.

Port Mayaca Hurricane Memorial (Canal Point). Courtesy of noaa
.gov.

Shelter (Canal Point). Courtesy of City of Pahokee.

Shana (Broward). Courtesy of Randy Temkin.

He was everything (Broward). Courtesy of Randy Temkin.

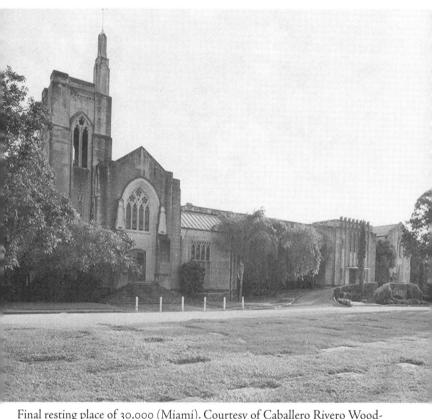

Final resting place of 30,000 (Miami). Courtesy of Caballero Rivero Wood-lawn Funeral Homes.

Grave of a child who fell out a window (Key West). Courtesy of the University of West Florida Archaeology Institute.

Woman in Bondage (Key West). Courtesy of Carol Tedesco.

Angel watching over (Key West). Courtesy of Carol Tedesco.

9

WINDING OAKS FARM
RACEHORSE CEMETERY, OCALA

Every family I know has at least one member interested in genealogy. Some people enjoy the challenge of fill-in-the-blanks.
Others research names, dates, and geographical settings as a
prelude to finding stories. But for most of us, I think it would
be fair to say, ancestor tracing may be absorbing but it's still a
hobby.

By contrast, genealogy is essential to racehorse owners because bloodline is one of the few things a potential owner or
trainer has to go on when deciding whether or not to invest in
a given horse. Lineage is important because it suggests a prospect's potential for speed. In the case of stallions it also affects
how much the horse will bring at stud.

All of the above explains why the gravestones at Winding Oaks cemetery list parentage in so much greater detail
than any human grave would. That racing is a business also
explains why so many inscriptions mention the number of
places a horse took and the amount of money it earned its
owners. What if we approached our memorials that way,
shunning verses like the one beginning "Remember me as you
pass by" and heartfelt tributes like "Susan, gone to angels" in
favor of inscriptions along the lines of "Here lies John Smith
(1933–2004) out of Eric Smith and Becky Jones by Winston
Glicksberg" or "In his lifetime he earned $2,230,000 for his
grateful family"? Boggles the mind, doesn't it? But with racehorses, that's how it is. They may have been loved, but the
ones who were loved most earned their keep and then some.

Winding Oaks Farm, where most of the horses buried in this cemetery were born, is divided into intensely green fields with rounded corners (because horses don't see well, they tend to run into square corners). Though the land has been used for racing since the 1950s, its thousand acres became Winding Oaks only recently—in 2002, when Eugene and Laura Melnyk combined two older farms—Tartan and Mockingbird. In central Florida, where every inch of land seems to be in demand, a farm as large as Winding Oaks is unusual, and visually strange, its fields rising as they do from the side of a road lined with subdivisions, malls, and fast food joints.

And yet, drive only a few hundred feet in and the hustle of SR-200 seems far away. Here you're wrapped in restful green, sloping gently upward and worlds of pasture, dotted here and there with stables and other farm buildings.

I stopped at the office to meet Phil Hronek, the farm manager who had offered to take me to the cemetery. All I knew about him ahead of time was that he's polite to strangers and that he has the gravelly voice of a radio detective. In person, he turned out to be a small weathered man in a white T-shirt, shorts, and a baseball cap, with something in his aspect that screamed that horses were in his blood. And they are. By the time Hronek started high school he was exercising gallopers at Hollywood Park and dreaming of becoming a jockey. When he was drafted for Vietnam in 1968 and came back heavy, he decided to become a trainer. And, though he's not a boastful man, I could tell from Hronek's aspect and obvious level of responsibility here that I'd been lucky enough to meet one of the best in the business.

On a farm this large, you drive. Phil hopped in his truck and gestured out the window for me to follow him. At the turns we made arcing up the hill, I noticed that the roads were neatly signed and, as you might have expected, named for horses. I memorized the first few turns, then lost count. After passing several barns, Phil pulled off the grassy verge beside a stable, which, he told me later, is used for brood mares in foaling time. He cut his engine. I followed suit and we both got out.

I was puzzled. I hadn't seen a single horse along the way

and there were none in sight now, which didn't jibe with Phil's comment to me on the phone that there were 506 of them currently in residence. When I asked Phil about that, he explained that the horses were at lunch. Apparently, like the businessmen and women they are, they go inside to eat. He added that I wouldn't have seen any horses until I got well into the farm anyhow, because so many drunk drivers had smashed through the fences that border SR-200 that he and the management had decided to leave those fields permanently empty.

The cemetery consists of a three-quarter round of neat memorials next to the stable. Each memorial carries two stones, one upright, one horizontal. I was thinking how lovely it was that departing generations are laid to rest beside the place where new horses come into the world when Phil cut in. The original owners had chosen the site for two reasons, he said: because it lies at the highest point of what was then Tartan Farms and because of the beauty of the live oaks growing here. And the trees *are* beautiful, like tall mothers spreading their branches across the grass.

In the center of the memorials stands a gazebo. When I asked if anyone played music for the horses Phil said no but that the gazebo has been used for the funerals of people who'd worked on the farm and wanted to be sent away surrounded by what they'd loved. He added that weddings could potentially take place here too, but he couldn't remember any that had. Of course, the owner's children are little yet. One can imagine them in their twenties or thirties, looking out over all this while they take their vows. It's especially easy to imagine since Winding Oaks' current owners' children live most of the time in Barbados, where they have to be guarded because their family's wealth makes them such obvious targets for kidnappers. The kids love it here, Phil said, because it's safe for them to be outside running around.

Many human cemeteries are limited in their occupancy. Some accept only people who live in a particular place (Micanopy), others only decedents of a particular religion (Tolomato in St. Augustine). Still others are open only to people who happened to have died rich (Woodlawn Park North in Miami). In Winding Oaks, burial is by merit. Every horse here either died a champion or was the sire or dam of a champion. And whereas common racehorses are cremated, all the winners that died here and were accorded space are buried whole (except for one that died elsewhere so its grave contains only its heart and hooves).

The tenants of Winding Oaks include the great champion Dr. Fager, who died of colic in 1976 early in his stud career; Dr. Fager's sire Intentionally and his sister Ta Wee, both of whom were sprint champions; and Fager's son Patches, also a sprint champion and the last of the Tartan Farm horses who died here—in 2002 at the ripe age of thirty-two. Also buried here is Preakness Stakes winner Codex, who had started a successful career at stud when he died in 1984.

In the case of racehorses, giving birth to star progeny can up your status almost as much as being a star yourself. And it makes sense. After all, would you rather mate your prize mare to an unknown stallion or to one whose colt romped home in the Preakness? It's too bad that's not true in the human world. If only I could take credit for my kids (I can't; I adore them but otherwise I had nothing to do with it), there's no question I'd be as revered as Gabriel Garcia Marquez by now.

SPOTLIGHT: THE SPEEDING TICKET

In November 1968, after an emotional sendoff, Dr. Fager was finally retiring. As his van entered Marion County after the long drive from New Jersey, he was no doubt anticipating the moment when he would pull into the oak-lined drive at Tartan Farms. But his homecoming was not to be so easy. No sooner had he crossed the county line when deputy sheriff Don Moreland pulled him over and, flanked by photographers, presented the doctor with a summons to appear in court. The charge was "reckless speed." This incident would have been routine (after all, speeding on I-75 is common) if Dr. Fager hadn't been so young—only four—and more important, if he hadn't been a horse.

As it happens, since Dr. Fager was one of the fastest horses racing had ever known, a citation for "reckless speed" was the perfect finis to a stellar career. He was the only horse of his time to have received all four titles: Horse of the Year, Handicap Horse, Sprinter, and Turf Horse. And—pride of place—he was a Floridian. He had been born at Tartan Farms and when he died, he would be buried there.

When Dr. Fager was born, no one expected much of him. Though his dam Aspidistra's bloodline had included the great champion War Admiral, she herself had run so poorly that she'd been retired after only three races. She arrived at Tartan as the staff's present to the owner on his seventieth birthday. They'd chosen her mostly because at $6,500—which was all they had to spend—she was a bargain.

The doctor's sire, Rough'n Tumble, hadn't looked promising either. John Nerud, who ran the farm's day-to-day operations, had gone after the big stallion despite the fact that he had a plastic foot. Most people thought the foot would keep him from breeding because it would be bound to hurt when he came down on it. But Nerud believed Rough'n Tumble's farm manager who said that though coming off mares probably did hurt, the horse mounted them anyway. At the time, people in the racing industry laughed at Nerud for what they thought was his credulousness. But the joke—Dr. Fager—turned out to be on them.

On April 6, 1964, Aspidistra was moved to a small paddock because she was looking ready to drop her foal. Late that morning—unusually, because brood mares seldom give birth in the middle of the day—her water broke. By the time the farm manager, John Hartigan, arrived, the mother-to-be had been moved to the foaling barn where at 12:55 p.m., she delivered a bay colt.

The colt didn't look good. He was skinny, with unusually long legs and two club feet from an abnormality in the joint of the coffin bone. Much later, Nerud said that when Dr. Fager was born, "he wouldn't have brought five thousand dollars."

When the colt was one day old, his trainers started getting him used to the lead. One trainer would guide Aspidistra around the old plum tree in front of the barn while his partner led her colt in the other direction. When the two met in the middle, the trainers would restart the process in the opposite direction. The colt proved to be such a quick learner that after a couple of days, he was walking around toward his mother by himself.

Dr. Fager (his name would come later) grew fast. Eventually he would reach sixteen hands two inches. And though in his first workouts he tended to trip, by the end of his first spring training season his style had become so fluent it was almost honeyed. His exercisers were impressed. This horse could run.

Though the doctor would turn out to be fire-eyed in public, he was always in his private life a sensitive guy. If you scolded him, his feelings would be clearly hurt. He was also kind to other creatures. When a litter of kittens was born in his stall, the minute he was free of his bridle, he would walk over and nuzzle his little ones—for all the world like a father back from work—before heading to his trough for dinner. When the mother cat finally carried her kittens off, the big horse moped for days.

Around this time, John Nerud had been riding after a runaway, ironically one of the stable's cheaper horses, when his own horse shied and threw him. When a month passed and Nerud was still blacking out, he and his wife flew to Boston for medical attention. By the time they arrived at their hotel, Nerud's speech was so slurred that the clerk refused to register them because he was convinced Nerud was drunk. It turned out that Nerud had a massive blood clot on his brain. A Dr. Charles Fager who headed neurosurgery at the Lahey Clinic, operated to remove the clot. A few days later, when Nerud began suffering spasms, Dr. Fager operated again. If the second operation didn't work, he told his patient, and it might not, there was nothing else medicine could do.

Nerud rejected the possibility of failure. He was so determined to pull through that he went back to work from his wheelchair in the hospital corridor, with an IV drip still in his arm. His first task was to name Tartan's new crop of yearlings. The farm's prime prospect became Minnesota Mac, after Tartan's owner, William McKnight, chairman of the board of 3M. Aspidistra's colt was next. When Dr. Fager walked by, Nerud handed him an almost illegible note. The note gave Nerud permission to name the colt after him. Fager looked at it cursorily then scribbled his name on it as if the note had been a prescription, which was exactly what it turned out to be: a prescription for success.

Dr. Fager the colt continued to develop, both as a runner and as a personality. At two he did something which showed him to be as ingenious as he was headstrong. His barn was next to a paddock which the doctor greatly preferred to the confinement of his stall. So every day after he'd been brought back from his workout, he'd lie down and work his head and part of his body under the webbing that served as a gate. Then he'd get up, thereby ripping what was left of the webbing out of the wall. Then he'd hustle over to the paddock and have a high old time running around until someone found him and took him back. Joe Dimitrijevic, who ran Nerud's Hialeah operation at the time, finally broke the doctor of that trick by tapping his nose with a broom every time he stuck his head under the webbing.

Dimitrijevic's was a small victory, but the big one went to Dr. Fager. As long as he lived, he ran races his own way. More often than not, he would romp down the home stretch with his jockey sitting, hands still, on his back.

Because Nerud didn't believe in overworking his horses, the furthest he would run them in training was half a mile. The resulting lack of distance information frustrated clock-ers and bettors because Nerud's charges' workout times didn't tell them how fast his horses might run in an actual race. They so disliked this about Nerud that, at least in New York, the clockers called him the "half-mile sonofabitch." In any case, now you know why in the spring of 1966 when Nerud brought Dr. Fager to New York for the first time, no one had any idea how the horse might do.

Dr. Fager made his debut on July 15 at Aqueduct. With an apprentice jockey named David Hidalgo on his back yelling unsuccessfully "Whoa!" he breezed to the finish, winning eas-ily. The doctor's next race was a six furlong in Saratoga. This time the competition was stiffer. When the race came to the stretch with Dr. Fager ahead by a length, Hidalgo decided to use his whip. This made the big stallion up his lead to six lengths before Hidalgo could get his hands back on the reins.

Though Hidalgo won the race, the incident revealed a potential problem because the moment the horse had felt the whip, he had ducked sideways, a dangerous move in a crowd of horses. Nerud also thought Hidalgo had run his horse too hard—Fager had won the race by an unnecessary eight lengths, and it had taken him half a mile just to calm down. So for the doctor's next outing, Nerud replaced his apprentice jockey with Manny Ycaza, who was more experienced. Never, Nerud told Manny, let Dr. Fager open up if the way ahead was blocked because—Manny could believe it or not—once this horse started running, he couldn't be stopped.

Toward the end of the doctor's first season, Nerud replaced Ycaza with Willie Shoemaker. But Shoemaker turned out not to be a good fit. On his first ride, he used his whip, causing his charge to run into a wall of horses. On his second, he let the doctor drift in the stretch and lost the race to a horse called Successor, whom Dr. Fager had recently easily beaten. After that race, the year's last, Shoemaker told Nerud that the big horse was too much for him. Dr. Fager's loss to Successor turned out to be only a minor blip in a stellar first year. Charles Hatton, writing in the *Daily Racing Form* described him as an "astonishing performer," a horse that leaves his rivals "breathless."

The doctor's next season turned into a classic rivalry between him and a speedster called Damascus. At their first meeting, Willie Shoemaker on Damascus faced a reinstated Ycaza on the doctor. Though Damascus tried hard, the doctor beat him by a half-length. Ycaza said afterwards that he could have won by much more. After this, the call went out to enter Dr. Fager in the Derby or the Preakness, but Nerud demurred because, he said, those races were for a certain kind of horse and Dr. Fager wasn't that kind of horse. Pressed on the point, Nerud lied and said the doctor was injured.

For Fager's next race, the Withers, Nerud had to go to a jockey named Braulio Baeza because Ycaza, who tended to roughness, was temporarily suspended from riding. After Fager won that race by six lengths, Baeza, a prominent rider not given to impetuous outbursts, called him a machine.

The following race saw Ycaza back in the saddle. But Nerud

was worried because one of the race stewards was known to dislike him (Ycaza). Dr. Fager won easily enough, coming within three-fifths of a second of the track record. However, during the race Ycaza had cut in front of the pack, and an inquiry sign went up after the results were announced, the issue being whether Ycaza had caused the horses behind him to bump into each other. When the decision went against Ycaza, Dr. Fager was disqualified. Both Nerud and Ycaza protested, saying their horse had never touched another at any time in the race. However, the results stood, handing Dr. Fager his second loss.

The rest of 1967 went easily until the Woodward stakes, run in Saratoga Springs, New York. This was the only time Dr. Fager and Damascus would meet that year. The field in that race also included the defending Horse of the Year, Buckpasser. Because three stellar horses would meet in the same race, the Woodward was the subject of unprecedented publicity, attracting a record crowd of over fifty-five thousand. On that day, Buckpasser was favored to win, with Dr. Fager and Damascus twin seconds. But both Buckpasser and Damascus used rabbits (fast starters whose role is to tempt contenders to run too fast early in the race) so the race proved not to be a straight showdown. The rabbits caused Dr. Fager to lose the race. He blew by all of them except one, Hedevar, immediately, then blazed past Hedevar in the opening three-quarters. But at the quarter pole, he tired and Damascus overtook him, winning by ten lengths while Dr. Fager, in spite of a heroic last effort, was edged out for second by Buckpasser.

Nerud was so frustrated with the result of the Woodward that he approached the chairman of the New York Racing Association with a proposition for a two-horse race: Damascus versus Dr. Fager, jointly backed by the Association and Nerud, with Damascus putting up nothing. But the chairman turned him down.

One other 1967 race is worth mentioning, not for its outcome—Dr. Fager won easily—but for a pre-event occurrence that reveals the dark side of the racing world at the time. The race in question was the mile and a quarter Hawthorne Gold Cup, run in Chicago. Nerud didn't think his regular night watchman would be enough security given the way that town operated, so he hired Robert Carey, the son of the race's managing director, and told him "Don't come empty." That evening, a limo carrying several men in business suits showed up at Dr. Fager's barn. When Nerud's regular watchman told the men that they couldn't see the horse, the men pushed past him and started toward the doctor's stall. But before they could reach it, Carey stuck a gun in the first man's belly. "You heard what the man said." And the intruders got back into their limo and drove away.

By the end of the year, Dr. Fager had won seven of nine races. This record, coupled with the fact that over his first two years his average victory margin had been five lengths, earned him the title of Champion Sprinter in the *Morning Telegraph/ Daily Racing Form* poll.

The next season, 1968, would be Dr. Fager's last, but by the end of it he'd have set speed records that would stand for almost thirty years. In the off-months between his second and third seasons, Nerud stopped cutting Dr. Fager's mane and foretop, thinking it would make the horse look more ferocious. Whether or not this was a factor, the doctor won his first race—at Aqueduct—by three lengths, carrying a heavy 130 pounds, and would have won by much more had the jockey not been trying to hold him back. He won the next too, in California, also carrying 130, beating an exceptionally fast horse, Kissin' George. No horse had ever won that race carrying so much weight.

In June of 1968 soon after the California race, Dr. Fager came down with colic, a disease his mother and all her colts had been susceptible to. At first, the pain made him thrash wildly about in his stall. Then he tired. It took several men to stop him from going down, but it was necessary because, as everyone in the riding world knows, when a horse is allowed to go down, he seldom gets back up. Finally, the vet gave him triple the normal dose of relaxant and he recovered. The only damage done was that he was sidelined for a couple of weeks.

On the fourth of July, Dr. Fager was set to meet his old rival, Damascus, at the mile and a quarter Southern Handicap. Both horses would be carrying significant weight—Damascus

133 pounds, the doctor 132. When word came that the rabbit Hedevar would be running as well, Nerud put it out that Damascus's handlers must think he couldn't beat Dr. Fager on his own. At the track before the race began, Nerud found out that Frank Whitely, Damascus's trainer, had scratched Hedevar. Whitely didn't deny why he'd done it, so Nerud knew his comment had hit home. In his mind, the race was over.

It turned out to be much closer than Nerud had thought— or hoped. Damascus and Dr. Fager rounded the quarter pole side by side. The cheering crowd rose to its feet. Then Dr. Fager opened up a two-length lead and ran to the finish with Baeza on his back, as relaxed as if he'd been out for a Sunday drive.

Damascus and the doctor's next, and last, showdown happened at the Brooklyn Handicap. This time, Damascus was assigned 130 pounds and Dr. Fager 135. The combination of the weight and the returned Hedevar bested the doctor, who came in two-and-a-half lengths behind his rival.

But Dr. Fager was far from through. Several wins later, he set two world records. First, he ran the fastest quarter mile ever run in a race of any length, and second, in a ten-length victory at Arlington he bested Buckpasser's world record, also set at Arlington, by finishing the race in an unbelievable 1:32 1/5. The track announcer's spontaneous "Wow!" came through loud and clear. He'd been so excited he had forgotten to turn off his microphone.

After one more memorable outing, this one on slick grass, which Dr. Fager carrying 134 pounds fought all the way and won by a nose, Nerud picked a seven-furlong race called the Vosburgh Handicap to finish his horse's career. Dr. Fager was assigned 139 pounds for that race, against Kissin' George's 127. The night before the race, Fager started acting colicky and Nerud stayed up with him until two in the morning, dosing him with baking soda (conventional medication might have caused the horse to fail the drug test). Luckily, by post time, Dr. Fager was fine, and despite his heavy load he blasted out ahead of his rivals, breaking the track record and missing a world record for the distance by only a fifth of a second. It was a fitting close to a great career.

Nerud must have had tears in his eyes as he left the horse he'd lived with so long in the care of Tartan's farm manager, the same John Hartigan who'd seen Dr. Fager born only four years before.

In August of his last racing year, the doctor's stud value had been syndicated at $3.2 million, the third highest ever, behind Buckpasser and Vaguely Noble. For purposes of comparison, Damascus was syndicated at only $2.5 million. Dr. Fager's first few years at stud didn't live up to his reputation but in 1974 several of his progeny started winning and by the end of that year, he was the ninth-leading sire in the country. There was a reason for the delay: most of the doctor's best offspring were fillies, who tend not to hit their strides until their second or third racing seasons.

In August 1976, at the end of the doctor's eighth breeding season, the night watchman at Tartan Farms noticed that the big horse was acting oddly. The doctor had had colic a few times since he arrived home and each time recovered quickly. This time was to be different.

The vet, Dr. Ruben Brawer, arrived sometime after nine. When the usual treatments—mineral oil mixed with a sedative and pain killer, an anti-gas drug called Tercapsol, and an injection of muscle relaxant—made no difference, Dr. Brawer repeated the procedure. When that didn't help either, three more vets were called. By now the doctor's pulse was racing. He was trembling and sweating. He was also in obvious pain. The vets punched him with a trocar, an instrument used to relieve bloat. It didn't work.

Dr. Fager thrashed about, swelling tighter and tighter, and banging into the corners of his stall. At 11:30 p.m., he lay down and died.

The cemetery where the great horse lies sits on its hill overlooking Lake Ta Wee (named for Dr. Fager's half sister). Beneath Dr. Fager's headstone is a flat granite slab reading: "Racing's Grand Slam . . . 1968 Horse of the Year, Handicap Champion, Sprint Champion, Grass Champion . . . World record for a mile." But this doesn't sum up the doctor's life. What should have been on his stone is something the late racing writer David Alexander once said of him: "The memory of him is the memory of the wind."

PART III

CENTRAL AND WEST CENTRAL FLORIDA

﹌﹌﹌﹌﹌﹌﹌﹌﹌﹌﹌﹌﹌﹌﹌﹌﹌﹌﹌﹌﹌﹌﹌﹌﹌﹌﹌﹌﹌﹌﹌﹌﹌

10

UPSALA CEMETERY,
SANFORD

In the late nineteenth century, many Swedes left their impoverished homeland in hopes of finding a better life. Possibly because of the proliferation of "land of opportunity" recruiting information in Sweden at the time, most of them traveled to the United States. In any case, a census taken just before World War I revealed that one-fifth of all the Swedes in the world were living here.

It's a commonplace that there are lots of people of Scandinavian descent in states like Wisconsin and Minnesota. What's not so well-known is that, as the migrations went on, significant numbers of Swedes either went directly to central Florida or ended up there.

The first group of immigrants from Sweden settled in the general area in the 1850s, but the bulk of the population came later—beginning in 1871—to work in Henry Sanford's orange groves. Sanford, who had been ambassador to Belgium under President Lincoln, went to Florida in 1870 because he thought there was money in citrus. After looking around, he decided that the central part of the state would be best for his purpose so he bought 12,500 acres on the south side of Lake Monroe. He began by planting an eighty-six-acre grove (named "St. Gertrude" after a thirteenth-century German saint) just west of what is now downtown Sanford. When St. Gertrude's soil turned out to be inhospitable Sanford had the trees moved to another grove, where he'd already installed seven hundred banana trees and four thousand orange seedlings. That grove,

"Belair," still exists as an agricultural experiment station. Belair's biggest claim to fame is that its manager, Carl Vihlen, developed the Valencia, which would become the mainstay of Florida's citrus industry via a strain of orange from an English import called Tardif-Brown's Late.

Sanford started his citrus business by hiring locals. When they turned out to be unreliable, he imported sixty blacks from Madison, in northern Florida. But soon after the new workers arrived, a group of whites armed with shotguns swarmed into the camp where the blacks were housed and drove them away. Whether anyone was killed is a matter of dispute but the incident certainly proved that the two-race solution wasn't going to work.

Sanford then considered importing Chinese labor but decided against it. Finally, an entrepreneur named Wilhelm Henschen, who called himself "doctor" because he had a PhD from Uppsala, persuaded Sanford to try Swedes. Henschen knew central Florida well. He had emigrated there himself, planning to start an agricultural community at Lake Jessup, but his wife rebelled so aggressively at the pioneer life that he moved the family to New York where he worked for a shipping company and started a Swedish language newspaper.

For the recruitment process, Henschen teamed up with his brother Josef, who was then still living in Sweden. The Henschens charged Sanford $8.75 a head plus expenses. The first group they brought in, some thirty-three people, a few of them children, earned them $300. The Swedes were allowed into the country under the Contract Labor Law, a federal statute— essentially indentured servitude—that offered immigrants citizenship in return for a full year of work. The idea was that by the end of the year the immigrant would have repaid the cost of his passage and would then be free. But in practice many new Americans ended up working under substandard conditions and for periods considerably longer than a year.

Sanford, though, at least intended to be fair. The agreement he made with his first group of workers was that in return for the year's labor, they would be housed, fed, and their children would be educated. Later, justifiably worried about losing his help, Sanford offered the Swedes five acres if they would promise to stay with him for that many years. Those original land grants were the beginning of the settlement of New Upsala (from "Uppsala," a town in Sweden).

The first recruits came in steerage across the Atlantic. Seasickness was rampant in the unventilated conditions below decks. Even if you weren't sick yourself, the odor from those who were must have been overwhelming. From New York, the workers-to-be were given deck passage in three stages: to Charleston, to Jacksonville, then up the St. Johns to Mellonville, where they finally arrived, weak-legged, with at most one foot-locker's worth of possessions.

There were glitches with Sanford's handling of this first group. To begin with, the one-room frame structure he'd had built (at a cost of $300) to house the new workers was so small that about half the floor space originally intended to be divided between men and women ended up mixed-sex. There weren't enough beds either, so many people had to sleep on the floor. Sanford also lacked understanding of the effects of traveling so far and to such a different climate. The Swedes had arrived at the start of summer but instead of giving them time to adjust to their new environment, Sanford put them straight to work. The men were assigned to clearing land while the women cooked, sewed, or did laundry.

It wasn't long before the workers complained that their living conditions violated their contract. Sanford responded by giving them some straw for bedding and some clothing (much of what the immigrants had arrived with was now beyond use and many of them were without adequate shoes). He also offered them credit at his store for tobacco and provisions. But despite the fact that the Swedes' potatoes, beans, rice, and beef (they did their own butchering) were costing Sanford less than $6 per person per month, he charged them so much that many of this first group were forced to extend their contracts.

Early on, the skilled workers in that first group (most of the men) had complained about being made to clear land, but they were such fast workers that the problem soon took care of itself. In only six weeks, they'd finished that work and were reassigned to projects more suitable to their backgrounds: a store, a hotel, and a church.

By the time a second group of twenty Swedes arrived in November of 1871, life in the groves had settled down. The new arrivals were assigned to a new twenty-by-forty-foot bunk house and after a few days of supervised adjustment, they were given the supplies the first group had been forced to demand.

There was considerable local prejudice against the Swedes. Contrary to the way most of us perceive Scandinavians, one of the complaints most often lodged against the new arrivals was that they were dirty. The main reason the community didn't like the Swedes though—and this should sound familiar—came down to jobs. One morning a note appeared on the door of the church under construction threatening to burn the place down if Sanford didn't get rid of the "foreign labor." Happily, the threat turned out to be a bluff. Sanford ignored it and the church, at the time the most elaborate in that part of Florida, was completed without incident.

Though most of the Swedes stayed where they arrived, from the beginning some single men had been running away which, given their indentured status, made them fugitives. By 1872, the Swedish equivalent of the Underground Railroad had grown up to care for the escapees: a safe house in Charleston, followed by spiriting away back to Sweden.

In 1873, Sanford gave seventeen of his workers five acres each in New Upsala, a colony just north of Belair. As time passed, more and more Swedes settled there, and by the late nineteenth century, it had become the largest Swedish settlement in Florida.

Life in New Upsala wasn't physically easy. The weather for most of the year was steamy—not ideal for women dressed in Victorian clothes. The terrain too was so wet that a swamp split the settlement in two, upper and lower. Still, for the unassimilated, New Upsala was a comfortable place to be. The grocery store—supplied by a car hand-hauled by narrow gauge from Sanford—sold such familiar specialties as lutefisk and salt herring. There was a local school where children who spoke Swedish at home were in the majority. For social life, there were two Lutheran churches.

One of the churches was accessible only via a foot-wide boardwalk through the swamp, which made attending service a teetery business for ladies who would not think of not wearing long skirts and high-button shoes, not to mention hats susceptible to catching on overhanging branches. Sometimes gentlemen would wade alongside them to be sure they didn't fall in. One of those gentlemen, a Mr. Larsen, was said to have caught consumption from repeatedly sitting through services with wet feet.

It was whispered about in those days that the boardwalk was haunted since often when the lanterns people carried at night reached a certain point—always the same point—they would flicker and go out. Loud splashing would follow, to the accompaniment of eerie noises. Some ladies would faint under the strain and their gentlemen escorts would be forced to carry them home. A few skeptics suggested that the young men had invented the ghost to soften up their girls so that when they proposed to them, they'd be accepted, but that uncharitable contention was never substantiated.

In 1894 and 1895, back-to-back freezes dealt a one-two punch to the citrus industry. The first, in December, caused a good deal of damage. Then, in the predawn hours of February 7, just as the groves were beginning to recover, there was a second hard frost. Many of the trees cracked loudly as expanding sap burst their trunks and branches. By morning, there were virtually none left alive. Since citrus had supported nearly everyone in New Upsala, all but sixteen families were forced to leave. The churches, now without full-time pastors, cut their Swedish-language services to once a month. Happily, within ten years, many of the families that had left returned, and as time went on, other Swedes joined them. By the 1920s, the town had a thriving population of over five hundred.

Among New Upsala's early inhabitants were my ex-husband's grandmother Helen Malm, and her family, which consisted of her parents and eight sisters. Helen, who married the Sanford postmaster, lived on Sanford Avenue in a house whose yard was filled with huge citrus trees planted from seed when she was a young, just married, woman. The last of the Malm sisters, Aunt Alma, was recruited along with other Swedes to work for the telephone company. She worked there all her life, and her daughter after her. Aunt Alma lived in a tiny Cracker house out of town until she died. She was one of the sweetest people I ever met, and despite her numerous privations I never once heard her complain.

Sweden is still a presence in the Sanford area. Although Swedish is no longer spoken in New Upsala and most of the original buildings are gone (with the exception of the Presbyterian church built in 1892, which still stands on the corner of Upsala Road and 25th Street), the many local descendents of those original settlers still dress up at Christmas time to commemorate St. Lucia. The St. Lucia tradition involves the youngest daughter in the house getting up first on Christmas Day. Then, having dressed all in white and put on a crown of candles—these days, they use Christmas lights—she serves her family coffee and sweet rolls. Though it isn't commonly known, a love of strong coffee is as traditionally Swedish as a partiality to lutefisk.

Upsala cemetery is located on twenty-five acres Henry Sanford gave the Swedes to use as a worship center and burial ground. The first church they built there (now gone) was, naturally, Lutheran since Lutheranism is the state religion of Sweden and native-born Swedes may leave the church only by formally disaffiliating. But though services were conducted in Swedish by a Lutheran minister, the original congregation decided not to affiliate with the national organization. Instead it called itself the Scandinavian Society.

The original congregation took back its withdrawal and reaffiliated with the Swedish Lutheran Church in 1892, when some of the younger Swedes left what they saw as their antiquated religion for Presbyterianism. This situation has caused some confusion as to the age of the cemetery. It's been erroneously dated from the beginnings of the Scandinavian Society's formal affiliation with the Lutheran Church. Actually the earliest burial there was in 1831.

It says something about Swedish nature that the young people's departure to Presbyterianism didn't cause a rift in the community. Instead, people in New Upsala would go to both churches, attending the Lutheran service in the morning and the Presbyterian social in the afternoon. And no matter what their affiliation, any local Swedes who died were buried in Upsala, on the land Sanford had donated.

Upsala—announced by a historical marker—lies along Upsala Road just off State Road 46 from Sanford. To get there, you pass a mix of farmland and older houses interspersed with gated communities that look out of place in this rural setting. The church that used to front the cemetery is long gone, and the land is being cleared to make way for its (still Lutheran) replacement. In the course of the land clearing, though some large trees were left, many others were brutally cut, so to get to the cemetery you have to traverse a balding area. You would think all this destruction would have ruined the atmosphere of the cemetery. But you'd be wrong.

The place is a jewel. Because there are still trees and a row of jasmine bushes shielding it from the partially constructed church, it feels so remote that the sight of a truck driving by on the road seems as dissonant as a freighter suddenly looming over the top of a canal embankment. Doves call from the horseshoe of woods of oaks, palmetto, and cabbage palm that cup the grounds on three sides, the way a mother's hand might present water to a thirsty child. Native grasses carpet the area. Appropriate to a place sheltering pioneers and their descendents, there are no grandiose monuments, only simple stones, sometimes only markers left by a funeral home recording births and deaths.

As you come in, there's a small grove, bamboo at the back, fronted by a tall bush with spiky red flowers sheltering a wooden fence with an undated sign that says "Angel Joy, Beloved daughter of Joyce, loving you always." In front of the fence is a lovely, thoughtful planting of bromeliads, several of which were, the day I came, in pale pink bloom. There's also a small statue, almost hidden by jasmine, of twin angels into whose laps flowers have fallen.

The antiseptic beauty of golf-course-quality maintenance seen in other cemeteries is completely absent here. The grounds feel intimate and natural, as if the woods were slowly reclaiming their own. Unswept leaves lie gently on some of the graves. It feels as if people who would come to such a place would come not for pride's sake but simply to kneel and remember.

There are many family plots with names like Lundquist (beginning with John, born in 1885, all the way to the twins Joanne and Gerald born in 1933, who lived no years and nine years, respectively), Erikson, and Bengtson (Christina, born in 1839, Erik, 1836, Elias, 1844, and the last of the Bengtsons, Edward, born in 1881). There are also Tyner (including Leonard in 1906 and his sister Gussie, who followed him four years later, neither of whom reached a second birthday) and Stedt (Carl, b. 1841, and Emma, b. 1871). The Stedts' graves and Frank Erikson's (b. 1848) were originally together, described by a rectangle of iron pipe interspersed with irrigation pockets—they look like stone pots—taken from farms. Similar pockets can be found all around the cemetery.

Some of the graves are so hidden by vegetation that one needs to kneel to see them properly. One of these belongs to Patsy Ann Holloway, b. 1935, who lived only two years. The letters on Patsy's marker are intact but grown over, so you have to find out who she was by using your fingertips—a perfect metaphor for the way we find the past, as if we were in a dark room, descrying its boundaries and stories with our hands. Patsy's parents, Walter and Jossie Holloway, lie nearby, just on the other side of the tree.

Another of the nearly hidden graves is John Borell's, born 1857, died 1943. His wife, Christina, lies in a depression nearby, her place marked only by a funeral home marker under cracked glass now almost impossible to read. Christina, it says, lived ninety years, ten months, and twenty-nine days, a way of marking time usually limited to children, and making her birth date, April 9, 1870, available only by subtraction. John Borell's grave is concealed differently from little Patsy's. Hers lies under the arch of a large palmetto, his is sheltered by bushes at the foot of a very tall tree that was almost surely not there when John was laid to rest.

A couple of the women in this yard—and probably many more—deserve particular mention: Christina Bengston, for example, came to Florida in the early summer of 1871, part of the first group of Swedes Henry Sanford imported. When the family arrived, she and her husband, Elias, had two small children. Twelve years later, when Elias died, she had ten. Eleven mouths to feed yet she persevered, and did it alone. She must have been a saint. Among Christina's descendents buried here are her daughters, Augusta, who married a Fry, and Matilda, who married a Tyner. Finally, there's Christina's granddaughter Eunice Martin, "Aunt Eunice" to the Swedish community. Eunice was born in New Upsala in 1901 and lived almost 102 years. Late in her life, she joined a social club called the Birthday Girls, made up of direct descendents of New Upsala's early settlers. The activities of the club consisted of periodic gatherings for coffee and sweet treats. At the time the club was founded, almost all its members were in their eighties.

When you visit New Upsala, you will find yourself inadvertently walking over many sleepers under the ground because what you see is far from all there is. Somewhere between twenty and thirty no longer marked graves have been located so far but, considering the population of New Upsala and the fact that almost anyone who died locally was buried here, there must be many more

Before you leave, take a moment to stand in the center of the grounds Sanford gave the Swedes those many years ago and breathe in the peace that surrounds you—the bird that calls somewhere out of sight, the spirits of the people who lived and died on this land, and the spell of Florida: the palm and jasmine and palmetto that outlasted them and will outlast us all.

SPOTLIGHT: VOYAGE TO AMERICA

Sofia Charlotta Sjoborg sits, so tiny beside her cousin Wilhem that she seems almost another race, in a Henschen family portrait taken in Sweden in 1868. Three years later, at the age of sixty-six (at a time when forty was considered elderly), she emigrated to Florida. Seven years after that, she began—by herself—homesteading 140 acres. Homesteading in those days involved five years of living on, and farming, the land you wanted to claim, then having witnesses substantiate your work. In August of 1833—she was seventy-eight—Sofia completed all those requirements and received title to her land in a document signed by then president of the United States, Chester A. Arthur. Sadly, her achievement came at a cost. She died three months later and—though her marker has not survived—was buried in Upsala Cemetery.

This piece, though, isn't about Sofia's later life, because beyond the bare facts there isn't much documentation of that. It's about her journey from Sweden to Florida as recorded in her travel diary, only recently translated from the Swedish.

Sofia and her cousin Esias left her home in Upsala for Stockholm on April 18, 1871, to join Esais's brothers Wilhelm and Josef and some others, a group of about fifty in all. From there, the emigrants boarded the train to Gothenberg. Though interrupted briefly by a broken rail, they arrived in plenty of time to meet their ship, which was scheduled to depart two days later. On the morning of departure, after Sofia finished her coffee with her friends Charlotte and Lotta, she proceeded to the dock, only to find that the ship's 1:00 p.m. launch had been delayed. The reason for the delay—that the police commissioner was refusing to clear the emigrants for departure until he had finished dinner—annoyed Sofia and some others enough that they got on the ship anyway. The ship's captain was annoyed too, so much so that he thumbed his nose at the commissioner by taking up the gangplank and leaving shore. Unfortunately, this left the bulk of Sofia's group behind on the dock. Some of the women were crying, and their sisters on the ship, according to Sofia, were uselessly reaching out their arms. It was a tense situation, with the emigrants begging the irascible captain to go back to the docks and take on the rest of his passengers. But it ended happily because in the end, he did.

The first night out, Esias helped Sofia and some of the other older women to their bunks at about six. They fell asleep as they could, given the thuds of the younger passengers dancing "Franciskas" and waltzing "as long as they were able" to tunes played on a harmonica. Sofia reports that she woke feeling queasy enough that she spent most of the next two days in her bunk. Finally, the ship reached Edinburgh and the emigrants traveled by train to Glasgow, where Sofia and her companions pronounced both the food—steaming coffee and sweet rolls—and accommodation much more to their liking than what they'd encountered in Gothenburg. The group then proceeded to enjoy a couple of days visiting parks and shops which sold "every imaginable kind of thing, especially beautiful small hats, flowers and feathers, birds of paradise, etc etc."

On their second day in Glasgow, one of Sofia's traveling companions, a Mrs. Janson, became so ill that the local doctor who visited her advised her (through an interpreter) to stay behind. But Sofia and others carried the day by arguing that for their friend to remain among strangers in a place where she couldn't even speak the language would only aggravate her condition, and under the care of W. Erlund, a fellow emigrant, the lady was allowed to leave.

The *Anglia*, the ship that would take the travelers to America, put out from Glasgow on April 29 with five hundred passengers, and took on two hundred more in Ireland. Mrs. Janson spent the whole voyage in the ship's hospital, in the company of a girl with lockjaw who had been, before she was roused by large doses of cognac, given up for dead.

On the group's first day at sea, a Sunday, Sofia's brother Wilhelm read a sermon for the Swedes. Sofia, who was devoted to her Lutheran faith, reveled in his message, and entered in her diary afterwards that she was determined not to be corrupted by American Christianity which she saw as indistinguishable "from the secular world in its participation in pleasures." Listen to her describing her happiest moments on the voyage: "someone reads aloud from the New Testament, and those who like to listen gather around . . . and Julia and Esaias and sometimes some of the Vustmanland girls join in a spiritual song." "Then," Sofia continues, "I lie for awhile on sacks of sawdust [she would have slept in a featherbed at home but she never presents the sawdust as a hardship] surrounded by dear Christian sisters, most of whom I have not seen before but have known in the spirit, and I feel my hand pressed by the others at the more beautiful and lively stanzas."

Sofia's piety—though as you've just heard, she found it a comfort—didn't keep her from enjoying secular pleasures.

The passage in her letter describing the hymn-singing continues like this: "Freedom then comes into its own; soon thereafter appear the harmonica players who begin to sing lusty songs . . . the English waiter comes in, dancing in time with the music and hands out the butter dishes, boys wrestle with each other, throw their caps against the ceiling . . . Laughter and noise but all in friendliness."

The first week out the weather was stormy enough that many of the ship's passengers, including Sofia, were seasick. She says, "I cannot eat . . . I lay down most of the time." Her discomfort was probably exacerbated by several facts. To begin with, every time she or one of her companions tried to get some air, the waves washing over the decks would soak them and force them to retreat. Then, there was no light below decks and the sleeping arrangements were so crowded that passengers had to lie pressed up against each other. There would have been no escaping the rocking, or the sounds of retching amid odors of sick and excrement. And this with all comers mixed in: married people and single people, desirables and undesirables. Sofia particularly mentions one woman and "her two filthy kids."

The negativity of that last comment was unusual for Sofia, who was not a complainer. Her statement that within "a few days" most of the travelers recovered and began to enjoy themselves was typical and has to be weighed against other reports that suggest that the entire group spent the trip deathly ill.

On Sunday May 7, some people out on deck spotted an iceberg but Sofia didn't manage to dress quickly enough to see it. After services, she passed the time as she did most days, talking quietly with friends and making such plans as devising garden layouts for when they should arrive.

When, four days later, the American coast came into view, Sofia hurried down to the hospital to tell Mrs. Janson. The day before the lady had been sitting up in a chair and had asked for and drunk a glass of soda water but this morning she seemed much weaker, so weak that Sofia wondered at first if she were breathing. Promising Mrs. Janson she'd return, Sofia went up on deck, where she saw the pale green hills of New York, as well as many steamships. When she went back to the hospital, she found her friend in apparently deep sleep, her hands and forehead cold. The ship's doctor lit a candle to examine the lady then said, a few minutes later, that she was dead. What was left of her was shrouded in an English flag and lowered into the sea.

In New York harbor, American doctors boarded the ship and led the immigrants "back and forth on deck like a flock of sheep." At dusk, everyone entered Castle Garden, once a 2,000-seat theater where Jenny Lind, the Swedish nightingale, had sung. Germans, Scotsmen, Irishmen, and Swedes were separated and their goods inspected. After that came a meal of cheese, bread, and milk, and a sleep on mattresses laid out on the floor.

Sofia was lucky to have arrived at Castle Garden. If she'd emigrated only a few years earlier, she'd have been left to the untender mercies of the predators who thronged the docks on the southern tip of Manhattan. The worst of these were said to have been the "runners" whose job it was to entice immigrants to overpriced run-down boarding houses. Some of the worthies were so aggressive that if a family proved recalcitrant, they would seize a baby or a pretty daughter's wrist and take off through the crowd. When, by whatever means, families ended up at the runners' boarding houses, the exorbitant rates often left them penniless before they could get established. In that case, their landlords would strip them of their belongings and do one of three things: turn them out on the street, send them to work in a brickyard, or shanghai them onto a ship. For years, the police were more or less helpless to stop such abusive practices because the docks at which the immigrants were landing stretched out over such a wide area— three or four miles. Finally the government decided to handle the problem by centralizing the immigration process, so it converted Castle Garden to a reception center. Once the Garden was in full swing, the only immigrants who were preyed on were the ones who, in spite of being warned, listened to the hustlers who assaulted them as soon as they walked out the gates.

Processing the crowds who came to Castle Garden wasn't simple because the immigrants came from such different places. But early on, according to a contemporary article in *Harpers*, customs officials came to recognize the nationalities of new arrivals by their dress. Englishmen wore Scotch caps; Germans sported dark blue woolen coats, brass-buttoned vests, and flat caps; Bohemians wore scarves; Norwegians asymmetrical stiff grey jackets, and so on. The author of the article singled out the Swedes—whom he said made excellent citizens—as particularly easy to distinguish, not just by their clothing (tanned-leather breeches and waistcoats) but also because they had a very specific body odor, a mix, the author thought, of leather, salt herring, onions, and perspiration.

Recognizing the country of origin of an immigrant, though, isn't the same as communicating with him or her, so language-based misunderstandings often made for slow processing. It often happened too that someone would arrive knowing only the name of his destination city which, since American city names aren't unique, could require a good deal of probing before the new arrival could be directed to the railroad ticket office.

Sofia's group presented no such problems. Not many Swedes did, since, compared to other immigrants, they tended to be highly educated. After being cleared, the Henschen party decamped to one of the boarding houses (room and board typically between $6 and $9 a week) permitted to solicit within Castle Garden.

Over the next day and a half, Sofia went often from her new rooms to see traveling companions depart, while Wilhelm spent his time making purchases in anticipation of his group's journey south. Finally, at two in the afternoon on May 13, their own time came, and Sofia and her party embarked for Charleston on the *Champion*. This was a much lighter boat than the *Anglia* had been, and was crewed mostly by Negroes whom Sofia pronounced "older and more serious" than the crew of the *Anglia*. As the ship steamed toward its destination, where it arrived two days later, the Swedes shed their traveling clothes in favor of what they imagined more suitable to warm weather.

Charleston proved to be a busy place, with mules and Negroes unloading cotton and other cargos, and when Sofia embarked on a walk, she found herself enjoying its beautiful streets, especially its flowers. Soon though, she got lost and had trouble figuring out where she was since with no English she could neither explain what she wanted nor understand what people were trying to tell her. In the end "a kind old Negro" guided her to her third and last ship, the *Diktator*, bound for Savannah.

The bare facts of Sofia's description of her journey gibe with other reports: the party left Sweden for Edinburgh, Ireland, and finally New York. But her cheerful diary entries belie the tone of her shipmates' letters that tend to stress bad weather, the omnipresent sickness, and the poor conditions on the ship. The contrast between Sofia's and her companions' descriptions is so extreme that, reading her side by side with anyone else, you'd think she had made a different journey which, of course, she hadn't.

This kind of filtering applies as well to what Sofia says happened when the party settled into their new home. For months, she reports, she lived in a tent (remember, she arrived in June, the most humid, oppressive part of the year). And since Sofia wasn't the kind of woman who would have stripped down to stay cool, she must have endured the heat in the kind of heavy black dresses she wore for her family picture back in 1868. And her accounts don't even mention mosquitoes—and as anyone who has ever been to Florida in the summer knows, there must have been plenty. The closest she got to complaining was her comment, after she'd proclaimed her tent "an excellent place to live," that "it [the tent] is somewhat cramped and warm at night, when the walls are shut tight." I should think so.

11

MANASOTA MEMORIAL PARK, BRADENTON

In the early 1920s, circus magnate John Ringling's secretary purchased a forty-acre celery field. She thought she was buying investment property, something to hold onto until land prices rose. But her boss, ever the deal-maker, persuaded her to let him build a family crypt on it. Once the crypt was built, he reserved the land around it for his family and employees and christened the resulting area Manasota, a combination of "Sarasota," the winter home of the Ringling Brothers Barnum & Bailey Circus, and "Manatee," the county in which the land lies.

Not long after Ringling's pink marble crypt was built, Manasota opened its burials to the general public with the exception of the area Ringling had reserved for circus people (by which, incidentally, he meant not just performers but the extended Ringling family, all the way down to custodians).

Finding Manasota involves facing the hard truth of sprawl, since like so many once-isolated Floridian institutions Manasota has been affected by development. When it was founded, it lay in a bucolic haze of fields. Probably, too, since this is Florida, there were lowlands nearby where frogs sang at night. Today however, it's split by the six lanes of Highway 70. Two-thirds of the cemetery lies on the south side, the rest on the north.

Ringling and his people are buried in the southern section. The northern area consists of a half-empty field where some lovely oaks intersperse with a scatter of built-in vases of fading artificial blooms. Fronting the north section, facing the highway, is a brand new funeral home. The original office, a two-story white frame house across the road, seems to be used now mostly for its garage where the maintenance people keep their equipment.

If you're approaching from I-75, getting into the interesting part of Manasota's grounds is a little tricky. The large sign announcing it is on your right (the north) as is the cemetery's official parking lot. But the historic section is on your left, the other side of the road. And since to cross this particular highway on foot would be to risk acquiring your very own headstone, it's more prudent to drive. To do this, go left out of the parking lot, and turn right at the first light. The elaborate sandstone affair flanked by towers on your immediate right after the turn is the entrance you want. You'll need to make your visit in daylight hours because the wrought-iron gates between the towers are closed after dark.

Facing you as you enter is a sign listing the many activities Manasota prohibits. You can't plant flowers, shrubs, bushes, or trees, for example. And you can leave such items as potted plants, wreaths, baskets, and flowers on your loved one's grave only if it happens to be Christmas, Easter, Veterans Day, Memorial Day, Mother's Day, or Father's Day (presumably grandparents are out of luck). Anything you put there on any of those days except Christmas will be removed within a week—which the sign renders as "seven (7) days." Christmas flowers and decorations get a break; they can be left until January 31. In other words, Santa Clauses and mistletoe get five times more stage time than items left, say, for your mother.

But that's not all. You can't put boxes, toys, ornaments, chairs, benches, trellises "and/or similar articles" near a grave. Nor may you enclose it, meaning no family plots. In case you don't get the idea that the bottom line is "no anything" the sign finishes its list, rather ungrammatically, this way: "Personal items such as poems, pictures, letters, etc. shall be removed immediately by cemetery personnel."

A young man who happened to be cutting the grass that day explained that most of the prohibitions are economically driven. First, the management doesn't allow nonstandard tombstones because it wants to maximize sales of its in-house memorials—dull-looking flush-to-the-ground markers with built-in vases. Second, any decorations impact staff time, especially mowing time. Now, though flush memorials may be standard these days, many of the other prohibitions aren't, and from the entrance the uniformity of the grave sites felt stifling. Luckily, as you'll hear, when I made my way farther in I found evidence of the truism that no matter how repressive a regime, there's no stopping the human spirit.

John Ringling, of course, had his crypt built here long before there were any prohibitions and its large pink marble edifice with R I N G L I N G engraved above the door cuts an impressive figure as you enter the cemetery. Three steep steps lead the eye up to a wrought-iron gate flanked by two wide marble bowls whose size so strongly suggests water to me that I wondered if Ringling had intended them as fountains.

Though John had intended the crypt for himself, in the end he was buried in Sarasota and his wife Mabel, who was originally here, was eventually moved to lie by John. But John's brother Charles—the circus's manager and advance man—was buried here and never moved which keeps the Ringling name from being a hollow boast.

"Ringling" is the Americanized version of John and Charles's name. They were born Rüngeling, the sons of a German immigrant and harness maker. Charles and his five brothers grew up doing vaudeville. Then one night in 1884, they decided to bill their act as a circus. Their timing was excellent since the period straddling the turn of the twentieth century was the golden age of the circus in America. Circuses were so popular with the public in those days that by 1900 more than a hundred were touring the countryside, drawing, especially in rural areas, as many as twelve thousand spectators at each performance.

The Ringlings were ambitious; witness the grandiose monikers they tried out in their first three years: "Ringling Bros. United Monster Shows"; "The Great Double Circus"; "The Royal European Menagerie"; "The Museum, Caravan, and Congress of Trained Animals." Such names must have convinced someone because they did so well that around 1890, they joined the elite—the thirty or so circuses that traveled by rail. From the beginning they were toward the top of that elite: their engines pulled eighty-four cars (Buffalo Bill's Wild West Show, by comparison, traveled with fifty-nine). At their peak in the early 1920s, the Ringlings' trains had one hundred cars and they were using tents that could accommodate more than ten thousand. Such massive shows required so much land (a full fourteen acres) that as the population urbanized, their venues declined. In 1932—the end of an era—the circus passed out of Ringling hands.

The first fifteen years of the brothers' careers as circus owners presaged none of this. By 1900, they had absorbed so many smaller operations that their only serious remaining competition was Barnum and Bailey. In 1907, for the sum of $400,000 they gained control of that too and became America's indisputably biggest show.

What distinguished the Ringling brothers from other circus owners besides their business acumen was that in contrast to the profanity, crooked gaming, and short changing that were foisted off on the public by many traveling circuses, they ran a clean operation. In other words, their circus was the kind of event to which a family could take a child of tender years without worrying over what Mama and Daddy might have to explain on the way home.

The Ringlings' modus operandi was to tour between late April and early October (performing in over 150 cities per tour) then spend the winter resting and working up new acts. Its first winter home was Bridgeport, Connecticut but in 1927, the now-named Greatest Show on Earth officially moved to Sarasota, Florida. Charles Ringling in particular loved Sarasota. He lived there (in a mansion now owned by New College), donated land to the county to build a courthouse, founded Sarasota's third bank, the Ringling Bank and Trust, and served as president of the chamber of commerce. When he died of a cerebral hemorrhage, the whole town mourned.

You might look for Siegfried "Freddy" Kursawe, who died at seventy-three in 2003 and was buried in the Ringling area. Kursawe was a member of the Six Frielanis, a cycling act I remember seeing when I thought all this was sorcery.

Arguably the most famous circus occupants of Manasota, besides Ringling himself, are some members of the Flying Wallendas, whose magical act I was lucky enough to see when I was a child. The Wallendas aren't (as you'd expect them to have been) buried in the Ringling area, so finding them took some searching. I finally located their plot straight back from and a little to the left of Ringling's, set out behind two trees, one of which is a palm which leans precipitously, no doubt courtesy of some hurricane.

A wide granite slab proclaims "The Wallendas" and underneath the name, "Aerialists Supreme." That the family is not forgotten is evidenced by several unfaded bouquets of artificial flowers leaning against similar older ones along the base of the memorial. The Wallenda plot is marked by short pillars, but though the chains that joined the pillars are still here, some disrespectful person—probably a cemetery worker—has unhooked them.

Three generations of Wallendas lie here, including the clan's patriarch, Karl, known as The Great Wallenda, who fell to his death in 1978 while navigating a high wire across a street in Puerto Rico. A photograph on Karl's grave shows him wearing a purple vest and pants, and a yellow shirt. He's balancing a long stick. His feet are out of sight but you can almost feel the way the wire sags under them. Karl is still handsome in the picture though he must have been in his forties or fifties when it was taken.

The circus people share Manasota with a number of early baseball players. The most colorful of them may be Hall of Famer Paul Waner, who played outfield for Pittsburgh in the 1920s and '30s. Paul, who was born in 1903 and died in 1965 was nicknamed "Big Poison," and was something of an alcohol aficionado. Casey Stengel said of Waner's graceful base running that "he could slide without breaking the bottle on his hip." Another of Paul's alcohol-related claims to fame was his legendary ability to hit while hungover. And he hit well. Only in the brief period when the team persuaded him not to drink did his batting average fall. Paul Waner and his younger brother, Lloyd "Little Poison" hold the record for career hits by brothers, ahead of both the Alous and the DiMaggios.

You may wonder how the Waners got their names. The way I heard it the names date back to a game in 1927 when a Brooklyn fan was said to have blurted out, "Them Waners! It's always the little poison on thoid and the big poison on foist!" Of course, like many stories of this kind, this one may be too good to be true.

Another Hall of Famer here in Manasota is manager Bill McKechnie, born 1886, who led three teams—the Pirates, the St. Louis Cardinals, and the Cincinnati Reds—to National League pennants. Other early major leaguers are "Butch" Henline, born 1894, Johnny Cooney, born 1901, and Jack Burns, born 1907.

Wrapping up the list of Manasotans whose lives were remarkable in the conventional sense of that word is William Grove who, in 1899 at the age of twenty-seven was awarded the Medal of Honor for his courage during a battle in the Philippines. His citation reads: "In advance of his regiment, he rushed to the assistance of his colonel, charging, pistol in hand, killing seven insurgents, and compelling surrender of all not killed or wounded."

Unlike the baseball players and war heroes, the Masons buried here have their own area—the only non-circus group that does. In the center of their space three God-sized pink marble chairs arranged in a "U" face a dais with a Masonic symbol. On the dais a Bible is spread open to the words "May the souls of the righteous through God's mercy rest in peace and light perpetual shine upon the world."

Except for those two set-aside areas, Manasota's aspect is generally uneventful. For one thing, there's a minimum of landscaping and except for the planted palms that line the roads, very few large trees (not surprising when you remember that the cemetery is an ex-celery field). Still, the paucity of shelter means that most of Manasota's occupants rest in the mean sun. If one sees the sun as reality this makes metaphoric sense, though even so, I think that after a few years I'd long for shade.

There's very little statuary here either, perhaps because statuary and unusual memorials were prohibited early on. Or maybe the explanation is that Manasota was opened rather recently, in 1929, long after the Victorian fashion for statuary had passed. In any case, if you sight across the tops of the graves, what you'll see is an ocean of shortish granite markers only a few of which are topped with anything. The only exceptions I noticed (though of course there may be more) were a stone cupid sitting on the top of a child's grave and a headless Virgin Mary in front of the memorial to a couple named Damasco.

Manasota's plainness isn't limited to its stones. The inscriptions here yield many fewer facts than usual and fewer heartfelt tributes or farewells. Even the Wallendas refrained from commenting anywhere except on the stone that refers to all of them.

There are heartening exceptions to the numbing sameness: two side-by-side graves in a family plot behind the Wallendas, for instance. On the first is scrawled in cursive: "Hattie." On the second, in a completely different style we see: "Jeremy." No surnames in either case.

I noticed a few grave sites too, with defiant decorations (which may by now have been removed but seemed to have been there for some time). One stone reading "Mother-Granny" prominently displayed four prohibited items: two poems addressed to "Grandma," an angel, and a plaque containing a Bible verse. Another grave, of a man who'd died at thirty-six—I came in April—harbored a faded Santa Claus. There were also two older memorials with undisturbed—albeit untended—shrubs planted through stone holes built into the slabs.

But the prize example of spirit, the grave that for my money gets the title of "Flower of Manasota," belongs to Maryam Mora, a clearly beloved mother. The back of her standing marble slab is decorated with twenty or thirty blue dolphins that probably started life as refrigerator magnets. Around the bottom frolic crystal dolphins, plastic dolphins, dolphins reflected in mirrors, dolphins swimming at every possible playful angle, and to top it all off, a couple of sitting teddy bears to match the teddy bear engraved on her grave. A portrait of Maryam herself, a smiling dark-haired woman, is affixed to the front. She looks happy.

When I came across Maryam's spectacular memorial, I worried that the family who put it there was going to come back to find all this gone, but I needn't have been. When I knelt for a closer look I discovered that every single item had been firmly glued. *Firmly* glued.

Before I left Manasota, I went to the back to look at the mausoleums. Whereas in some cemeteries, mausoleums resemble palaces, these look like nothing so much as 7-11s. Or maybe units intended for self-storage. They're gracelessly flat-roofed and arranged like an apartment complex whose occupants' name plates face, for the most part, not gardens but each other. I didn't stay.

You might wonder whether, given the way I've described the place, Manasota is worth visiting. Actually, it is. I firmly believe that the chance to pay tribute to the Wallendas, who came as close to flight as anyone who's ever lived, shouldn't be passed up. And it wouldn't be a bad idea either to visit Big Poison and picture him, still half-drunk, slamming the ball out of the park. Besides, when surroundings are spare, the exceptions to that spareness give all the more pleasure and by the time you visit, new rebels will have arrived to delight your imagination. They always do.

SPOTLIGHT: BEING ON THE WIRE

> *Life is being on the wire, everything else is just waiting.*
> Karl Wallenda

The earth of Manasota shelters eleven former denizens of the air, representing three generations of the Flying Wallendas. Given the fact that all these people regularly performed high above the ground without a net, it's surprising that only the family's patriarch Karl aka "the Great Wallenda" and three others died of falls. Of the remaining seven, one died of accidental electrocution, four passed away in their beds, and two, both third generation, died young of disease, one of AIDS, the other, Angel, of cancer.

Angel's story is of particular interest. She didn't begin training as an aerialist until she was seventeen, the year in which she married, and perhaps also the year she assumed her prescient name (her birth name was Elizabeth). By the time Angel was nineteen, she had lost her right leg to cancer. Two years after that, the disease claimed parts of both her lungs. Then, when surgeries and treatments had done all the good they could, she returned to the circus, becoming the only person ever to walk the high wire with an artificial leg. Finally, the cancer came back so virulently that she was forced to retire. Six years later, she passed away, leaving behind a true lesson in courage.

The Wallendas are in at least their eighth generation of circus tradition. The family performance history begins in Bohemia in the 1820s with an itinerant troupe of Wallenda acrobats, jugglers, clowns, aerialists, and animal trainers, traveling by wagon and living on what they could make by passing the hat. After Germany absorbed Bohemia late in the century, the younger generation reinvented themselves as Germans.

Karl's father Englebert, a brutal man known for his agility on the trapeze, deserted the family when Karl was very young, leaving him and his brothers on their own. In good weather, they performed in beer halls, worked as clowns, and from time to time as behind the scenes technicians in various small circuses. But every winter, the supply of performance jobs would dry up and in order to survive they had to mine coal. All of them hated that, spending the day in the dark.

In 1921 when Karl was sixteen, he answered an ad requesting someone who could do handstands. Since his best trick at the time was a handstand on top of a stack of chairs, he was sure he'd be a natural for the job. But when he showed up for the audition, he found out that though the job required only a single handstand per performance, there was a catch: the handstand had to be done balanced on the foot soles of a man lying along a wire almost fifty feet in the air. Karl thought that the job was too risky no matter how much it paid, so he refused it. But halfway to the train station, he remembered how tough times were and how unpleasant it was to mine coal every winter and he went back. That job was the beginning of his highwire career.

After some time, Karl took his new found skills and began

touring in various circuses with his brother Herman and some other family members. At one of these, the Wallendas were performing simultaneously with several other acts when Karl, annoyed they weren't getting the attention he thought they deserved, drew a small pistol out of his waistband and fired it repeatedly into the air. Though that kind of flamboyance must have annoyed the other performers, it was popular with audiences and the Wallendas began to get a reputation for being idiosyncratic. This they later cemented by abandoning the aerialists' traditional skintight glitter in favor of sailor suits. Around this time, Karl married a fifteen-year-old named Martha, who had joined the circus as a dancer. Martha never did walk the wire. Instead, she used her highly developed sense of balance to arch over a bar while she was rotated elegantly around.

In 1927, the Wallendas went to Cuba to perform in the Circo Santos. Their act caused such a sensation there that the proprietor of the biggest circus in America, John Ringling, traveled from Florida to see them perform. But he didn't succeed, at least not at first, because Circo Santos's manager didn't trust Ringling, so he dropped the Wallendas from every performance the intruder was known to be attending.

In a few days, Ringling was seen boarding a ship for Miami. When the ship was safely at sea, the relieved manager put the Wallendas back onto the program. But Ringling had outsmarted him by getting off the ship before it sailed, so when the Wallendas performed that day, Ringling was hiding in the wings. What he saw impressed him so much that he hired the family immediately and took them to the United States to headline in the Greatest Show on Earth.

The Wallendas debuted for Ringling in the spring of 1928 at New York's Madison Square Garden. Their big draw was to be a three-level pyramid, with Helen (destined to be Karl's second wife; Martha would remarry the circus vet) at the top. But a problem arose. The pyramid was dangerous and the Wallendas' net (all performers used nets back then) hadn't arrived from Cuba by the time the sold-out crowd was filing into its seats. Karl pondered whether to downgrade his trick or risk his family's lives. He decided to go ahead with his original plan. When the Wallendas finished their act that night, the audience leapt up and gave them a fifteen-minute ovation complete with stomping and whistling. Since in Europe this kind of crowd reaction would have meant disapproval, it horrified Karl so much that he ordered his performers off the wire immediately. Then, instead of taking bows, the whole family fled the arena to recover from the humiliation they thought they'd suffered.

The Wallendas, ever more successful, had tried out various names for themselves starting with "The Wallenda Brothers." By 1934 they'd settled on the not-very-charismatic "The Wallenda Troupe." But an accident that year would give them their final name. What happened was this. As the performers were mounting their pyramid their main cable loosened so suddenly that everyone went tumbling. On other occasions like this, Wallendas would lose their lives but on that particular night all the performers managed to grab wires, with the happy result that bruises were the worst of their injuries. A reporter later wrote that they'd fallen so gracefully they seemed to be flying, and "The Flying Wallendas" they were from then on.

In 1936, Karl and Helen bought a house in Sarasota where the circus had been wintering. Many other performers followed suit, with the result that generations of circus children were born and raised in that town. 1936 was also the year one of Karl's brothers, Willi, had a fatal accident in Sweden. Willi had been using a net but he bounced out of it and hit the ground. Karl's grandson Tino who still performs with the circus argues that nets, far from increasing performers' safety, may actually cause accidents. He reasons that a net can undermine a performer's commitment to absolute focus every single minute he or she is on the wire because it subconsciously implies that falling is possible and may even be recoverable.

According to Tino Wallenda, aerialists keep their balance not with their feet but with their eyes. The rule of thumb is never to look down or to the side but only at a small point on the platform toward which you're walking. The effectiveness of this kind of focus is illustrated by the time in the mid-1960s that an electrician accidentally plunged the arena into darkness while the Wallendas were rehearsing the seven-man pyramid. You'd have expected someone to have fallen, especially because the situation must have brought back memories of the tragic 1962 incident that had killed two troupe members. But the performers kept their focus so perfectly that afternoon that when the lights went on they were all still looking at the point they'd been locked into when the electrician made his mistake.

In 1944, the Ringlings replaced their leaky flame-resistant Big Top with an old-fashioned tent waterproofed with paraffin and benzene. On the sixth of July that year, the Wallendas were performing before a crowd of seven thousand in Hartford, Connecticut when the tent caught fire. The minute the band saw what was happening it struck up the circus disaster tune, "Stars and Stripes Forever" and employees led the horses, lions, and elephants out of the tent and the Wallendas came down. At least two of them, Herman's son Gunther and another troupe member named Phillip, rather than seek safety helped put the fire out and were credited with saving many lives. In spite of their efforts, 168 people died that day, and 400 were seriously injured, either by fire or by being trampled.

Three years after the Hartford fire, Karl Wallenda, who'd been less and less happy with the management since John Ringling died in 1936, decided to go out on his own. He had in mind to launch his new venture with an impossibly daring feat: an eight-man pyramid. But when his brother Herman convinced him that using eight men would be too risky, Circus Wallenda opened in 1947 with the number dropped to seven. The pyramid was a huge success with audiences but Karl's economic timing hadn't been the best so his circus struggled and finally folded. When it did, Karl split his Sarasota property and gave his performers home sites in lieu of the money he owed them. Many of those performers' families still live in that original neighborhood.

The pyramid, now eight men, outlasted the circus and came to be the Wallendas' signature act. Four men would stand on the bottom with Karl Wallenda in the anchor position calling each move. Two more would climb onto the shoulders of the first group, placing themselves between positions one and two, and three and four, and holding a bar between them with a chair balanced on it. A woman would then climb onto the chair and at the end of the routine she would stand on the seat.

In 1962, the Wallendas were performing the pyramid in Detroit. Dieter Schepp—a twenty-three-year-old in his first week as a member of the troupe—was on the bottom tier. He was only five steps from the platform when he suddenly shouted in German "I can't hold it" and fell. Above him one person after another lost his balance. Karl managed to grab the second wire and catch the woman on her way down, holding her until the frantic people below could improvise a net (she left circuses forever after that). Dieter Schepp and Dick Faughnan, Karl's daughter Jenny's husband, died at the scene. Karl's son Mario was paralyzed for life. Karl himself broke his pelvis and suffered a double hernia.

The accident didn't stop the act. Herman and Guenther performed the matinee the following day. And Karl, against his doctors' advice, checked himself out of the hospital so he could appear that night. He would refuse surgeries until the season was over. But though the show did go on, Karl ordered the eight-man pyramid discontinued. However, less than two years later he changed his mind and began training new walkers. His daughter Jenny called him a murderer for it but Karl refused to listen and soon his signature act was back on the program.

Besides his circus work, Karl performed many spectacular skywalks, the most famous of which took place in 1970 when at the age of sixty-five he walked across Tallulah Gorge in Georgia. The gorge is 1,000 feet deep and 975 feet wide. The two-inch cable Karl needed to cross it was almost triple the diameter of circus cable and had to be installed on poles flown in by helicopter. It was guyed by twenty thousand feet of additional cable stretched at intervals from the walking wire to the ground. Close to a quarter of a million people witnessed the eighteen breath-holding minutes it took Karl to cross the abyss. During that time he paused twice, put his pole on the wire, and stood on his head. His second headstand, he dedicated to the troops in Vietnam. The pole weighed thirty pounds so part of this maneuver was to give his arms a break, but the rest was pure spectacle.

There was something else unusual about the Tallulah Gorge crossing. Karl was carrying a surprise for his grandson Tino in his pocket—a letter from Tino's girlfriend Olinka—that he delivered to the boy as he stepped off the wire.

Karl made many other successful skywalks in the course of his career. He traversed the Astrodome, walked across Busch Stadium, and over the King's Dominion fountain in Virginia to name a few, but eight years after Tallulah, it would be a skywalk that killed him. This particular walk was scheduled to take place 120 feet in the air between buildings in Puerto Rico. It's never been established whether Karl fell because of improperly anchored stabilizing wires or because of the wind, which at the time was approaching thirty miles an hour. In any case, as he reached the halfway point, the wire under his feet began to sway violently. Karl lost his balance. As he went down, a horrified crowd saw him grab for the wire, miss, hit a parked taxi, and bounce to the ground. His body was so badly crushed by the impact that he would be buried in a closed casket. The second Wallenda troupe, performing in Detroit, heard the news by telephone. At first they couldn't believe it. Then they did.

Given his history, it's appropriate that Karl is buried under a stone that, aggressive as a circus poster, announces "The Wallendas." You can almost hear the crowds. In his final publicity picture, posted on his grave, he stands resplendent in purple vest and pants holding a balancing pole and leaning to one side. The pose is so graceful he seems almost to be dancing. It's clear he's walking a wire but how far above the ground he may be doesn't matter because like every aerialist, like anyone in this life who happens to take risks, the Great Wallenda knows not to look down.

PART IV

SOUTH FLORIDA

12

PORT MAYACA MEMORIAL
GARDENS, CANAL POINT

The 1928 storm that devastated the southeastern side of Lake
Okeechobee was called simply the Great Hurricane because
back then there was no international storm-naming conven-
tion. In 1953, one was established, and for a very practical reason. The fact that storms couldn't be individually identified
was making weather data radioed from off the coast difficult
if not impossible to interpret. Until 1974, when men's names
were added, the storm roster included only women. The original practice was sexist of course, but whether the 1974 addi-
tions were made in an effort to correct that, or simply because
more names were needed I don't know.

Though hurricanes were nameless in the United States
until 1953, the Spanish-speaking Caribbean had been nam-
ing them for centuries. So when the Great Hurricane made
landfall in Puerto Rico on Thursday September 13, 1928, it was
christened "San Felipe" because it arrived on that saint's feast
day. Before it reached the island, San Felipe had killed over
one thousand people. It would add to that total in Puerto Rico
and in the process destroy over half the island's homes, leaving
seven hundred thousand without shelter. Oliver Fassig of the
U.S. Weather Service there estimated storm winds had topped
200 miles per hour but, he reported, he couldn't be sure of
the exact figure because his gauges had broken when the wind
speed hit 150 miles per hour.

Somewhere on its way to the United States, San Felipe
lost its name, so when its winds made landfall in Palm Beach

County, they arrived anonymously. The storm hadn't been expected to reach Florida. Weather reports from Miami and Jacksonville the day after it hit Puerto Rico (Friday, September 14) were predicting it would arc away from land. Even on Sunday, when the erstwhile San Felipe had veered enough to strike the Bahamas, Florida officials were still considering the storm warnings they'd posted precautionary.

Since in the 1920s not everyone had radios or read the newspapers, storm warnings consisted of flags and that Sunday they were flying up and down both coasts, one of the few times that had ever happened. Many east coast Floridians—especially people who lived in Palm Beach directly in the projected path of the storm—remembered earlier storms and took the warnings seriously. Because they did, though the extent of property damage to Palm Beach—$16 billion in today's currency—sent Florida into the depression a year ahead of the rest of the country, the storm's death toll on the coast was only four. Still, one of those deaths tugged hard: a baby boy, swept from Fred Nelms's arms into the water as he and his wife Anna were fleeing their house as it collapsed around them.

The coast had been relatively lucky, at least in human terms, but the six thousand migrant farm workers living on Lake Okeechobee's south shore, forty miles inland, wouldn't share that luck. Nearly half of them would perish.

Three factors, two weather-related, one human, led to the huge loss of life. The first was that the hurricane arrived at a time when Okeechobee's water level was unusually high. 1926 and 1927 had been wet years. Then, in August 1928, a thunderstorm struck the lake's north side. The rain was so heavy that groves were cut off from land and fish were swimming in the streets of flooded towns. By mid-September, local rainfall had reached forty-seven inches. Before the end of the month, the figure would rise to eighty-eight inches.

The second reason the Great Hurricane was so devastating was that it approached the lake from the already-saturated north. The resulting surge of water breached the four-foot mud dikes that had never been intended to protect the population but only to keep rain from flooding farmland (a project to build more substantial dikes had stalled in the courts) and pushed an eleven-foot wall of water toward the towns on the southern edge of the lake.

Besides the high lake level and the direction of approach of the storm, the third reason for the high death toll was that forecasters had been so wrong about the hurricane's path. You can't blame them though because in the days before satellites and hurricane hunters, the only information they had was what ships at sea radioed in, and in this case those reports turned out to be incomplete.

Here's what happened. On Friday the fourteenth, the day after the storm hit Puerto Rico, people living around Lake Okeechobee were told that it wasn't coming their way. A Dr. Buck, the only doctor around those parts, didn't believe the reports, so he sent American Legionnaires out in trucks to carry people to high ground. The Legionnaires brought around forty Negroes and poor whites into town but when nothing happened, most of them went home.

Again in fairness to the weathermen, given the direction from which the hurricane came, when it finally did arrive residents on the southeast corner of the lake would probably have been trapped anyhow because the only two roads from the south side of the lake ran next to water. Highway 27, which might have gotten residents with cars safely to the coast, would have been impassible too because it was under construction and the crews hadn't yet dumped the dirt they'd planned to build it up with to bring it above the floodplain.

In any case, when the hurricane did hit Okeechobee three days later, it found almost everyone home. We don't know how high the winds were because the local gauges broke at 96 knots, but we do know that this hurricane's barometer reading—27.43 millibars—was the fifth lowest ever recorded in an Atlantic storm.

Conditions must have been terrifying—the wind screaming, trees cracking like rifle shots, rain blowing blindingly sideways, and the only illumination the lightning that split the black sky then did it again.

The flimsy houses and businesses in Belle Glade, Pahokee, and South Bay—and most were flimsy, these were poor people—gave way immediately and the families huddling inside them drowned. The majority of the more substantial homesteads finally tilted too and fell into the raging water, carrying their terrified occupants with them. Though desperate hymns, calls to God, and later, the cries of the drowning, must have rawed the throats of many, whatever sounds they made must have been blotted out by the fury of the gale. In their desperation, people did anything. They climbed water towers. They clung to cross bars of power poles, to pieces of attic ceiling grabbed as the roof blew away, to boards whose nails must have protruded, even to the bloated bodies of cows. Mothers strapped themselves and their children to trees then witnessed the branches give way. Thousands, many of whom were never found, were carried off that night.

The day after the hurricane, would-be rescuers came upon scenes of devastation. Where land had been they found a lake in which floated pieces of shacks, random household goods, and the bloated remains of people and livestock. The rescuers buried black corpses directly but put the bodies of whites into donated pine boxes and trucked them to gravesites on higher ground. Corpses that were too swollen to fit into boxes ended up stacked like cordwood on the backs of trucks. One of these was the bloated corpse of a man who had in life weighed 110 pounds.

All this burying and carrying was what rescue crews started out doing. But they couldn't keep pace with the bodies that kept floating up from back canals and swamps, and by the fifth day the untended corpses were rotting so rapidly that the health department ordered them burned. Bandana-swathed volunteers, including survivors having to handle the corpses of people they knew (one man recognized a two-year-old who just days before the storm had shown him the bracelet she had received for her birthday), piled the bodies up willy-nilly then burned them, using driftwood and poured-on oil so the fire would start hot.

For weeks after the storm, bodies were floating up from the swamp. Many of these were never identified. In all, about 1,600 of the nameless were brought by cart and railroad car to be buried on high ground in Port Mayaca. Scores of others were laid to rest in makeshift graveyards in roadside ditches.

Still others ended up in West Palm Beach: sixty-nine white people buried in pine boxes and 674 blacks, unceremoniously dumped into an unmarked twenty-foot hole in the city's pauper cemetery.

At the time, the official death toll of the Great Hurricane was about 2,500, but the true number would have been much higher since the area was populated mostly by migrant workers with no one to report them missing. And no one knows how many bodies simply disappeared into the swampy waters of the Everglades. In 2003 the official number was raised to 3,000, which makes the Great Hurricane the third most costly disaster in American history in terms of loss of life, behind the 1900 Galveston hurricane (that took an estimated 6,000 to 12,000 lives) and the 1906 San Francisco earthquake and fire (3,000 to 6,000).

Today, the area around Port Mayaca is still agricultural. Coming from the north along 441, it's a long way between houses and the only commercial establishments are occasional gas stations. The land is flat and open and populated mostly by cattle, in pastures punctuated with the palms and pines that grow wild here. A cloud-shot sky so big it could engender nothing but wonder hangs above.

As you approach Okeechobee, dikes to the right of the road rise so high they completely hide the water. But periodic signs point you toward a scenic drive at some tiny distance— ½ mile, ¼ mile—so you know it must be close. Then, suddenly, you cross a rainbow-shaped bridge arcing over a corner and you see the lake for the first time. Okeechobee is an ocean. It's awesome. And the sight of its power can do nothing but fill you with compassion for the towns that once lined the south shore, waiting for the hurricane to tuck them in.

Along Route 76 approaching Port Mayaca from the west, the only buildings you pass look closed-up. There are no obvious houses. In a few miles, Memorial Gardens, a field of flat markers, each punctuated by a bouquet of fading artificial flowers, appears on the right. A sign asserts: "Nothing is allowed on the graves except flowers" and warns that trespassing mementos will be removed.

A little farther on, a second entrance leads to the original part of the grounds, the part that is home to the unnamed victims of the 1928 disaster. The memorial for those fallen consists of a large granite slab at the foot of a flagpole. The inscription on it reads: "To the 1600 pioneers who gave their lives in the 1928 hurricane so that the glades might be as we know it [*sic*] today." That the deaths of these people are couched in such heroic terms speaks to the fact that as a direct result of the Great Hurricane, huge dikes were built to confine the waters of the lake. Though there's some doubt as to the environmental wisdom of those dikes there's no question they make the population safer.

The cemetery at Port Mayaca was established specifically because of the 1928 disaster, the site chosen because it lies on relatively high ground. The cities of Pahokee, Belle Glade, and South Bay operated it jointly until 1992, when Pahokee took control.

Other than the mass grave, this side of the Memorial Gardens seems to be populated mostly by ranchers and white Crackers. However, its monoculture is about to change. The bodies of Hispanic farm workers and owners used to be returned to Mexico or Guatemala for burial, but now more and more Hispanics see this part of Florida as home, and are expressing a desire to be buried here. Because of this, the city of Pahokee plans to establish a special section to accommodate them. The first idea was to set up a dedicated Catholic section. But since not all Hispanics follow that religion, the current thinking is to set up a Spanish section instead.

Now, the 1928 memorial, while memorable, isn't the only reason to come to Mayaca. If you look around, you'll find many others. I noticed a stone, for example, that carries an especially touching tribute to fatherhood. It says: "Boughman" then "Anyone can be a Father but it takes someone special to be a Dad." And there's more. Besides the inscription, the stone carries an oval carving of a stag standing proud with mountains behind him, and around the oval, hovering pine branches, needles, and cones, graceful as angels.

There's another carved stone here, I would think by the same artist. It's also oval and depicts a night lake with mounded shores. There are cattails in the foreground, a moon settling into branches on the left, and a duck flying toward it from the right. The inhabitant of that lake is named Carpenter.

To the right of the entrance stands a chapel Vinson Henderson erected in memory of his wife Louise. You may not recognize it for what it is at first, since what Louise (and now her husband) preside over is a marble structure with approximately the dimensions of a large car wash. It's open to the air at both ends and on its shiny inside walls are mounted other, often very personal, memorials. The tone of the postings—mostly handwritten notes and family pictures—reminded me of the Vietnam memorial in Washington. I found two of them particularly moving. The first was a cluster of photographs of a handsome, smiling, African American man, together with a note from his wife in the shape of a valentine, to the effect that if God hadn't called him home, today, the fourth of July, would have been their seventeenth wedding anniversary. The other consisted of two snapshots of a weather-skinned blonde man in a tractor cap. I'd have guessed he was in his fifties. Next to the pictures was taped a handwritten message: "You are the love of my life."

As graveyards go, this one is neither gorgeous nor bleak. The grass looks prosperous and a number of trees, mostly palms and pines, grace the grounds. The most spectacular of the trees stand near the entrance: two huge ficuses whose roots are twining around each other. It seems to me that those trees are the outward and visible sign of the way people here have built community.

Next door to the Memorial Gardens is the 26,000-acre Du Pois Nature Preserve. I stopped at the visitor's center, where a pretty blonde young woman was on duty. She grew up around here, she said, adding that among the old Cracker families, most of whom still ranch this land, everyone knows everyone. I believe that. What makes what she said all the more affecting is that the 1,600 unidentified dead that lie here may never be known to anyone but each other.

In spite of the fact that in her novel, *Their Eyes Were Watching God*, Zora Neale Hurston iconically described the 1928 hurricane, I felt I had to find my own story. I know the quality of my prose isn't up to Zora's, but to limit such a large event to only one account seems ungenerous. Besides, I believe Minnie and Washington deserve to be remembered even though their tale is quieter than Janie and Tea Cake's. It doesn't signify, by the way, whether they were really called Minnie and Washington or whether what happened to them happened exactly the way I tell it. What does matter is that everything in their story is, from the heart, true.

Minnie and Washington grew up on neighboring tenant farms in Georgia. They were fifteen and sixteen in 1924 when their white landlord combined five farms into one. With so much less land, their parents couldn't feed themselves let alone their children, so when a man in a pickup truck showed up at the feed store promising jobs harvesting potatoes in New York, the two of them thought God had come down and passed a miracle and they went right along. By the end of their first season up north two things had happened: they'd fallen in love and they'd had a baby called Martha. But they hadn't saved enough to go home, so they followed the crops south and ended up harvesting winter vegetables on the fertile muck lands bordering Okeechobee.

For the next few years they traveled up and down the coast, making four dollars on good days, and things went along pretty much the same except they added two more children to the family: Duncan and James. Also, somewhere along the line Washington had developed a drinking problem. Sometimes Minnie would go to work alone while Washington lay around, his bootlegged bottle never far from his dangling hand. There didn't seem to be much future for them in the normal sense. On the other hand, edge-living was all they'd ever known, and the children were healthy, and when Minnie looked at Washington, she still felt that low-down heat.

By the time they arrived in Belle Glade for the fourth time in August of 1928, migrants had swollen its population to nearly five hundred. Minnie and Washington didn't live in farm housing or in a tent or in a makeshift lean-to as so many did, because they'd always managed to put enough money aside—five dollars a week—to stay in a boarding house in Colored Town. It was a nice place, with a water spigot and toilet on each floor and rooms that came with some furniture: a card table, two folding chairs, and a single bed. One of Minnie and Washington's mattresses went on the bed, the other went on the floor for the kids. They had the rest of what they'd need with them—a footlocker of assorted clothes and cooking utensils and a two-burner stove—and once they nailed a crate onto the wall for their food and a broomstick across a corner to hang things on, they were set for the winter.

They also liked this particular boarding house because they had the same neighbors every year—Katie from Tennessee with her four kids, and Chester from north Georgia. Chester was a pious, quiet man who used to take them to hear Brother Weston preach when his tent revival came through.

Every day in Belle Glade sang the same tune as the day before. Up north, people usually worked in crews but here in Florida they tended to freelance, so around six in the morning after some grits, with butter if they were flush, the whole family would walk down to the loading place. The kids were too young to work in the fields but Minnie took them anyway because she thought they'd be safer where she could see them than back in town. The work the family did on any given day depended on who was offering what. Minnie and Washington (or just Minnie if Washington happened to be on a tear) would go from truck to truck listening to offers and when the seven o'clock whistle shrilled, they'd climb into the back of the truck whose pay looked like the best deal. Most of the roads were sand so if it hadn't rained lately, they'd be coated in fine white powder by the time they got to the fields.

While Minnie and Washington worked the beans or peppers or potatoes, five-year-old Martha's job was to watch the baby, which in practice meant that she and Duncan spent most of their time running around in the dirt with the other kids who were too young to pick. At the noon break the family would look for shade—usually there wasn't any but they always looked—then sit down and unwrap their sandwiches. Sometimes, they'd treat Duncan and Martha to bottled drinks from one of the bright-skirted women who traveled with the pickers. Martha liked soft drinks—her favorite was the bright orange one—because they made her burp. She and Duncan had burping contests but no one ever won because right in the middle, they'd start laughing.

On Friday September 14, the family passed the time after their backbones, rice, and cornbread with Minnie mending and Washington putting the final touches on a fish he was carving for Martha from a bit of scrap wood. Martha herself was sitting on the mattress playing bailing-twine cat's cradle with Hallie from downstairs. The other two children were playing together, Duncan popping up at James from behind the footlocker or from under the table and James screeching in delight until the two of them got so loud that Minnie had to tell them to hush. Around eight, Minnie and Washington put the children down and went out to sit on the front steps. They treasured those moments because they were about the extent of their private time.

They talked about Dr. Buck and the bunch of Negroes and poor whites he'd carried into town because he hadn't believed the forecasters. But they dropped the subject pretty soon since by now everyone had gone back home. Besides, they'd heard on the radio just that morning that they didn't need to worry and since neither of them could read, they'd have had no way of knowing that as they spoke, the Palm Beach newspaper was busy contradicting the radio by printing a small box that said the hurricane was "likely to strike." It didn't say where, just "Florida."

So it wasn't surprising that Minnie and Washington were more interested in the details of last night's fight than they were in the storm. Neither of them knew the man who'd been stabbed, all they'd heard was that he was called Jacques and he was from Haiti, but they knew those things happened. Besides, it was gossip and they both liked gossip.

The next day, Saturday, the weather news coming into Belle Glade was about the same but the Seminoles, who remembered the hurricane two years back, were leaving for high ground. They'd noticed how quiet the air had fallen and that snakes were on the move and animals were scuttling into burrows and climbing trees and that the only birds to be seen were seagulls. Inland, that meant rain.

If Minnie and Washington had left when the Seminoles did, they might have survived. Instead, they sat on the steps until it got dark then put the children to bed. Later, when they thought the little ones had fallen asleep, they reached for each other in the dark, trying, as always, not to make too much noise.

Sunday morning brought armies of clouds scudding across a sky which alternated schizophrenically from black to sun. By noon, coastal residents knew the hurricane wasn't going to miss Florida after all.

But Minnie and Washington didn't. They also didn't know that in the last twenty-four hours the water level in Okeechobee had risen by three feet, or that by six o'clock that night, the first waves would breach the dike.

As the day moved on, the wind began to gust. When rain began, first sporadic then relentless, Minnie, Washington, and the kids went to the top floor of the boarding house. By dusk, they were joined by everyone else who could cram in. Huddled around a crackling radio, they all heard the announcer's voice suddenly turn as he heard that the wild winds he'd just finished saying were forecast to miss Florida, were, as he spoke, striking Palm Beach.

The sides of the building began to shake. Minnie was cradling James on one side and Martha, who had regressed to stroking the corner of her blanket with her thumb, on the other. Duncan, who'd always been afraid of lightning, had climbed up onto his daddy.

While all this was going on, the first houses were being washed off their foundations at Chosen and pitched into the canal. A few people survived by cutting holes in the roof or by diving out windows. Others, though, rode their careening homes all the way to the Belle Glade Bridge where the houses broke up and the people inside either drowned or clung to something, anything.

The depth of the water on the streets of Belle Glade had

stayed constant at only a foot or two. But this would change. As the storm approached so did the winds, until they were gusting over 150 miles an hour. Then, slowly, they changed direction. When they finished, their cone was pointing straight at the already-breached spot in the dike. Slowly at first then faster, the dike began to melt, releasing wind-whipped walls of watery muck.

Inside Minnie and Washington's boarding house it was pitch black. The flimsy walls were shaking out of control, like someone at a revival, speaking in tongues. Lapping waves reached the top of the staircase and lapped higher. The wind was deafening. Minnie and Washington and the others stacked whatever they could find, and standing on the teetering pile worked the trap door to the attic loose and lifted the children through it. By the time the last of the adults followed, the tower they'd made only a few adrenaline-laced minutes ago was collapsing into the rising water. In the attic, scores of people huddled to keep warm.

Brother Silas started a hymn which even the ones who didn't believe sang until their lungs burned. It didn't matter they couldn't hear themselves over the storm. Suddenly everything went still. Washington told Minnie he loved her. They hugged the children. Then the eye passed over.

The roar outside was punctuated with snapping trees. The boarding house roof shivered twice, hard. Then the nails that had held it down pulled free and the roof lifted away and sailed into the street. The people inside were drenched, choking. They cut their hands grabbing at anything they could find. Minnie lost her balance. As she fell to one side, Robert flew from her arms. She tried to grab at him but he was gone. She screamed for Washington but he didn't answer. She couldn't see past her own whipping hair. She held onto Martha, hard. Then what was left of the building tipped and fell into the wild river the street had become.

A rescuer came across Robert the next noon, trapped between two splayed boards. The man had a baby of his own at home. He shivered and slid the little corpse onto his shovel where it felt lighter than the possum he'd killed the other day because it was getting his chickens. Three days later Minnie, naked and minus an arm, bobbed up through the muck along with pieces of boarding house wall, broken tables, splintered beams, a shattered lantern, a doll, and some dead chickens. She'd been swept into the lake, miles from Colored Town. The worker who'd pulled her back behind his boat had had to study on her body to make out its race because so many of the white people who had drowned had turned black. In the end he decided correctly and set Minnie to one side, away from the pine boxes built for whites.

Martha's bodily existence ended in a field of saw grass beside a long stick with a white flag floating out among dozens of other flags. Half-submerged, she had swollen out of her clothes. By the time she was found, four days after the hurricane, her skin had become so sodden it disintegrated at a touch. Because there was no one left to say who she had been, a worker who had primed himself with whiskey to dull his stomach and heart dumped her in the pile to be doused with coal oil and burned. The thick black cloud would be visible for miles. Washington and Duncan were never found.

Martha's ashes and Minnie minus the arm and Robert whole lie under the marker in Port Mayaca with the bodies and ashes of others who are, perhaps forever, nameless. Something of what happened on the Okeechobee shore that day and what rescuers had to face afterwards has been told. There are stories of heroism and stubbornness among those tales, and the telling of them is good. But the nameless blacks and whites who moved with the season have only a few such stories. Zora Neale Hurston wrote one. Here, humbly offered, is another.

‚‚‚‚‚‚‚‚‚‚‚‚‚‚‚‚‚‚‚‚‚‚‚‚‚‚‚‚‚‚‚‚‚‚‚‚‚‚

13

BROWARD PET CEMETERY, PLANTATION

I was having dinner with some women friends the other night, when one of them mentioned she'd just lost her cat Tooley. She went on to say that she felt a little sheepish about it but she had to admit that Tooley's death had been more devastating to her than the loss of some relatives she could name. This remark elicited supportive comments up and down the table. Sidney, for instance, told us that even though her own cat had died nine years ago, having reached a ripe old age, she still thinks of her every day.

That being the case, it's not surprising that many people bury their pets somewhere they can visit them. My grandmother's best friend in Pennsylvania had a pet cemetery on her farm where she laid to rest all the dogs she and my grandmother (with whom she lived for thirty-five years) had owned, each dog with its own stone. When I'd be taken to visit her, we'd go to the cemetery to leave a bone on the grave of Dooley the mastiff who, she told me, had stood fierce guard over me when I was a baby. My grandmother's friend had had the luxury of land. But since most of us don't anymore, a network of pet cemeteries has arisen to fill the need we have to memorialize our furry loves. Broward Pet Cemetery, in Plantation, is one of those.

The cemetery with its flowers, its grassy walks, and its large palms and oaks, several hung with enormous stag horn ferns, fell on hard times before it became the labor of love you see today. It was founded in 1967 by the bereaved owner of the dog buried under the statue that greets you as you enter. After 1978, when that person died, the grounds were abandoned to weeds except for an area dedicated to anonymous burials. But in 1986 Dr. Ernest "Pete" Seiler, a retired veterinarian, bought and rescued the place. The first thing Dr. Seiler did was clear the land. Then, since the original cemetery had kept no records he put ads in area papers, asking anyone who had buried a pet here to contact him. As a result of the ads, around eighty graves were re-marked, though not perfectly because many people could remember only approximately where their pet's spot had been. Once Dr. Seiler had done what he could for the cemetery's original inhabitants, he landscaped and planned out the rest of the area. Broward Pet Cemetery is today, oddly enough, the only pet cemetery in heavily settled Broward County.

I don't know what the environs of the cemetery were like in 1967 or 1978, but I'd lay odds the area was country. Now though, a pet looking across the street would see a McMansion with a yard worth a good romp and flower displays that would be irresistible to anyone who enjoyed digging.

The cemetery is beautifully maintained, and studded with often-elaborate memorials. There's a lot of marble here, for instance, and a lot of rose granite, both flush and upright. There are also more portraits on grave stones than in most human graveyards. Some of the images are photographic, printed on metal, of the pet surrounded by his humans; others are carved. Flowers abound, all of them left by families. Sandy Ketchum, who manages the cemetery, pointed out a particularly elaborate family grave site as belonging to a Miami woman who owns a string of florist shops. Sandy added that the woman changes the displays on her pets' graves on a seasonal basis. The January day I visited, for instance, the area sported bright red splashes of poinsettias. When the florist's husband dies, said Sandy, she's planning to bury him here with her other pets.

You'd think it would be hard to take decedents named "Lotta Pooping" or "Pumpkin" seriously but it isn't, not when you consider the emotional involvement implied by the tributes on the graves. The people who owned these animals were true and loving parents: Mom, Mommy, Dad, Daddy, Papi, Nanny, Poppy. One stone reads: "My son, my love, my life." Another: "Sammie, our little boy in a white suit." Another: "Our sweet faced little girl." Another: "We loved you madly." Another: "My baby. We miss you so much." When I mentioned to Dr. Seiler how touching I found those memorials, he said that the worst case scenario—and it's a pattern—goes like this. There's an old couple and they have a dog. One of the spouses dies. Then the dog dies. Then the other spouse dies.

Besides generic inscriptions like "Forever in our Hearts," there are many highly personal tributes. One gravestone of several that display a Star of David (stones rest on these graves the way they do on human Jewish graves) reads "You have been with us since the beginning of your journey and will follow us to the ends of ours." Some people have written poems to their pets, wishing them blue skies and sunsets in their afterlives. One poet-at-heart wrote "Asleep in the sun forever."

There's more than the usual amount of statuary here. Besides the traditional St. Francis, Mary, and Jesus you'll find stone angels, cupids, even winged dogs, but for some reason (or I didn't see any) no winged cats. Besides the statues, the cemetery is awhirl with spinning pinwheels—pets must have liked to watch them—and toys like stuffed animals. In the cat area, there's even a bird feeder complete with plastic birds. It must be torment to the cat lying under it.

All the items I've described would be interesting enough to prompt a visit. But they weren't the most surprising things I saw. What I found most impressive was the plethora of Christmas memorabilia (this was the end of January). I saw wreathes, miniature Christmas trees, elves bearing presents, fake gift boxes with big bows, and waving Santa Clauses. There was even a Christmas card shaped like a dog, whose inscription read "I miss you but I'm being very brave."

George, who works on the grounds and digs graves when that's called for, told me that every Christmas people set up full-size trees complete with lights and balls on their pets' graves—bigger, he said, than the one he has at home. Often too, they leave wrapped presents under the trees as if their pets could wake up and open them.

George told me that beside dogs and house cats, Broward houses monkeys, birds, ferrets, even a civet cat. He also told me about the day Jackie Gleason came to bury his dog. Gleason was very private about his grief, George said. He didn't want the dog's grave marked and he didn't want anyone to know he'd been here. He buried him then went away.

George likes working here. As he explained why, he lit up: he thinks of this place as always full of animals, both live and dead. He tells me about the rabbits (he calls them "bunnies"), squirrels, and birds that grace the grounds in the mornings and says that he can measure the passage of the seasons by which birds are singing. He thinks the pets under the ground must be happy in such a natural setting.

Broward Pet Cemetery isn't especially easy to find; you have to work your way around the canals that vein the area. But maybe that's part of its charm. Landscaped on all four sides, it feels like a secret garden. When you come in past the stately dog statue, to your left is an open, markerless, field. If you didn't know otherwise, you'd think the wide grass was intended simply as a park for future occupants of the cemetery to run in while their owners visit the graves of their predecessors. And it is that, but under that smooth sward it's also a Potter's Field for the hundreds of unnamed cremated animals the county buries here. Not all the animals here are in the earth. A memorial erected by the Humane Society next to the office contains the cremains of at least four hundred cats and dogs.

In front of you and to the right, you'll see the marked graves I've been telling you about, and—you can't miss them—the flowers. It occurs to me that those might be the reincarnations of the flowers that the pets that lie under the stones had, in fits of puppy or kitten fun, loved to dig up. Some of the flowers are the sort that require tending, so the fact that they're in such beautiful shape implies that someone comes to give them what they need. In the process I should think, that someone remembers the daily walks where Bob or Jenna would crisscross the trail then vanish into the bushes in hot pursuit of a wayward squirrel, then run back to them, panting heavily; or the trips to the dog run, where every morning Jib or Pogo found friends to play with. Stooping to tend flowers is analogous too to the gesture a parent might have made while taking a wet stick from Mattie, whose tail used to wag so fast and circularly that it threatened to helicopter her off the ground. Or perhaps the woman with the trowel is simply thinking of the way Mickey the cat used to circle before he settled in her lap while she watched the news, or the way Jack would push her over to her own side of the bed because he was bound and determined to have his.

These imaginings aren't fanciful. If the toys and so on didn't already suggest it, Sandy, Pete (the owner), and George all said that people often come to sit by their pets' graves. Sometimes they leave a dog biscuit or a cat treat behind. Sometimes they spend a few minutes in the white vine-covered gazebo that stands three-quarters of the way back in the cemetery before they go.

I asked Sandy, because she runs day-to-day operations, how funerals here work. First George will dig the grave, she said. Then the animal is brought out and laid into it. If the bereaved family is Jewish, they may say Kaddish. Otherwise, if no particular kind of service has been requested, she'll read a nondenominational prayer.

Sandy added that before a pet is buried some families like a viewing. She took me to a darkened room where a small gray and black tabby, whose funeral was scheduled for eleven (it was ten), was laid out in a white coffin. Her sweet-looking face rested on a satin pillow. A satin sheet was pulled over her to tuck her in. Her toys were piled beside her (anything that will fit into the coffin is allowed). Some families choose a supply of their pet's favorite treats, others photographs, others a leash, and so on. The cemetery will clean pets for viewing, Sandy explained, but not embalm them.

She showed me the available coffins. They run the gamut from double-wall fiberglass to single-wall fiberglass to plain wood. Some of the fiberglass coffins are plain; others are embossed with flowers. She also showed me some urns: antique brass, wood, onyx, cloisonné, and so on. One style of urn offers "a big screen TV photo" of your pet. She said that more people are opting for cremation than before, and also more often than before, are choosing to take their pets home rather than inter the cremains in the flowery area outside she calls "The Columbarium."

When an owner wants a pet cremated, if it's not too large, it's done here. When whoever has done the cremation is finished, he grinds what's left in a blender before he puts it in the urn. I asked Sandy whether the cemetery accepts horses and if so how they cremate them. She said Broward has four horses but that they were cremated elsewhere. The crematoria that take horses (Broward doesn't) have to saw the corpses up first because no cremation oven is big enough to accommodate them whole. When she finished, I went to look for the horses. Only one of the four horse graves here is marked. The inscription on it reads, poignantly: "Gold Bond, our friend to the end. He served the Miami Police Department faithfully for 14 years. The mounted patrol will truly miss him."

As I was approaching Gold Bond, I noticed a family plot with three graves—two labs and a shepherd, each with a carved portrait. One of the inscriptions reads: "Best dog I ever trained." There's an area here for service dogs—guide dogs for the blind, police dogs, drug-sniffing dogs, and so on, but it's been set up so recently that it's yet to be occupied.

When we were in the viewing room, Sandy told me that the owners of the little cat had requested its funeral not be disturbed. She suggested I wait in the gazebo because of the vines that conceal whatever is in it from the outside. So just before eleven, I went there and sat down. It was so peaceful among the flowers there that I slipped into a meditative state.

I woke up to a fresh rectangular grave rimmed with Astroturf to keep it from collapsing. The dirt that would fill it had been piled on a plastic sheet beside it. In a few minutes, Sandy came out of the office, followed by two middle-aged women in single file. The more stooped of the two was wiping her eyes with a Kleenex. In her role as minister, Sandy went to the head of the grave and all three of the women stood still.

I kept my promise to myself not to eavesdrop so I don't know what was said. At the conclusion of the ceremony, Sandy and the mourners went inside while George filled in the grave and packed turf over it. Eventually, the cat's widows came back out and walked around the cemetery. They seemed to be studying tombstones. Maybe they were trying to get inscription ideas but I wondered why they hadn't come knowing what they wanted to say. Maybe they were just picking out materials.

While I was watching the women, Dr. Seiler, the cemetery's owner, joined me in the gazebo. He's a very warm person and I could see how helpful he must have been to bereaved clients. Just in case I should need it, he volunteered that the Humane Society offers grief counseling and gave me some leaflets to take home. When the women had gone, and I was no longer a potential intruder, I thanked the kind doctor and went away.

SPOTLIGHT: HAUNTED BY A DOG

Christine Rodriguez and her husband had read somewhere that Broward Pet Cemetery was open to the public 24/7, so when they found themselves in the area in September 2003, they decided to check it out. Christine is a parapsychologist with a degree in psychology from the University of Florida, so she has a special sensitivity to atmosphere, but she didn't see her visit to this particular cemetery as anything more than a pleasant way to spend a bit of time.

She and her husband had trouble finding the place at first because of the canals. But they persisted, and finally came on the wrought-iron fence and whitewashed brick wall that mark the boundaries of the cemetery. It was the middle of the afternoon and they could see from the entrance that, in spite of the cemetery's contention that staff was available during daylight hours, the office was deserted. They saw no one else either, not anywhere. The parking lot was empty and no one was out mowing the grass or setting flowers straight, nor were there any other visitors walking through. They were alone with the graves, the oppressive heat, and the clear blue sky.

But the gates were open, so they went in. They'd gone maybe ten feet and had paused to look at the statue of the founder's dog, Christine said, when a sudden wave of energy almost knocked her over. It felt like animals running all around her, jumping up and down. When it faded, the wave left such deep sadness behind that Christine began to cry. And once she'd started, she couldn't stop. She felt as if the world had ended. Yet even in the grips of her sorrow, Christine had the strong sense that she wasn't the one crying. Being a parapsychologist, she knew what to do: tell the energy to back off. When it had gone, she asked her aerospace engineer husband if he'd felt what she had, and he said no. But since Christine's husband hadn't spent years learning to detect energy fields, the fact that he didn't feel anything didn't mean that it hadn't been there.

Three or four rows into the dog graves, Christine found another hot spot. She took forty or fifty pictures there, she said, before they went on. There seemed to be no activity in the cat area, and Christine got nothing from the rest of the dog area either, nor did she sense any emanations coming from the open field. The only other part of the cemetery that yielded anything was an area around a memorial toward the back, where there were no individual markers. That energy, according to Christine, felt different. It felt good.

Whatever had been near the statue near the entrance gate seemed to have gone by the time Christine and her husband left, but as they walked out, she turned around, half-looking, and snapped some pictures anyway. When they got home the next morning and Christine downloaded the pictures to her computer, all of them looked routine except for one, on which there was a dark spot. It could have been a flaw in the lens, a bug, a shadow, almost anything. But when she zoomed in on the spot, it shaped itself into a black dog. But that was impossible because there hadn't *been* any dogs. And no life-size stuffed animals that could have been taken for dogs either. In the first instance, Christine would have noticed. In the second, as she discovered later, at the time she visited, stuffed dogs and cats weren't allowed (other stuffed toys yes, but not those).

She called her husband over, pointed out the enhanced spot, and asked him, "What do you think this is?" He said "Well, it certainly *looks* like a dog." She followed up with "Do you remember anything out there that looked like that?" to which he answered "Absolutely not." Then she closed Photoshop and told him to forget she'd asked. No matter what it looked like, it couldn't have been a dog. Maybe if it had been late at night, some stray might have snuck into the picture without her seeing it, she thought—but not at two o'clock in the afternoon. The spot must have been on the camera lens, or maybe a trick of the light. She was all ready to let it go.

At breakfast the next morning, her usually skeptical husband said "Remember the picture of the dog you showed me yesterday? You need to go back to the cemetery and take another one in the same place at the same time of day, see if it might have been a shadow." She told him she didn't want to, it was probably only dust on the lens and besides, it was a long drive. He said well, it looked like a dog to him, and he kept at her. It took her a couple of days to relent, but she finally gave in and took several more pictures of the spot at exactly the same angle, exactly the same time of day. Nothing. Huh, thought Christine. The original picture must have been authentic.

But she was busy with other projects at the time, so she posted the picture on her web site and put the phantom dog out of her mind. Then she got a phone call from a film producer. Someone at *Ghost Magazine* who'd seen the photo had given him her name. This man told Christine that he'd heard from locals that a black dog had been seen a number of times running across the road by the cemetery, and that when drivers swerved to avoid it the dog had vanished into thin air. Apparently, this non-dog had caused several near accidents.

The call got Christine interested enough to follow up, so she called the cemetery office. The minute she asked about the black dog, the woman who answered the phone went on defense. She wouldn't say she'd seen anything. She wouldn't say if the lawn man had seen anything. What she did say, over and over, was "We don't have anything going on in here." When Christine offered to show her the picture, the woman's response was "I don't want to see any picture," then, without prompting she volunteered: "I don't know anything about ghost dogs." The final comment the woman made was a telling one: "I have to work in this office."

Christine did find out one more thing about Broward, from a vet tech via another vet tech—that the cemetery was known for its strange lights and strange noises, even when there was no one there. Further calls yielded no more information, so there the matter rests. But the black dog may not be resting so be careful as you approach, and if it runs across just in front of your car, drive straight ahead because, don't worry, you can't kill it, it's already dead.

14

WOODLAWN PARK NORTH CEMETERY, MIAMI

Woodlawn Park was established in 1913 on what is now called Calle Ocho. Unlike most cemeteries with "park" in their names, Woodlawn deserves that designation. Its founders— a hotelier named William UrMey, an attorney named Clifton Benson, and a developer named Thomas Wilson—decided to make it into the kind of tropical garden that would attract discriminating families. To that end, they imported thousands of dollars worth (a fortune in those days) of rare tropical plants and trees, among them the first shefflera (umbrella tree) and mahogany trees ever brought into the United States. They planted their purchases not randomly but according to a site plan drawn by William Phillips, whose resume included Fairchild Tropical Gardens in Coral Gables, the Bok Tower and Sanctuary in Lake Wales, and the Biltmore Forest in Asheville, North Carolina.

In 1926 the founders commissioned a prominent architect, McDonald Lovell, to design a mausoleum. The result, covering more than a city block at the back of the cemetery, resembles a Gothic cathedral. Its coral rock exterior features crenellations, rose windows, arched entrances, and stained glass. Its marble interior contains two chapels and thousands of crypts and niches.

I arrived at Woodlawn on one of those days so unrealistically hot that you know it's going to rain. I parked at the entrance, opened my umbrella against the sun, and walked between two huge wrought-iron gates. I was immediately met by a dark, round pool surrounded by low shrubs and flanked by a broad semicircle of wise men—enormous banyan trees. A sign in front of the pool proclaimed the area a bird sanctuary. A bird sanctuary in the heart of urban Miami! I was entranced.

At the entrance to the cemetery proper, I stopped to look around. Besides a number of family mausoleums spread over the wide lawns, I noticed many white statues. The most common presences were Catholic: the Virgin Mary and Jesus of the Sacred Heart, as well as a few saints and two or three life-size Jesuses kneeling in prayer. I saw many trees too— oaks, banyans, and palms, and several I didn't recognize. Thus oriented I wandered, perusing the ethnic mix of names on the stones. People finishing out their lives in this beautiful city seemed to have had begun them almost anywhere in the world. Among recent burials, I saw many Hispanics, but also Poles, Germans, English, and Scots. There's even a Seminole, Billy Osceola, the great-grandson of Chief Tigertail.

I had been crouching to study the stones of a husband, a wife, and a grandson, all of whom had died before I was born, when a cemetery worker who'd been barreling back and forth cutting the grass reached my row. I stood up, and seeing that I wanted to talk, he cut his engine. This was Cedric, a large African American man with striking green eyes. After a few preliminaries he volunteered that from the day he began work in Woodlawn, he'd felt welcome, and that every day here is a day of rejoicing for him. There's something about this place, he said. He told me too that almost every work day he spends a few minutes alone in the mausoleum chapel. Being surrounded by so many who died before him, he told me, gives him the sense that we're all family, because though in life we may stand taller or smaller, in death we're the same. He added that when he passes visitors who seem especially sad, he makes sure to tell them not to worry, that God will help them.

When Cedric fell silent, I asked him if he knew the name of a particularly spectacular tree behind us. He squinted at it then said it was called a monkey-can't-climb. He got off the tractor to show me why: thorns projecting from the roots that curved several feet out from, and at least two feet up, the trunk. After Cedric had gone, I noticed that the monkey-can't-climb's roots circumscribed several flush-to-the-ground markers, including Juan Fernández's, who'd been born in Spain in 1895 and died in Miami in 19-something. I tried scratching the soft leaves off the rest of the date, first with my foot then with the flat of my hand but it had been reclaimed. Jessie Byers lies here too, a root away. She died in 1926. Later I noticed another tropical tree, whose smooth roots encircled graves not defensively like the monkey-can't-climb but tenderly, the way a mother might put her arms around her children.

On an open area of grass, I rescued a small white plush rabbit. It had been there at least overnight because it was soaking wet. Cedric had moved to the far side of the grounds by this time and had his ear protection back on, so I had to stand in front of him to flag him down. When I held the rabbit up, he said he'd seen a woman and a little girl leave it on a grave. He couldn't remember which grave, so he asked me to leave the rabbit by the water spigot closest to where I'd found it, because when the woman and child came to refill their vase (they'd been carrying flowers), they'd find their rabbit and put it back. Feeling oddly comforted, I propped up the rabbit at the base of the spigot.

After awhile, I began to realize that other than the statuary there's relatively little detail on graves here: very few verses and almost no information about anyone's life. The only specifics I could recall afterwards were a few Masonic symbols, the legend "juntos para siempre" between the graves of August and Lucy Atenen and one other couple, a few praying hands, and a single spray of pine.

That said, over the years Woodlawn has welcomed some interesting people, like Desi Arnaz, musician and TV star, Fernando Bujones, a Cuban ballet dancer enshrined in the Florida Hall of Fame, and Ramon Santamaria, the percussionist known as "Mongo" who wrote "Afro Blue" and performed the 1963 hit "Watermelon Man." *MAD* magazine cartoonist Antonio Prohìas is also buried here, as is the briefly but spectacularly famous AIDS activist Pedro Zamora, who left MTV's *Real World* for the quieter world under the grass. Woodlawn also shelters a couple of major league baseball players and, to keep them company, Matt Gribble, an Olympic gold medalist in swimming.

Many of Woodlawn's famous residents were involved in politics somewhere in Latin America. Anastasio Somoza García, the notorious Nicaraguan dictator, is buried here as are two former Cuban presidents, a Cuban general, and a former head of the Cuban House of Deputies. Here also lie two historically important Cuban Americans: Manuel Artime, who led the ill-fated Bay of Pigs invasion and Jorge Mas Canosa, who was for many years and through several U.S. presidencies the most prominent Cuban in America.

Most of the family mausoleums are traditional, white one-roomed buildings fronted by pillars and iron entrance gates. Several of them are fitted with stained glass inside so colored lights can shine on the floor and, when the sun is right, shine obliquely along the marble side walls. Somoza García owns one of these little houses; the Bacardi rum family another; and the Miltons who built the Fontainbleau Hotel, another. There is only one conspicuously unusual mausoleum here: a ten-foot-high sandstone pyramid fronted by a sphinx, erected for Mary Hecht by her husband, who later joined her there.

In the part of the cemetery devoted to veterans are two interesting monuments. The American Legion erected the first: a stepped square white pedestal topped by four larger than life statues—a soldier, a flier, a sailor, and a nurse, each facing in a cardinal direction and each painted mostly red and blue. The second is dedicated to the unknown soldiers who fought for Cuban freedom. Every Veterans Day, the cemetery management lays an American flag on each identifiably veteran grave, and conducts, gratis, a ceremony to honor those who died in service to their country.

Toward the back of the grounds (though only a few of its victims are buried here) is a memorial to the casualties of the 1930 Key West hurricane. In front of a mausoleum belonging to a Mr. Phillips is a large Masonic monument you visually can't—and emotionally shouldn't—miss. It carries this legend: "Let every dawn of morning be to you as the beginning of life, and every setting sun be as its close. And then let every one of those short lives leave its record of some kindly thing done for others." The sentiment seemed to me something to take home.

When I reached the back of the cemetery, I entered the mausoleum by climbing a few steps. Inside, the lack of natural context—no sky, no grass, no trees—and the absolute silence left me breathless. Too, the fact that the mausoleum holds the remains of over thirty thousand people felt emotionally overwhelming—wall after facing wall three or four slabs high, interrupted only occasionally by the gated alcoves reserved for families. I thought: there must be miles of walls. And there may really be, since this multistory building encompasses an entire city block, and except for two small chapels, is entirely occupied by crypts.

There's something else too, something that would give any sensitive visitor an unexpected frisson: because the memorials in the mausoleum haven't deteriorated since the day they were chiseled, all the deaths they memorialize feel recent. Walking among them, I viscerally understood why Cedric feels kin to these people.

It's also easy to identify with what's in here because the many personal objects laid out on the ledges that frame the slabs haven't deteriorated either, not like the little rabbit outside, doomed to mildew and finally fall apart.

Here are some of the many touching displays I saw. Remembering Silvio and Consuelo Álvarez who lie side by side on the top row at the end of a hallway are a tiny stuffed koala, two vases of live flowers, two empty dime store drinking glasses, two framed photos (one of an older man, one of an older woman), an empty perfume bottle, a candle holder, a tiny plastic princess figure, a filigreed metal box, and two figures of black saints. To the left and a row down from the Álvarezes, on the ledge belonging to the Kavell family stands a miniature castle from whose crenellated tower rises a blue and white flag.

Around the corner to the right from the Álvarezes and Kavells, set into the middle tier and separated by one slab are Janeene and Stanley Mykytka. On each ledge is propped a card containing a child's handprint and a little poem that ends "If I could pick my grandparents, I'd pick you."

Sighting down facing halls of the mausoleum is like driving a road lined with floating flowers because of the small vases at random heights holding vivid reds, whites, light blues, every color a flower can be. I came across some unusual legends here inside such as Peter de Bagniewski's (d. 1949): "Decorated with Poland's Golden Cross of Merit" and proclaimed a "Knight of Gregory the Great."

In the center of the building is a funeral chapel. I sat a few minutes before starting out again. On my way out the niche where three Brickells lie (d. 1908, 1918, and 1922 respectively) brought to mind the softly moonlit night my friend Margarita and I had walked the avenue named for them. On my way out of the building, I came across the second chapel. There was an intimacy about this one not entirely attributable to its size (it's no bigger than the average living room). Maybe it was to do with the way sunlight from its stained glass windows was casting quivering blues and reds onto the floor. I settled into one of the simple wooden pews and contemplated the unadorned wall in front of me. What seemed like a long time passed. When I finally stood to go, I noticed a huge copy of a painting by Raphael—Jesus surrounded by awed angels—set above the door leading out. I hadn't seen it coming in.

SPOTLIGHT: SPY VS. SPY

Late in 1959, Fidel Castro stood on the steps of the presidential palace jabbing angrily at a cartoon by Antonio Prohìas. The cartoon showed El Jefe (Fidel's nickname) surrounded by smarmy yes-men. By the time Fidel finished his diatribe, he had the crowd shouting *Paredón por Prohìas*! Execution for Prohìas! This wasn't an idle threat on Fidel's part. In his first six months in office, he had ordered 550 people, most of them associated with the former (Batista) regime, to be put to death. (There were trials but real defense wasn't part of them). As time went on, he became more and more paranoid with the result that anyone he perceived as opposing his regime was at risk of imprisonment or worse.

When Fidel assumed power in January 1959, almost the entire Cuban press—twenty-nine national newspapers, thirty-six radio stations, and eleven television stations—including Prohìas, arguably the most prominent editorial cartoonist in the country at the time, had backed him. But when Fidel began edging toward dictatorship, a few of his original backers, also including Prohìas, reacted accordingly.

Though Prohìas was never officially indicted, after the scene at the presidential palace the family started getting threatening phone calls. Soon, his regular venues began to shut him out. Some fired him outright; others left him on staff but stopped publishing his work. Finally only *El Mundo* was printing him. But many of the cartoons it accepted were censored before they could appear. The few that did see print were accompanied by lengthy censor-written *coletillas* accusing the artist of being if not a CIA operative, at least a traitor.

One day without warning, Prohìas's colleagues accused him of working for the CIA and demanded he resign the presidency of the Cuban Cartoonists Association which, since he had no real choice, he did. After that, Prohìas, once the most famous cartoonist in the country, found himself unable to find any home for his work at all.

Even so disgraced, Prohìas wanted to stay in Cuba. He tried sign painting to replace his lost income. But even lying as low as this, he couldn't escape notoriety. People who recognized him on the street, eventually even his former friends, started shouting "*Contrarevolucionario!*" at him and spitting ostentatiously on the sidewalk where he was about to step. There was more and more talk about how he was a traitor and how he deserved death. Finally, he gave in to the inevitable and in 1960, just as Castro was consolidating his control of the press by taking over *El Mundo*, the once-eminent artist boarded a plane for New York. Never again would he set foot on home soil.

He rented a studio apartment in a cheap hotel, the Hargrave, and worked a full shift ironing sweaters at a clothing factory. Also, just as he had done back in Havana when he was sixteen, he drew at night. Almost immediately his cartoons found homes in *El Diario* and *La Prensa*, the most prominent Spanish language newspapers then operating in the United States. The tone of Prohìas's new work was noticed in Cuba.

About two months after he arrived in New York, a fellow journalist commented on Radio Havana that the revolution "is so generous that it allows Prohìas's children to walk the streets." Afraid now for his family's safety, Prohìas sent for them, and the very next day they too boarded a plane for New York.

Antonio Prohìas, according to himself, was born as an artist in 1929, when his fourth-grade teacher enlisted his help in teaching his classmates to draw. As he matured, though his parents gave lip service to his talent, both of them, especially his lawyer father, expressed in no uncertain terms their opposition to his pursuing art as a career. This didn't stop the young Prohìas from drawing but it did drive him to do it in secret. At sixteen he stopped hiding. He quit school to work a menial job in a fertilizer factory by day and draw by night. In only a year he achieved his first publication. After that, he worked steadily, first for *El Dia*, then during World War II, for *El Diario de la Marina*, where he began doing editorial cartoons.

In 1946 when Prohìas was twenty-five, he won the first-ever national prize for cartooning, an award he'd win a total of six times. The prize was $1,500. The day the news came out in the papers, his father phoned him to ask him to stop by the office. When Prohìas did, his father asked him for a loan of $500. Prohìas offered him $800; the loan never took place. Later, Prohìas would tell another cartoonist, Bill Janocha, that he was convinced this episode was his father's way of admitting he'd been wrong.

After that first prize, Prohìas's career went from strength to strength. Eventually, he became the chief editorial cartoonist at *El Mundo*, Cuba's most prestigious daily newspaper. At one time, he was working regularly for five different newspapers and magazines. During the Batista regime, he developed a villainous character called El Hombre Siniestro. The strip was a huge success and enhanced its author's already stellar reputation for biting satire.

When Fidel first seized power, Prohìas supported him but then information officials at the American embassy showed him convinced him that El Jefe wasn't as independent as he claimed to be. A 1959 effort depicting Castro as a sheepskin draped over a hammer and sickle was the first of many

Prohìas cartoons linking Fidel and communism. And though Castro more than once sent word through intermediaries warning him to knock it off, Prohìas wasn't the sort to take to muzzling—hence the scene at the palace.

It may seem strange that with all his visual assaults on the regime Prohìas never actually *said* anything against Castro, either out loud or in writing. But it isn't strange at all when you know that he had seen words as far less powerful than drawing ever since he was a child. As a result, the adult Prohìas had developed the ability to communicate at a high level without resorting to language. It was this visual skill that would allow him to reach millions of American readers in spite of the fact that he never really mastered English.

Before Prohìas left Cuba, he had been experimenting with a strip directly inspired by Fidel. If Fidel insisted on calling Prohìas a spy, why then Prohìas would draw one—not Fidel, just a spy. He iced the storyline by creating a second spy to go with the first. The beauty of Prohìas's conceit was that since the two spies didn't represent any particular person or ideology, no one would care what happened to them. He settled on two nefarious spies, one black and one white, each trying to outdo the other. Eventually he would invent a gray spy: a woman. It says something about Prohìas that when this female spy turned up, she usually came out on top.

In any case, when Prohìas decided his black and white spies were ready for prime time, which happened to be July 22, 1960, he took his portfolio to twenty-five-cent cheap *MAD* magazine at 225 Lafayette Street near Little Italy. He brought his fourteen-year-old daughter Marta with him (it was her birthday) because though she'd been in New York only a few days, she spoke better English than he did. Better didn't mean functional, though. Marta's English was shaky enough that *MAD*'s editors found themselves having to resort to what they could remember from high school Spanish.

On their first visit, Prohìas and Marta came into a foyer occupied by two associate editors, competing for space at the same desk. The editors looked over Prohìas's sketches, told him they weren't in the market for new material, and suggested some other magazines he might try. Prohìas then took a chance. He told the editors that if he couldn't publish *Spy vs. Spy* in *MAD* then he wouldn't publish it at all, and he started to tear up his cartoons. The editors jumped on him before he could do too much damage. Then they asked him to draw something. The minute he picked up his pencil, they stopped his hand and hired him. Prohìas and Marta left the office that day with $800 and a contract for freelance work.

Soon, Prohìas's freelance assignments grew so frequent that *MAD* gave him his own desk. He would work there until he retired. Still, though he relished the supportive atmosphere he found at the magazine, Prohìas was never comfortable with the cultural differences between America and Cuba. Cubans dressed for work, for instance, whereas at *MAD* such items as neckties, though omnipresent at the time elsewhere in New York, were pretty much unknown. In Cuba too, you stand when your boss comes in to the room. But every time Prohìas tried to do that, his boss, Al Feldstein, would push him back down.

Prohìas and his wife divorced in the early 1960s and she moved to Miami, but she and Prohìas stayed friends and he would visit her and the children for a couple of months every year. His Miami trips became more and more frequent until finally he just didn't go back to New York. He died in Miami in February of 1998 at the age of seventy-seven.

By the time he did die, Prohìas's pen had left an indelible mark on his adopted country. *Spy vs. Spy* had appeared in almost every issue of *MAD* since the morning its editors had hired him (it had been ghosted since 1988 but only because of his declining health). Nine collections of the strip had made the best seller list. Both Milton Bradley and Nintendo had put out *Spy vs. Spy* games. The black and white spies were even used in Altoids ads.

When I was growing up, almost every boy I knew relished *MAD*, and most of them would have told you that *Spy vs. Spy* was the best thing in *MAD*. In fact every time I mention Prohìas to a male friend (I usually have to tell him who

Prohìas was since people tend not to notice authors' names), what I get back is *Spy vs. Spy*! I loved that strip!" And, judging from the glow in his eye, the man still does. For the record, I don't mean to exclude girls but in my generation at least, more boys than girls seemed to spark to *MAD*'s raw approach to humor.

Looking at *Spy vs. Spy* in retrospect, it's clear how politically advanced Prohìas's vision was. Here was an artist who, working against the atmosphere of his times, abandoned the world of superheroes in favor of two bad guys, the black and the white. And like many modern antiheroes, both black and white were happy only in the throes of some twisted plan to inflict pain and suffering, preferably on each other but if some bystander ended up victimized instead, not a problem. Also, in *Spy vs. Spy*, Black would be up for awhile, then White, then Black, the point being that in the real world, no one ever finally wins. Furthermore, as is sometimes the case in real life, the spies weren't very good at their jobs. Witness the fact that the only secret the White Spy ever stole was the plan for the 1963 Edsel, a notorious bomb of a Ford model.

In plotting his strips, Prohìas was careful to vary his backgrounds and never to repeat a device. A 1970 interview lets us into his methods. First, he'd set the spies up on opposite sides of a controversy. Then, he'd design some Rube Goldberg contraption for one of them to use against the other. Once he had those particulars worked out, he'd draw the frames in pencil on a piece of typing paper and submit them to the editors for comment. Once the script was approved, he'd ink it on illustration board in the "twice up" size that was the standard for cartoonists.

When he wasn't drawing, Prohìas enjoyed scotch, good cigars, and coffee. He called everyone *m'hijo* or *m'hija* because, according to his daughter, he couldn't remember names. He was known for his kindness to strangers, especially children who, he was convinced, deserved to be supported in their dreams. He used to buy supplies for young artists he met, commenting that "you never know." He once sent an eight-year-old who'd mailed him a drawing, some books and a personalized birthday card. Twenty-five years later, that eight-year-old wrote to say he was still grateful. Prohìas's nickname was El Flaco, the thin man, but his spirit was anything but that. On the contrary, it was as *ancho* (wide) as the skies he might have seen at night when he was sixteen, with dust in his hair and only dreams in his pocket.

15

KEY WEST CEMETERY,
KEY WEST

Though Ponce de León had claimed Florida for Spain in 1513, Key West was remote enough and the Indians there were fierce enough that there wasn't a serious European presence there until three hundred years later.

Key West was originally called Cayo de los Martires, "cayo" being Taino for island and "martires" Spanish for martyrs, the latter commemorating an incident in which the local Indians killed some Spanish missionaries. By the late 1700s when the island debuted on maps, its name had morphed to Cayo Hueso (Bone Key).

Some say "bone" refers to human bones early explorers found on the beaches; others trace the word to an apple tree whose name in Spanish also happened to have been *hueso*. Whatever its origin, most agree that *cayo*, pronounced with a hard "c," eventually morphed to "key" and *hueso* to its phonemic cousin "west."

The European settlement of Key West began—appropriately enough, considering the way a lot of later Florida was settled—with a land scam. Juan Pablo Salas, an army officer from St. Augustine who'd been deeded the island in 1815 by the Spanish governor of Cuba, sold it to John Strong in exchange for a sloop valued at $575. Strong then sold the island to George Murray who in turn sold it to John Geddes, a former governor of South Carolina. Meanwhile, back in Havana, in January of 1822 Salas sold his title again, this time to an American businessman named Simonton, for $2,000. Finally, after six years of controversy, Congress ruled that Simonton (who happened to have more influence in Washington than Geddes) was the legal owner.

When Simonton acquired Key West, it was still legally North Havana, Spanish property. But Simonton had no intention of living under Spanish rule so he argued in Washington that his island would give the United States what it had heretofore been missing: a deep harbor between New Orleans and Norfolk. Accordingly, on March 25, 1822, the navy sent Matthew Perry on a schooner appropriately named *The Shark* into Key West harbor to plant an American flag in the sand. When the Spanish didn't protest Perry's act, the deed was done. To seal it, Perry renamed Key West "Thompson's Island" after the then-secretary of the navy.

Almost immediately after that, Washington established a customs house in Key West. But it swiftly became clear that before the new port could thrive something would have to be done about the pirates (Disney didn't make it up). So the federal government mounted an antipirate campaign, headed by a Commodore Porter. Porter was generally successful at beating the pirates back but he governed the island with such an iron hand that there was some question as to whether the pirates or the townspeople hated him more.

In 1830, Key West, covering an area of some 358 acres, was platted. Its population grew quickly, from 517 the year of the platting to 2,645 in 1850, to 9,000 in 1880, to almost 20,000 in 1890. At the start of the Civil War, it was the richest city per capita in the United States, and during that war it became the largest city in Florida, thanks to the decline of its only serious rival, Jacksonville. Growth continued in the twentieth century, but more slowly. In 1950, for instance, the island was home to 21,792, excluding military. But now in the twenty-first century, for the first time in its history Key West's population is declining, down 8 percent between 2000 and 2006.

Since Key West is an island, its growth potential has always depended on how easily people could reach it. Until 1912 when Flagler's railroad arrived (after filling 134 acres of wetlands to make room for a terminal), it was accessible only by sea. A keys causeway opened late in the 1920s helped, but getting to the island still involved forty miles of ferries. The ferry gap was a moot point at the time though since the South Florida land boom of the early '20s had been effectively arrested by the 1928 hurricane. The road to Key West was finally completed and ceremoniously traveled by FDR in 1939.

From its earliest days, Key West's nontourist economy has been driven by its geography. Many early Key Westers made their livings from the nineteenth-century equivalent of looting: wrecking. Wreckers would go to the beach in bad weather or at the rumor of a wreck, then rush out to foundering ships and strip them of their cargos. Many wreckers were murderers as well as thieves since they didn't always bother to rescue crew and passengers but would simply let them drown. As an example of the kinds of financial rewards wrecking could bring, Richard Fitzpatrick, who before 1828 was the only local auctioneer for salvaged property, took in more than $10,000 ($280,000 in today's currency) in a single year.

Salt production in Key West began in 1830 and brought in around fifty thousand bushels a year but the salt industry was dependent on rainfall—early rains could wipe out production—so didn't endure for long. Sponge fishing did though, and Key West came to dominate it. The earliest sponge fishermen were Bahamian immigrants, but as time passed more and more Greeks joined them. By the 1890s, a Greek named A. J. Arapian, aka "the sponge king," was bringing in close to half a million dollars in annual sales. Eventually Key West spongers lost their monopoly to the Greek community of Tarpon Springs on Florida's east coast, partly because a disease struck its sponges, partly because of the practicalities of transportation.

The military has always been important in the lives of Key Westers. First the navy was called in to combat pirates then Seminoles (Key West was untouched in the Seminole Wars but other keys were devastated). Then in 1845, the army built Fort Taylor (now a state park). When the Civil War broke out, the Union had so many soldiers in Key West that on January 13, 1861, a Captain James Brannan took possession of the town while it slept, and—though some contrarians flew Confederate flags—it remained under Union control for the rest of the war. The Union's blockade of the port made local businessman richer than ever from reselling goods that had been bound for the Confederacy. Some of the "goods," by the way, were slaves.

After the Civil War, the navy was built up four times: during the Spanish-American War (the *Maine* sailed from Key West), during World Wars I and II, and in 1962 during the Cuban Missile Crisis. The World War II military presence was especially significant because the navy built the first freshwater pipeline to Key West to serve its bases and constructed US-1 because it needed an improved highway to transport its equipment. The last military installation to be set up here was the naval air station, which is still in operation.

Besides wrecking, sponges, and the military, the cigar industry prospered in Key West from the time the first factory was set up in 1831 until the 1920s, when cigarettes displaced cigars as America's smoke of choice. So many of the cigar workers were Cuban that by the mid-1800s Spanish had become the island's second language. Starting in 1970 there was even a Spanish language newspaper, *El Republicano*. Fifteen years later though, a cigar workers' strike forced Vicente Ybor and others out of the keys to Tampa, thereby ending Key West's manufacturing monopoly.

During Prohibition, liquor smuggling became big business. Contraband beer and rum from Cuba and whiskey, rye, and scotch from the British Isles via Nassau flowed in and out of the harbor, enriching many Key Westers and, through their spending, the town as a whole.

The Great Depression hit Key West in two waves. First, tourism and its associated building industry dried up, then the navy reduced its presence to maintenance status. In 1934, the strapped city declared bankruptcy and threw itself on the mercy of the federal government.

Key West didn't really start recovering from its slump until 1949, when "pink gold," a new and profitable variety of shrimp, was discovered in the Marquesas and Tortugas. By the early 1950s around five hundred shrimp boats were plying the surrounding waters—a lot of boats for an island only two miles by four.

Tourism didn't pick up with the fishing. In fact, so few people were coming that in 1955 local motels began a price war, during which some of them even offered rooms for free.

One of the most colorful episodes in Key West history happened in 1982 when the U.S. Border Patrol set up a road block on US-1 near Florida City. The road block was supposed to stop drug running. It may or may not have done that but what it surely did do was back up traffic—as much as fifteen miles. The congestion, obviously, had a chilling effect on tourism. So on April 22 of that year, Key West seceded from the union. Tongues inserted firmly in cheeks, its citizens proclaimed themselves the Conch Republic and in their new capacity as an emerging nation applied for foreign aid.

Now despite their wild senses of humor—which you can't miss if you just walk around and look at front porches, potentially being assaulted along the way by one of the chickens that run loose in the streets—Key Westers, like the rest of us, die. And, like the rest of us, they have to be buried. The first town cemetery was close to Whitehead Point. But when an 1856 hurricane dragged many of its inhabitants from their graves and flung them every which-way—some ended up on sand dunes, others dangling from trees like weird Christmas ornaments—it became obvious that a beachfront cemetery hadn't been a good idea. So in 1857, the city moved its burying ground to the highest point in town: Solares Hill which, though it's a full eighteen feet above sea level, probably won't look like a hill to anyone but an ant. Key West's other historically important cemetery, an African American burial ground at Higg's Beach, was built over during the Civil War and has never been excavated so Solares Hill, officially called Key West Cemetery, is, as they say, the only game in town.

You won't have any trouble finding the place, since it's clearly marked on all the tourist maps. It's enclosed by an unclimbable (unless you're very, very drunk) wrought-iron fence, but has several entrance gates, at least one in each direction. Getting there involves a pretty walk through an older section of town: small, colorful if shabby, wooden houses, almost all of which have tin roofs.

The local tradition of tin roofing began after a series of devastating nineteenth-century fires destroyed a good deal of the city. Tin, Key Westers figured out, makes sense since unlike shingles or tar paper, it can repel sparks—a critical capability in a place where wood has been the building material of choice for centuries. Before the days of tin, local firefighters had a terrible time. Early in the nineteenth century, one crew got so frustrated trying to put out a blaze in a warehouse that they threw their equipment into the sea.

Solares Hill isn't quite twenty acres but in the middle of a town as small as Key West, it feels large. It also, for a major cemetery, seems awfully neglected. In early summer when I first visited, tall weeds abounded, breaking into straggly flower. There were also many statues missing heads, many broken gravestones, companies of broken vases, and legions of falling and faded plastic flowers. In contrast to all this disorder, the place is laid out like a town, in streets with names like Fourth Avenue and Violet Street.

As you may have gathered, I didn't find Solares Hill especially pretty and I don't think anyone would claim it's especially peaceful either. But that doesn't mean it's not interesting. For one thing, any graveyard that's home to 100,000 people piled on top of each other (some in stacked condos of ashes) and is still being added to is bound to radiate stories. And since this one is located in Key West, a famously quirky town, there are many.

Here, courtesy of one neighbor of the cemetery—a barechested, barefoot young man I found washing his car—is a good example. Locals who commit crimes habitually use the cemetery to get rid of the evidence, the neighbor told me, so there are guns and other, more miscellaneous, crime scene paraphernalia buried all over the grounds. In fact, he went on, just the other day a neighbor of his who's a convicted felon told the policeman who'd arrived to arrest him (someone had snitched) to look around, he didn't have any guns. Pressed, he admitted he'd had some but he'd buried them in the cemetery. When the officer asked him where, he just shrugged and said he couldn't remember, just "somewhere."

Another local anecdote involves the Arnold family. After their teenage son was hit by multiple cars as he was riding his moped, his grieving parents laid him to rest in their family plot under the kind of toy airplane a toddler might pedal around the yard. For years after the boy died, the slowly rusting airplane presided over his memory. When it was stolen, its loss caused such an outcry—this is Key West—that the thief relented and returned it.

I heard another, more recent, story about a woman who had moved into a house that was famous for its bright yellow rooms. She liked the color but, as she told her friends, there was something about it. Maybe what she was feeling had to do with the fact that, as several of them pointed out to her, yellow is often associated with depression. In any case, one day this woman's son, who was in high school at the time, went to the cemetery and killed himself. He lies there today.

The Key West Historical Society offers excellent maps of the Hill—you can print one off the web. But I'd suggest you not limit your visit to the official tour because there's a good chance that if you walk around on your own you'll come across graves at least as intriguing as any the map points out. I warn you though, finding your way isn't as easy as the street names imply, so you may get lost. I did. Just take it as part of the fun.

I'll start you out with a mini-tour. Close to the main entrance at the corner of Margaret and Angela streets (whose arch, charmingly, misspells "cemetery" as "cematary") you'll come upon a wrought-iron-fenced area featuring a bronze statue of a soldier presiding over the fifty-six victims of the 1898 sinking of the *Maine* in Havana Harbor. Beside the memorial rises a row of lovely palms. The grass here is an exception to the cemetery's general disarray. It's kept military-cut and because I visited close to Memorial Day, each marker was flanked by a bright new American flag. The *Maine* is one of two wartime memorials here. You enter the other by a metal archway, inside which is an obelisk and a book commemorating the Cuban patriots who died with José Marti in the unsuccessful 1868 uprising against the Spanish.

Down the way from the *Maine* memorial, turning right and on your right, you'll see a routine-looking slab remembering General Abraham Lincoln Sawyer. The general, who died in 1939, was a forty-four-inch-tall midget whose dying wish—here fulfilled—was to be buried in a full-size grave. Just past Sawyer is a tall urn-topped memorial to William Curry, reputedly Florida's first millionaire. His wife's name, Euphemia, seems to have been common in Key West because I noticed it on many other local gravestones.

Continuing along this same "street," to the left, in one of the stacks of vaults that are made for ashes, is an eye-level memorial I founded deeply moving. It consists of a heartfelt inscription to Gabriel Soler—*Papi, nunca te olvidamos* ("Daddy, we'll never forget you")—flanked by two hand-painted tiles. The first shows a handsome man in a crisp white shirt. The second consists of a guitar surrounded by a block plane, a hammer, a saw, and two pencils. *Gabriel, tampoco no te voy a olvidar,* says the other inscription, presumably written by Gabriel's wife. "I won't forget you either."

At the end of Seventh Avenue is one of Key West's most famous inscriptions: "I told you I was sick." You'll find it on a plaque fixed to a white crypt to the left of the arch marking the Jewish section of the cemetery. The possible (though in the end of course, not) hypochondriac's first name is offered only as initials. My life experience would suggest that those initials represent a man, since the women I know soldier on when they get ill but every man I've ever been associated with turns into a huge baby the minute a sniffle hits. The other most-often cited inscriptions in this cemetery, by the way, were commissioned by a wife ("At least I know where he's sleeping tonight") and a music lover ("Devoted fan of Julio Iglesias"). But I didn't happen to see either of those so I'll leave them to you.

There's a grave featuring especially enigmatic décor on the way to the aforementioned hypochondriac. It's on your left as you face the arch. Arranged on a slab are a Bambi (perhaps a pet), a small stone bear, and two bricks, each painted in three stripes, one red, white, and blue, the other red, yellow, and red.

Though, as I've said, Solares Hill tends to broken and/or neglected graves, it also includes some that are clearly loved. The Fernández family plot is one of those. It displays the only recent plantings I noticed and for good measure many vases of new-looking white cloth flowers. The Fernándezes even installed a functional hand pump for easy watering. The Albury plot too—whose first burial was in 1898 and most recent in 1969—is worth mentioning for its shivers of huge, also bright-white, flowers.

I particularly remember the family plot next to the Alburys, not because it's neglected but because of the story that may underlie a stone coming loose from its crypt. The stone remembers a thirteen-year-old, "My darling Anna Bell Patterson," and contains two dates, the last of which is 1943. Now the 1940s weren't pestilential years—yellow fever had disappeared by then and the polio epidemic hadn't come on—so when Anna Bell died, the odds are her family wasn't braced to lose her. But there's more. Since 1943 falls in the middle of World War II and the inscription on Anna's grave says "my" not "our," perhaps her father had already been killed, leaving her mother alone to deal with the loss of this child who might well have been all she had left of the man she'd sent off to war.

I don't want to give the impression that every statue in Solares is broken. You'll come across many intact ones, mostly Madonnas and angels rather than Jesuses. The largest I saw was an angel rising at least fifteen feet from its base. The legend reads simply "Gladys." There are some non-Christian images here too: an eagle for instance, and a sculpture known locally as "Bound Woman" on the tomb of Archibald Yates, who died in 1966.

A memorable pair of statues, a tall angel sweetly facing a smaller angel, was erected by the grieving mother of a child who fell out a window and was killed. When I visited in the spring of 2008, the larger angel's head was cut off and the stones were mutilated. But both have since been restored and, judging from the photograph I was shown, they're now one of the loveliest presences in the cemetery.

Something I don't think I've seen elsewhere is the shed roofs a number of families have erected over their plots. The effect makes me think of picnic shelters. And "shelter" is probably the operative word, since the roofs were clearly intended to protect the memorials underneath from Key West's often brutal weather. We're talking not only intense sun—you may not burn easily but if you don't cover yourself with sunscreen here, it's pretty much guaranteed that you'll end up looking like a molting lobster—but also driving wind and rain.

I didn't see much wildlife in Solares Hill, not even the stray cats Key West is famous for, but on one early morning walk I did hear a rooster crowing and on another, a flight of doves accompanied me, taking off like shaken souls as I neared, always landing just ahead. One of those forays into the air happened just as I was leaving a stone countenance of Jesus that happened to be flanked by stone doves like themselves. That monument, the Jesus and the doves, was dedicated to Yoyo and Paco, otherwise known as Georgina and Frank, a couple born respectively in 1894 and 1904. I had paused at their memorial, wishing they'd been my grandparents.

What will we have to say for ourselves when we die? Perhaps this: "Always dreamed of being someone. Still dreaming." The epitaph belongs to a James Richardson, born 1944, who died at sixty—earlier, I imagine, than he'd have expected. I knew a James Richardson once, a very talented writer. And I know he was born in 1944 and I know he died. Perhaps this stone was his shadow. I hope wherever he sleeps, these words will tell him he isn't forgotten. Jimmy, this is for you.

SPOTLIGHT: ALL FOR LOVE

Somewhere in the Key West Cemetery is an eighteen-inch square box containing the dismembered remains of a young Cuban woman. Her name was Elena Milagro Hoyos Mesa and she inspired the man who called himself Count Carl Von Cosel (he was born Karl Tanzler) to such a pitch of love that in October 1933 he dug her up and lived with her—in his mind as husband and wife—for more than seven years.

Von Cosel had emigrated to the United States from Germany in 1926, when he was forty-nine. In 1927 he left his wife and two daughters near Zephyrhills, Florida, and went to Key West to work as a radiologist at the naval hospital. He assured his family that the move was financially necessary and that it would be temporary. But when he met Elena, he was so distracted by his imagined relationship with her that in the next fifteen years his only letter home was a two-line birthday card.

When Von Cosel finally did go back to Zephyrhills, he went only because, he said, he could no longer endure the parade of tourists he'd been attracting since his release from jail the year before. Truth be told, he'd done nothing to discourage the traffic; in fact, he'd been profiting from it by charging a quarter (real money in those days) to tour his house and hear his story. He'd worked up a thriving souvenir business too. He sold his visitors screws from his laboratory, pipe organ parts, and relics of his lost Elena, offered as reverently as if she'd been a saint: photographs, scraps of her wedding dress. He even sold copies of her death mask.

Still, despite the side show atmosphere that swirled around him, much of the public believed that love and only love had motivated every strange thing Von Cosel had done, including selling souvenirs. You might not see the case that way, Elena's family no doubt didn't, but you can make up your own mind once you've heard the facts.

In his autobiography, Von Cosel claimed he first met Elena when he was twelve. He said he was asleep in the castle where he spent his childhood (a castle that, like the title he assumed when he left Germany, seems to have been a figment of his imagination) when an ancestress of his, a countess who had died in 1765, woke him up and presented Elena to him as his bride-to-be. Elena, Von Cosel said, appeared to him again years later when he was living in Australia (though there's no evidence he had ever been there).

Be that as it may, when in 1930 a dark-haired Cuban beauty named Elena Milagro de Hoyos appeared in Von Cosel's Key West office to seek treatment for tuberculosis, there was no question in his mind that she was the bride he had been waiting for. That both of them were married (Elena's husband had left her but they weren't divorced) never at any time in this affair, entered his consciousness.

Von Cosel showered his intended with presents: flowers, jewelry, wine, a silk kimono, even the elaborate bed on which he would one day lay her out, all of which Elena accepted though she steadfastly professed not to love him. When the treatments he thought she needed weren't available locally, Von Cosel offered to send her to a sanatorium at his own expense. But Elena refused to leave her family, so he built his own electroshock machine and began to treat her with it (at the time, many reputable doctors thought electric shock might alleviate tuberculosis). But the burns the treatments left were so deep and the treatments so painful that Elena began to miss her appointments. Faced with the specter of not seeing her, Von Cosel convinced Elena's family that she was improving and persisted until they allowed him to treat her at home. But all this effort came to nothing. Elena's case had been terminal from the day she and Von Cosel had met. The following October, she died.

Wild with grief, Von Cosel paid for Elena's funeral and all the expenses associated with it, including unusually elaborate embalming, a double coffin, and a cemetery plot. After a memorial mass at St. Mary's Star of the Sea, she was laid to rest. After the funeral, Von Cosel persuaded Elena's parents to rent him her room so he could sleep in the bed he had given her. Not content with living in Elena's house, he visited her every day in the cemetery. After a few weeks he got so worried about moisture getting into her casket that he bought the plot next to hers and commissioned an above-ground mausoleum so elaborate it looked like the house of a rich family of elves. During the three months it took to build the mausoleum, the doctor covered Elena's grave with a tarpaulin he had taken off the wingless airplane that would in only a few weeks be her home.

To move Elena's body to the mausoleum required both the state's and Elena's family's approval, both quickly given. The rest of Von Cosel's plan wouldn't have gotten anyone's approval. Once Elena was disinterred in preparation for the move, he bribed the management of a funeral parlor to leave him and a mortician alone overnight with her body. Once they were alone, Von Cosel and the mortician opened first Elena's vault, then her inner coffin.

The body they found inside turned out to have deteriorated to the point where its disintegrating clothing had to be peeled away strip by strip before anyone could even begin to clean it. After a few hours of this, it was clear that one night was not going to be enough so, as dawn broke, Von Cosel covered Elena with cotton saturated in cologne in anticipation of the next night the morgue would be free. In his second session, he finished cleaning his charge, slipped her into an incubation tank, and slid the tank and its contents into an elaborately sealed inner coffin inside an even more elaborately sealed outer one. By morning, Elena was safely at rest in the new home Von Cosel had described to her many times as he sat by her grave.

The doctor, by now seldom without his cane, had become the stuff of folklore. Every night he would be seen, deep in one-sided conversation, entering Elena's mausoleum. If inclement weather forced him to stay home, it was rumored he'd call instead, using a telephone he'd had installed for that purpose inside the little house. Von Cosel's visits had a routine. After he'd used the three keys that secured Elena's inner sanctum, he would lay his hand on her casket which, he said, felt warm. Then he'd talk to her for hours at a time. When he was ready to go, he'd lay out the night's presents—flowers, handkerchiefs, a fan—and ask Elena what she'd like him to bring next.

One Christmas night, Von Cosel said, he felt invisible hands caressing his face. On his next visit, a white-veiled apparition appeared at the door, stood in full moonlight a moment, and then vanished. The figure didn't appear again but as the moon's cycle waned, Elena began to sing her favorite song, "La Boda Negra" (The Black Wedding), in which on a stormy night, a lover disinters his bride, carries her home, lays her on his bed, then lies down beside her. Von Cosel took the song to be Elena's way of telling him what she wanted. How could he deny her? He'd never been able to deny her anything when she was alive and now that she was dead, he loved her more than ever.

In preparation for what he thought would be Elena's last move, Von Cosel rented a house just outside the cemetery gates. Then, on the night he'd chosen, he covered the fence with a blanket and loaded Elena's casket onto a wagon whose ends he'd padded with pillows. As he worked, he felt the souls of the dead all around him, cheering him on.

Unfortunately, just as he was trying to lift Elena's casket over the fence, it fell on top of him and leaked a foul-smelling liquid down his neck and into his clothes. His second attempt was more successful, and once Elena was safely out of sight, the doctor washed himself and his clothes with liquor from the bottle in his pocket (the house he'd rented had no running water), and went home.

A couple of nights later, Von Cosel moved Elena across town into the cockpit of the wingless airplane the commander of the navy base had allowed him to store behind the hospital. When he had settled Elena in her new home, he took her out of her coffin and washed her re-slimed body with perfumed soap and wine (at one point he was buying so much soap that the store clerk was beginning to wonder) and doused her with her favorite eau de cologne. Next, he flooded her innards with warm solutions, stuffed them with rags, and began to restore her appearance by splinting her nose and pulling her arms straight with pulleys. To restore—as he thought—Elena's skin, he coated first her face then the rest of her body with silk and beeswax. When he'd finished, he kissed her on the lips and blew into her mouth until, as he put it, "her bosom rose." Then he dressed her in her wedding dress and lifted her back into her coffin where she looked, he said, "more beautiful than ever."

Unfortunately, Elena's cockpit idyll didn't last long, because the understanding commander retired and his replacement told Von Cosel to move the plane (and all the other salvage equipment he'd accumulated) off the base. For Elena's new house, Von Cosel bought a shack on Rest Beach south of town and with the help of Elena's brother-in-law, divided the space into two. Half the space was to be a hangar for the airplane, the other half a laboratory/living quarters. When the renovations were finished, Mario, the brother-in-law, helped Von Cosel with the move. Because there was so much to relocate, the process required several trips, the last of which Mario spent squatting on the airplane to keep it from tipping as it was being towed behind a rental truck. Neither he nor any of the Hoyos who waved from their front porch as the procession slid by had any idea what was inside.

On Rest Beach, the doctor had a bigger working area than he'd had when he kept Elena in the cockpit, so it was here he began the process of what he hoped would be her resurrection. He thought resurrection was physically possible because he subscribed to his interpretation of a Brahman belief that if someone who died of an incurable disease were kept buried for a year, he or she would wake cured.

He started by laying Elena's naked body on a bed of white felt inside the incubation tank filled with a blood-temperature solution of oxyquinoline sulphate of sodium. After twenty-four hours, he drained the tank and replaced the sodium solution with the constantly circulating plasma bath in which she'd lie for most of the next two years (except for the few minutes every day when he'd take her out to rest, then treat her with radiation). After a few weeks of therapy, the doctor said, Elena's body filled out so much that he was often moved to kiss her lips, getting in the process "a liberal taste" of the solution in which she lay. All in all, those were happy days for him. Almost every evening, he would play Bach, Beethoven, or Wagner on his organ, partly for Elena's listening pleasure and partly to create the vibrations he thought would revive her. He played only "classical"—rather than "vulgar" genres like, for instance, jazz—because he believed that only worthy types of music had potential to reawaken the dead.

Sadly for Von Cosel, his Rest Beach retreat proved not to be permanent either. Before long, it was invaded by the WPA, which as part of FDR's jobs program was renovating the area for tourism. Where there had been only the sound of the waves, now one heard the shouts and hammer strikes of men building sheds and cabanas and cleaning up the flotsam and seaweed that were perpetually washing ashore. Around that time, the doctor took Elena out of the tank—she would never go back into it—and after recoating her body with beeswax, dressed her in wedding finery complete with gold crown and white gloves. He then laid her on her bed and surrounded her with flowers. Every night he slept on a cot by her side, leaving her only to get the mail. He had to get the mail, because that was where he got his money since, as came out much later, he had retired from the German navy.

In 1936 a major hurricane occasioned one of the most cinematic scenes of this whole strange affair: Count Von Cosel playing Wagner in the dark, the strains of his organ swelling as the wind rose and waves crashed over the deserted beach; the image of a desperate man playing louder and louder to protect, as he thought, his love who listened intently from her bed.

After the hurricane, the WPA came back in such force that Van Cosel was forced to move again. This move, which involved twenty truckloads of equipment and consumed a full two months, would be the last. Since his new house had no electricity, Von Cosel was forced to keep Elena exposed to the air. This necessity worried him because of its potential for insect damage and because he knew Elena might be mummified, but he consoled himself with the idea that in either case he'd eventually be able to reconstitute her by immersion. On the bright side, here, for the first time, he could sleep on the bed beside her.

Toward the end of July 1936, according to Von Cosel, Elena turned over on her side and began to get up. He counseled her frantically not to hurry because he was afraid she'd fall, having lain down so long. But his exhortations turned out to be academic because Elena's reanimation didn't last. One day soon after that though, she began to talk. Von Cosel had been adding a new layer of silk and wax to her skin to shut out the insects that had been tormenting her when he ran out of silk. Speaking up, Elena told him to finish the job with her wedding dress. He did, and when he was through he rewarded her with another, even more beautiful dress—this one gold to match her crown. He dressed Elena in the new gown and put her back to bed. After that she fell silent until September of 1940 when suddenly, on three successive days, she begged the count to hide her. On the third day, she began to tremble all over. At last, thought the count, my love is coming back to life! But it was not to be. By the time he kissed Elena's lips, her tremor had calmed.

Two weeks later, Von Cosel heard that Elena's mausoleum had been broken into. He hurried to the cemetery where he found both the sexton and the undertaker assuring Elena's sister Nana that Elena was safe because the inner casket hadn't been disturbed. But Nana was still anxious and insisted Elena's casket be opened anyhow so she could see for herself, a request the count, who had the only key, steadfastly and for obvious reasons, refused.

Two weeks later, Nana and the count had another confrontation at the mausoleum. The count accused Nana of having herself broken into Elena's tomb to steal her jewels. Nana responded by again begging him to open the coffin. She wanted to prove she hadn't taken the jewels, she said, but mostly she yearned to see her sister again. This time her plea touched the count's heart, so he took her and her husband Mario to his house, where he invited them in to see for themselves what good care he'd been taking of Elena. "See how beautiful she is" he said, as they stood beside her bed. Nana insisted that the mummified woman who lay in the count's house couldn't be her sister and again asked him to open the coffin. This frustrated Von Cosel. Hadn't he just proved he'd looked after Elena well? Not only that, but that he'd done it for years without asking anyone for anything. If he were going to reopen the coffin, he told Nana and Mario, he'd open it only when *he* decided it was time. After Nana left, the count, worried that Nana had been after Elena's jewels, took them off and hid them.

Four days later, the sheriff arrived, accompanied by some attendants with a hearse. When the count couldn't show a certificate legalizing his possession of a corpse, the attendants loaded Elena into a basket and took her away. Over the next few days, she would be exhibited at the funeral home and seen by nearly everyone who lived in Key West. Von Cosel spent the next week in the county jail, charged with desecrating a grave. On each of those nights, a band serenaded him to sleep. During the day, groups of women flocked to the jail, bringing food and support. At first the women were local but then a cadre of girls arrived from a cigar factory in Tampa. Later, people from all over the country would write letters in the doctor's defense.

At the preliminary hearing, the judge refused Von Cosel's plea to return Elena so he could finish reviving her. Then, after the hearing, a panel declared Von Cosel sane and able to stand trial. In the end, though, he went free. The two-year statute of limitations had run out on the first charge against him (grave molesting) and the court, perhaps giving in to the public outcry, dropped the second—unauthorized disinterment of a body.

In its ruling, the court allowed Von Cosel to keep Elena's jewels but the judge, along with everyone else in Key West, was determined to prevent his ever getting control of Elena's corpse again. To that end, the sheriff, a sexton, and an undertaker went to Solares Hill at three in the morning with Elena's hack-sawed body and buried it in a small box; exactly where has never been revealed.

Five hours after the doctor finally left Key West, an explosion destroyed Elena's mausoleum. Investigators couldn't find a timing device, so Von Cosel couldn't have been physically responsible. Who set the charge and why is still a mystery.

The rest is anticlimax. Von Cosel spent the rest of his life in Zephyrhills—a good deal of it in the cockpit of his airplane, writing his memoirs. They were, after all, the only way he had to keep Elena close by. Well, almost the only way. A replica of her was found with him in August of 1955 when neighbors noticed his mail piling up. By the time they called the sheriff, he'd been dead several days. The count's was by anyone's reckoning a strange case. But in the end, whether you admire the man for the depth of his passion or condemn him for what he did, or both, there's no escaping the fact that every step he took, no matter how apparently insane, he took for love.

APPENDIX I
CEMETERY ADDRESSES

Tallahassee and the Panhandle

The Old City Cemetery
Corner, Park Avenue and Martin Luther King Boulevard
Tallahassee, FL 32301

Mount Horeb Cemetery
2.9 miles north of Pinetta (Madison County)

Chestnut Street Cemetery
U.S. 98 (8th St.)
Apalachicola, FL 32320

Glendale Nature Preserve and Cemetery
On Highway 83, nine miles north of DeFuniak Springs

St. Michael's Cemetery
6 N. Alcaniz St.
Pensacola, FL 32501

North Central and Northeast Florida

Micanopy Historic Cemetery
Seminary St.
Micanopy, FL 32667

The Huguenot Cemetery
Between the Visitors Information Center and the Old City
Gate (across from Castillo de San Marco)
St. Augustine, FL 32084

Evergreen Cemetery
4535 Main St.
Jacksonville, FL 32206

Winding Oaks Farm Racehorse Cemetery
5850 SW College Rd.
Ocala, FL 34474

Central and West Central Florida

Upsala Cemetery
Upsala Rd. (Off C.R. 46A)
Sanford, FL 32771

Manasota Memorial Park
1221 53rd Avenue East
Bradenton, FL 34203

South and Southeast Florida

Port Mayaca Memorial Gardens
Canal Point, FL 33438

Broward Pet Cemetery
11455 NW 8th Street
Plantation, FL 33325

Woodlawn Park North Cemetery
3262 SW 8th Street
Miami, FL 33135

Key West Cemetery
701 Passover Lane
Key West, FL 33040

APPENDIX 2

FURTHER READING

General

Gannon, Michael. *Florida: A Short History*. Rev. ed, Gainesville: University Press of Florida, 2003.

Tebeau, Charles. *A History of Florida*. Coral Gables: University of Miami Press, 1973.

Subject-Specific*

Culhane, John. *The American Circus: An Illustrated History*. New York: Henry Holt, 1990.

Dewhurst, William Whitwell. *The History of Saint Augustine Florida, including a short description of the climate and advantages of Saint Augustine as a health resort*. New York: G. Putnam and Sons, 1881.

Gonzalez, Mrs. S. J. "Pensacola: Its Early History," *Florida Historical Quarterly* 2 (April 1909).

Hanna, A.J. *A Prince in their Midst; the Adventurous Life of Achille Murat on the American Frontier*. Norman: University of Oklahoma Press. 1946.

Harrison, Ben. *Undying Love: The True Story of A Passion That Defied Death*. New York: St. Martin's Press, 1997.

* Web sites are not included.

Haskin, Steve. *Doctor Fager, Racing's Top Record Setter*. Lexington, Ky.: Eclipse Press, 2007.

Hurston, Zora Neale. *Their Eyes Were Watching God*. Reissue Ed. New York: Harper Collins, 1998.

Kleinberg, Eliot. *Black Cloud: The Great Florida Hurricane of 1928*. New York: Carroll and Graf Publishers, 2003.

Mathis, James R. *The Making of the Primitive Baptists*. New York: Routledge, 2004.

Murat, Achille. Letters 1822–1841. Smathers Library, Special Collections Manuscripts, University of Florida.

Mykle, Robert. *Killer 'Cane: The Deadly Hurricane of 1928*. New York: Cooper Square Press, 2002.

Roux, Dolores. *Cemetery Tour*. Apalachicola, Fla.: Coombs House Bed and Breakfast, n.d. DVD.

Smith, Buckingham. *Sitiki: The Odyssey of an African Slave*. Edited by Patricia Griffin. Gainesville: University Press of Florida, 2009.

Von Cosel, Carl. *The Secret of Elena's Tomb*. Audio CD read by Jack Hans Pederson, 2003

Wallenda, Tino. *Walking the Straight and Narrow: Lessons in Faith from the High Wire*. Alachua, Fla.: Bridge-Logos, 2005.

Weiss, Rebecca. *A Florida Pioneer: The Adventurous Life of Josef Henschen, Swedish Immigrant in the 1870s*. Lulu.com, 2006.

INDEX

Lola Haskins has published nine books of poetry, most recently *Still, the Mountain* (2010), *Desire Lines, New and Selected Poems* (2004) and *The Rim Benders* (2001) as well as two of prose: *Not Feathers Yet: A Beginner's Guide to the Poetic Life* and *Solutions Beginning with A* (illustrated by Maggie Taylor). Among her awards are two National Endowment for the Arts Fellowships and four Individual Artist Fellowships from the state of Florida. Ms. Haskins retired from teaching computer science at the University of Florida and now teaches for the Rainier Writers Workshop, a low-residency MFA program. She lives in Gainesville. For more information please visit her at www.lolahaskins.com.